# THE SPIRIT
# OF THE
# MARATHON

# THE SPIRIT
## OF THE
# MARATHON

What to Expect
in Your First Marathon
and
How to Run Them
for the Rest of Your Life

(A companion volume to *First Marathons*)

## Gail Waesche Kislevitz

BREAKAWAY BOOKS
HALCOTTSVILLE, NEW YORK
2003

The Spirit of the Marathon
Copyright 2003 by Gail Waesche Kislevitz

ISBN: 1-891369-36-9
Library of Congress Control Number: 2003102250

Published by Breakaway Books
P.O. Box 24
Halcottsville, NY 12438
(800) 548-4348
**www.breakawaybooks.com**

FIRST EDITION

For Elijah and Anna, the two best moments of my life

# CONTENTS

**Part Two**
THE ELITES

**Part Three**
*FIRST MARATHONS* ALUMNI

**Part Four**
ADVICE AND SUPPORT

# FOREWORD

## Allan Steinfeld

# Why We Do It

Every year thousands of first-time marathoners participate in the thrill of a lifetime. Why do they do it? It's a good question and one that runners ponder themselves especially between miles 20 and 26. Every runner has his or her own specific reason for running the race. For the challenge, the athleticism, for the discipline, or simply because it's there. The marathon is a breathtaking, exhilarating, awesome experience. I can tell you this firsthand because every November I witness more than 30,000 runners crossing the finish line of the New York City Marathon and see it on their faces. Some are crying, some smile, some shout, others hold their arms high in a gesture of exuberance as if to say, *Yes, I did it!* The faces are stained with sweat and salt, sometimes soaked with rain, sometimes covered in road muck. No matter what condition they are in, they are all memorable to me because I see what's beneath.

I see the runner who gets up at 5 in the morning to get a run in before the kids leave for school. I see the runner who wants to get back in shape after sitting at a desk all day and runs in the dark with determination. I see the runner whose life is in need of repair and the marathon is the tool. I see priests, rabbis, police personnel, firefighters, foreigners, newlyweds, brothers, sisters, moms and daughters, dads and sons running side by side. I know the sacrifices they have all made over the past six months to get to the start and make it to the finish. Training to run a marathon is an all-consuming experience.

I know this because even though the marathon lasts for one day, for us at New York Road Runners it is a yearlong event. Most of the contact with the participants is through our clinics and races, but in my daily mail there is always a letter from a first-time marathoner about how the experience changed his or her life.

The marathon teaches us an invaluable lesson—the lesson of transcendence. The distance, 26.2 miles, is inconceivable for a person to run. On marathon morning, most runners will wake up to fear and trepidation at the daunting challenge that awaits them. After they have finished not only will they feel a tremendous liberation, but they are going to realize that they can do anything, anything, that they put their minds to doing. (Except perhaps walk downstairs normally the next morning.) The effort, the magnitude, and the energy of that day will change everyone involved. And if everyone takes the lessons and applies them to other areas of their lives, the success and impact of the race will continue to bring rewards for years to come.

Gail's interviews with first-time marathoners bring the race alive. For anyone who wants to know what it will be like to run 26.2 miles, these accounts are invaluable. You will struggle, you will hurt, and you may even hit the wall. But you will also know what it is like to fulfill a dream and achieve a personal best. And perhaps for the first time, you will come to know yourself like never before.

*Allan Steinfeld, Race Director, New York City Marathon*
*President, New York Road Runners*

# INTRODUCTION

# Catch the Spirit

If you have ever run a marathon, or are planning to, the usual question you are asked when word gets out about your goal is, "Why would you want to do that?"

It's hard to explain to someone who has never run one why we do it. The reason may be personal and intimate, such as a way of handling a midlife crisis or dealing with grief, or it could be quirky, such as losing a bet or no better reason than turning 40.

Why do we run marathons? For the spirit of it. Why do we continue to run more? To catch the spirit again and again. Webster defines the word *spirit* as "to infuse with energy." I doubt Webster ever ran a marathon, but his definition of that word hits the nail on the head. As you will see when you read these firsthand accounts of people's experience running their first, and sometimes second marathon and beyond, nothing compares with crossing the finish line of a marathon and knowing you achieved this once insurmountable goal all on your own. It's that spirit, that vigor, that animating principle of life that makes us run marathons.

Almost anyone can run (or finish in some fashion that resembles running) a marathon. It just depends on whether you are willing to sacrifice the time, the pain, relationships with your family and friends, the toenails, the cramping, the sleepless nights, running in the dark, the cold, the heat, the humidity and more, all for the sake of a five-cent piece of metal hanging on a tri-colored ribbon that becomes the equivalent of an Olympic gold medal and will proudly be displayed at home or the office.

Many first-timers cross the finish line and once they catch their breath, their first words are, "Never again." But a few weeks or perhaps a few months later, they find themselves picking up a running magazine, or bumping into their training partner, or glancing through the marathon pictures again and the seed that was planted at the first marathon begins to grow again. You didn't know that the marathon seed is a perennial? Some may view it more like poison ivy that starts to itch and needs to be scratched.

The training log comes out for a review and the questions start to haunt you. Maybe if I train harder I can better my time and break five hours? *Maybe if I run more 20-milers I won't hit the wall? Maybe I should run a different, faster, flatter course? Maybe this year I'll get into the New York City Marathon?*

That's when you know you've caught the spirit. You've caught the spirit when you are having a bad day and the only thing that cheers you up is a glance at your marathon finish-line photo sitting on your desk. You know you've caught the spirit when you attend another marathon not as a runner but as a spectator just to see and vicariously feel their contagious spirit. Or when you see a runner on the street and give the thumbs-up because you how good it feels. You know you've caught the spirit when someone asks your finishing time and you don't mind telling just how long it took because you accomplished your goal and that's all that matters.

The spirit of the marathon is found in Cathy Troisi, who has run 104 marathons since her first in 1992 and does most of them as a fund-raiser for cancer research. The spirit is also found in pioneer marathoner Kathrine Switzer for having the guts to run the Boston Marathon back in 1967 before women were officially allowed to run Boston and was almost physically knocked out of the race by the irate race director. She went on to become an influential spokesperson for women's rights on and off the track worldwide. Gary Mellor caught the marathon spirit, fulfilled a lifelong ambition to be an athlete, and finally exorcised the demons that haunted him since high school when he was always picked last for intramural sports. Abe Weintraub of Brooklyn, New York, ran his first marathon at 80 and set a world age-group record at 90. He embodies the spirit of the marathon.

And finally, the approximately 500,000 people who ran a marathon in 2002 all caught the spirit and lived to tell their tale over and over again.

## The Best of Times

Today an estimated 5.4 million Americans run at least three days a week, and major marathons are swelled beyond capacity and sell out in weeks. Keep your fingers and toes crossed if you want to get into the New York City Marathon or The Marine Corps Marathon, both of which turn away thousands of applicants.

In the U.S. there are over 300 marathon courses to choose from—and new ones are appearing every year. The Suzuki Rock 'n' Roll Marathon organization, which had its inaugural marathon in San Diego in 1998 and has since spread to other areas of the country, is predicting 30,000 registrants for the newest arrival in the series, the Rock 'n' Roll Arizona Marathon, scheduled for January, 2004.

The average age of a male marathoner is 38, and the female is 37. Males make up 60 percent of the field and females, 40 percent. The average finishing times are 4:10 for males and 4:38 for females. Overall, finishing times are continuing to show a slowing trend. For the five largest marathons in the U.S., Los Angeles averaged a finishing time of 5:14 in 2000 compared to 4:50 in '98; Chicago showed 4:26 in 2000 compared to 4:00 in '98; and Marine Corps showed 4:48 in 2000 compared to 4:38 in '98. The New York City Marathon and Honolulu stayed the same, 4:21:30 and 5:50 respectively.

Masters (runners over 40) make up 44 percent of the field, and their numbers have steadily increased by 2 percent per year. Our society is aging but also staying fit. This could be the reason for the slower finishing times.

To balance out the aging baby boomers, USATF Road Running Information Center researcher Ryan Lamppa sees a new trend in marathons towards a younger population. "A good sign for the growth of the sport is seen in a new population of under 30-year-olds who are running marathons, particularly themed ones like Rock 'n' Roll," says Lamppa. "These are the kids of the parents from the first running boom back in 1976. If this trend continues, as we think it will, there should be a new running boom in ten years that will equal or surpass that of the baby boomers."

Marathons are also becoming more family-friendly. Savvy race directors are making the run a destination for the entire family, not just the runner. Most marathons now offer half-marathon distances, fun runs for the kids, entertainment, celebrity autographs, and an entire weekend of marathon-related events. For many marathoners this is welcome news. But for some purists, this new focus is an albatross. Thankfully, there are plenty of both types to satisfy everyone. Want to compete? Qualify for Boston. Want to bring the family? Enter the Walt Disney World Marathon.

### A New Emphasis on Health and Fitness

The lifestyle of today's runner has evolved from the mentality of running through pain and 100-mile weeks to one that fits nicely into a hectic schedule complete with career, family, and other distractions. More and more, the impetus for running is fitness and fun versus high mileage and competition. Treating injuries has also gotten more advanced, with the main premise being to treat the cause, not the result, so that most running injuries are now curable. Most sports doctors agree that it is not how old you are that increases your chance of injuries but how well you prepare and stretch and take of your body that makes the difference in injury prevention. Finally, we are learning to run smarter.

### Own Your Running

Medical research has proven beyond a doubt that running is one of the healthiest forms of exercise. Some feel that a marathon may be an extreme version of the sport, but if you are inclined to go for it, do so. But what is more important than running a marathon is to make running your own. By that, I mean to embrace it and love it and nourish it as you would a best friend. Don't leave it at the finish line of your first marathon like a one-night stand. Don't give it up when the crowd disperses or your team-in-training pals go home and you are left with nothing but a hamstring pull.

Your goal should be to make running a life-affirming constant and stride through life with the same passion and commitment that got you running in the first place. As your connection to running change through the decades, accept them and work with them rather than ignore or resist them. Today, most Americans will live to approximately 75 years of age; by the year 2035, one in every four Americans will be over 65. As long as we are all going to live longer, why not make the most of those years? Will your times slow down as you get older? Probably. So what? The fact that you are running at all makes you more physically and mentally fit than most Americans.

Running serves as a positive force in our lives. Many runners describe having out-of-body experiences or define their running as a spiritual awakening, similar to going to church or the temple or wherever their faith leads them. Whether you refer to it as a runner's high, an endorphin fix, stress relief, private time, or just letting it all go after a long day's work, owning your running will make you a better runner because you are doing it for yourself. No one else, no other cause—just you.

So embrace the spirit of running and witness the spirit of the marathon as experienced by these runners who ran their first marathon and then some.

*Gail Waesche Kislevitz*
*January 2003*

# PART ONE

## MARATHONS AND BEYOND

The following 27 stories are real-life accounts of people's experiences running their first, and sometimes second, marathon. What I have attempted to do in this book, which is somewhat different from *First Marathons,* is to discuss what runners do after they've run their first marathon. Some of the stories concentrate on the second marathon, or perhaps a triathlon or other event. You will be surprised to find that as most runners cross the finish line of their first marathon, their immediate reaction is usually, *Never again*—like Gary Mellor, who had an excruciating time running his first marathon, or Jennifer Lou who whined the whole way home to her parents about what an awful time she had.

I don't want to give away the surprise endings, but they both went on to run more marathons. Why? It may take a few days or weeks or months, but at some point you start to wonder if you could have done better. Okay, the first marathon was a long shot. You did it, but maybe if you train differently, or harder or longer you can better your time. The other reason is to go for the goal again, to focus on something that takes months of preparation and gets you through some difficult times. If life is taking a nasty turn, run a marathon; you feel better afterward. And finally, after the pain goes away and you can walk normally, and the pictures and medal are still stroking your ego, you actually convince yourself that it wasn't that bad.

Not everyone sticks with the marathon. Some switch to other endurance sports like the triathlon or take up racing at shorter distances, like Sid Howard. Sid ran nine marathons but never felt comfortable, as if his body were rebelling and telling him to do something different. He quit the marathon and became a world-class miler.

No matter how many marathons people run, whether it's one or two or fifty or more, they all remember their first one. And when they stop running marathons, for whatever reasons such as health, or age, or moving on to something else, they always hold out one ounce of hope, one glimmer, that someday they may run another.

Here's a list of some of the things you can do after the glow of the first marathon has faded.

**Recover.** Take a few days, even a few weeks off from running. You and your body deserve it, even require it. Most muscle soreness comes on two or three days after the race due to inflammation or swelling in the muscle tissue, so you won't be going anywhere fast soon. But don't lose total sight of your running routine. A nice walk the first few days will help to get the muscles limber again after their epic effort. It's hard to get back into the swing of things if you idle too long. This may also be a good time to go for a massage, which will help stimulate the blood flow, stretch the tendons, and break up scar tissue, all of which help speed recovery.

**Write it down.** Record your memorable day in writing and validate it for posterity. You can also make a scrapbook of all your marathon memorabilia such as your race number, official finisher's diploma, all those great before and after race shots, and the congratulatory notes from family and friends.

**Resume running.** Slowly but surely resume your premarathon routine and get back into the swing of things. Enjoy that "runner's high" again after beating yourself up with long training runs. Remember, you are a true runner now so prove it by getting out there.

**Join a running club.** If you haven't already, this is the best way to preserve your training and be among people who will appreciate your efforts. Heck, they may even let you tell your marathon story again.

**Shorter-distance races.** Pick up the pace again with short-distance races like a 5K or a 10K. It will get you back in the pack, and it will feel great to cross a finish line again

**Cross-train.** Take a break from the pounding and pick up cycling or swimming to preserve your joints and bones. It's a great way to stay in shape, mix up the exercises, and not lose any cardiovascular conditioning.

**Do a duathlon.** Now that you've started biking, incorporate a bike and run race. It's fun and a great way to mix it up.

**Try a triathlon.** The hottest sport right now is triathlon. It is manageable and easier than a marathon at the shorter distances, such as the sprint triathlon, which is usually a half-mile swim, 14-mile bike, and 5K (or sometimes 5-mile) run. Get wet, ride, and run for some new fun. When you feel accomplished at this distance, move up to the Olympic distance, a half Ironman, or the whole enchilada, the Ironman.

**Volunteer.** Now that you are a spokesperson for your sport (all those marathon stories?), give back and help out at a local race. Learn what's it like behind the scenes.

**Another marathon.** Time to consider biting the big one again. This time, be different. Try one in a different state, or country. Some people get creative and decide to run a marathon in every state or region of the country or choose a goal such as running 26 marathons, one for every mile of a marathon. Others tend to savor the same course and run it repeatedly.

# THE (MARATHON) TRIALS OF HIS LIFE

**RICH BYRNE**

**D.O.B.: 10-17-64**
**RESIDENCE: SCIOTA, PA**
**OCCUPATION: MANAGER,**
  **THE RIDGEWOOD RUNNING CO.**
**FIRST MARATHON: 1984 NYC**
**MARATHON**
**AGE AT FIRST MARATHON: 20**

*Rich Byrne ran his first marathon as a cocky, self-assured kid and almost quit the sport for good after a disastrous run. Sixteen years later, with some maturing and better training under his belt, he decided to tackle the monster again and was rewarded with a strong and impressive finish. He credits running with keeping him focused and on track through some rough patches in his life. Now a manager at a running store, his running and his life are back on track. Especially since he just qualified for the 2004 men's Olympic marathon trials.*

I was a baseball player in high school. Never even thought of running. But the standardized physical fitness tests changed all that. When the tests were introduced and we all had to take them, I ran the 660-yard dash faster than anyone in the school—and that was on a terrible track. It had ruts and holes in it. It was condemned! It was like running on a beach, it was so sandy. So even under those conditions I ran the fastest time in the history of the school. I had no idea I could run like that.

The physical education teacher approached me and suggested I go out for cross-country. I had no idea what he was talking about. "What's cross country?" I asked him. He hooked me up with the coach and I gave it a shot but told him come spring, I was definitely going to play baseball. That was my game, not this running thing.

Being on the cross-country team was a new experience. It was painful and I didn't know what I was doing but I was hooked after the first practice. The first time I ran 5 miles it killed me but I loved it. I never went back to baseball. Running gave me a sense of personal accomplishment I never felt from playing other sports and it did wonders for my self-esteem. My home life wasn't always the happiest place to be and running saved me. It kept me out of trouble and got me into college.

I had a cousin who was one of the best runners in my county and he became my role model. Looking back on my high school years, I now realize if I hadn't found running I honestly don't know what would have become of me. Being on the team gave me that opportunity to take another path in life and I am very thankful I did.

I received over 30 scholarship offers and chose the University of Houston. The coach flew to my high school to meet me but the day he showed up I had cut classes. I didn't know he was coming and my guidance counselor finally found me at home. I was the first one in my family to go to college. This was a big deal, and I was excited but apprehensive at the same time. The level of competition was intense. Carl Lewis was my teammate; that's how good our team was. On top of that I was a poor student and homesick. I left after one year. In hindsight, that was the biggest mistake of my life. I returned home and continued running on my own.

In 1983 I watched the New York City Marathon and decided I could do it. As a runner I wanted to be a part of it and thought I could do well. At the time my longest run was 14 miles, so I worked out my own training schedule, which included weekend long runs up to 20 miles, one day of track workouts, and double-session runs three times a week. I averaged 90 miles a week.

By November I was ready. In fact, I was cocky. At the start of the marathon I was up front with all the elites and felt ready to burst. I still remember listening to the Alan Parsons Project blasting out of the speakers right before the gun went off. I was pumped. My goal was to run a sub-2:20 so I could prove to myself that I could run the Olympic trials qualifying standard time, which was 2:19:04 in 1984.

As prepared as I was, the one thing I couldn't control was the weather. That year was the hottest year on record for the marathon, 70 degrees at the start with high humidity. I knew to adjust my pace but I didn't know about adequate water intake. At the halfway mark my time was 1:10. I tried to take in water but it's difficult to get enough out of the little cups. So much gets wasted I probably only managed about 4 ounces for each water stop—and on a dangerously hot day, that wasn't near enough.

At mile 20, I hit bottom all in one shot. One step I was running, the next step I was walking. I didn't hit a wall; I hit a freight train doing 200 miles per hour. I was also delirious and dehydrated. I tried to eat anything I could get my hands on like orange slices and doughnuts. Sitting on the curb, my only thought was how I was going to get back to Central Park. I was so despondent I wasn't even angry or disappointed. I walked/ran the next 5 miles and then managed to run—sort of—the last mile. My only emotion was that I was happy to be alive. Although I finished in 2:39, I was so disappointed in myself I swore I would never run a marathon again in my life.

As soon as I crossed the finish line, I started vomiting; my friends had to carry me home. It took me one year to recover my overall health after that experience and another two or three before I could run with the same level of intensity. I suffered chronic stress fractures, ankle problems, the whole works. I ran a very stupid marathon. I only knew how to run fast and didn't take into consideration the potentially fatal effects of the heat.

For 16 years I never wanted to even hear the word *marathon*. I put it out of my thought process and just concentrated on getting my life together. I continued to run and started racing shorter distances with a passion and set times that placed me in the top 30 in the nation for the 10K. I was winning enough cash at the races to support myself in a very Bohemian lifestyle. Things were going well until I got injured and my running life crashed again.

In 1991 I joined the air force, got married, and went back to school to finish my college degree. By 1996 I was out of the Air Force, divorced, and working in a post office. I started racing again but not with any real spirit or passion for it. I was miserable; it was a low point in my life. The one constant was my running. And now, my running took on a different perspective. I wasn't racing; I was running while pushing my son, Mason, in a baby jogger. I had become a recreational runner and actually enjoyed it. For the first time, I noticed the scenery. There was no self-inflicted pressure to set goals or beat a time. Running was now immersed in all aspects of my life, not just a means to an end or obtaining a ranking. Going out for a 30-minute run with my son was the best part of my day.

I started coaching postcollegiate runners at a local college, and being around the runners got my competitive spirit going again. It was like my own self-help program. It brought back my self-esteem and gave me something to focus on besides being miserable, lonely, and goalless.

In 1999 I thought about doing another marathon. But getting time to train was near impossible with my postal job and the joint custody schedule for my son. In May of that year I ran a 10K and met a friend of mine who'd just opened up a running store and was looking for a manager. This was the perfect fit I needed. Taking that job turned my life around.

With my life back on track, I decide to run the 2000 Chicago Marathon. My hours at the store allowed for more training time, plus my running was encouraged! My boss liked the fact I was running a marathon. It's good business for a running store.

I approached my marathon training more scientifically this time around, not concentrating just on speed. My goal was to run fast and avoid beating up my body. Everything was going according to plan until three weeks prior to the marathon date when my knee started aching. I ran a 16-miler to make sure my knee would hold up and went to Chicago.

My goal at the start of my second marathon was to just finish. I was too worried about my knee to set a time. I went out slowly but at mile 14 a pain in my knee came on as if someone stuck a knife in it. It hurt so badly I thought about dropping out but I'd brought some pain medicine with me and decided this was the time to use it. As I pulled the tablets from my pocket, I dropped them and, in horror, watched them roll away into the gutter. There was nothing I could do. I kept running through the pain. One part of me wanted to drop out but the other part kept me going. Around mile 19 my knee went numb or I mentally blocked out the pain; I'm not sure which.

I finished in 2:32:10, and set a marathon PR (personal record). Despite the fact I couldn't walk, I was thrilled. As I crossed the finish line I promised myself I would never run another marathon again. A week later I was thinking how I could improve my time. I went to a surgeon to check out my knee and it turned out to be a tracking problem, nothing really serious. Exercises helped, and soon I was planning my next marathon.

I ran Chicago again in 2001 and finished 32nd overall, the seventh American to finish. That started me thinking that I had a shot at the U.S. Olympic marathon trials for 2004 so I set a new goal to qualify for the trials in Chicago in 2002.

I took my marathon training to an even higher scientific level. During training I had my blood levels checked every month to make sure my blood chemistry is where it should be for optimum results. I also got $B_{12}$ shots to combat fatigue and took iron supplements. I made a few dietary changes but still eat junk food. And depending on the monthly blood results, I altered my supplements or diet to meet the ranges I needed.

It all came together for me and I ran a 2:19:11 at Chicago and qualified for the U.S. Olympic trials in 2004 at the age of thirty-eight.

Running is my life. I work at a running store. All my friends are runners. It is how I identify myself. From the time I ran my first marathon at twenty years old to my second at thirty-six, I'd like to think I've matured. I can get over a bad race in a heartbeat whereas when I younger it would ruin me for weeks and months. I've learned to compartmentalize running so it doesn't take over. I don't even mind the five surgeries I've had from running-related injuries or the chronic anemia that saps my energy.

What I've learned over the years of running is that it is not so much the goal itself as the process to get there. I enjoy the long runs through the park in the early morning. I love the training and preparation for a race. I love coaching new runners and teaching them to love running as a lifelong sport. And I met my goal of being on the starting line of the 2004 Olympic Marathon Trials.

# WHAT IF I'M LAST?

**DALE CHRYSTOF**

**D.O.B.: 10/27/53**
**RESIDENCE: CHICAGO, IL**
**OCCUPATION: CARDIAC**
  **ULTRASOUND TECHNICIAN**
**FIRST MARATHON:**
  **2000 CHICAGO MARATHON**
**AGE AT FIRST MARATHON: 46**

*Dale is a classic first-timer. Never an athlete, she found herself teaching an aerobics class as part of her masters degree program. But first she had to get herself in shape so she could face the other younger, slimmer, fit instructors. That led to jogging, which led to running, which led to racing. Then she dragged her husband into the act and all hell broke loose as they both decided to run a marathon. Her biggest fear was not that she wouldn't finish, but that she would get lost and be last. Her account is filled with hilarious first-time mistakes they made and still had the ability to laugh at in the face of starvation and total exhaustion. Dale and her husband are two true marathon troupers.*

I began running around 1992 or so. I was starting a masters degree in exercise science and cardiac rehab and part of the program was to lead warm-up exercises for members of our community health improvement program. I hadn't exercised in years and hadn't done any running since grade school although at that time, I was pretty fast for a girl. I also had never led any exercise or warm-up group before. I occasionally participated in the exercise class but could barely get through it. I worried about whether I would even be able to lead an exercise class if I couldn't do the moves—unlike the other students who were younger, thinner, and experienced in the ways of fitness training. I hit the gym to learn how to use the equipment and to get fit. Then, since I had a lot of time on my hands between classes and there was an indoor running track near my classes, I started jogging. At first I jogged with a classmate but eventually she lost interest. I continued and soon was able to jog an entire mile without stopping. I confined my running to the track at first because I went to school at night and I was really only trying to get into shape and kill time between classes. Running in the evening also helped me clear my head of all the day's clutter from work (I was considering changing jobs) and home (our home was currently under renovation and I was not very organized).

Slowly my distance increased to 2, 3, then 4 miles. One of my colleagues suggested that I run in a 10K race. I had never run that distance before, nor had I ever been in a race before. Naively, I agreed to sign up. I was a bit apprehensive not only because I had never run that far before but also because I was slow and was afraid I'd be last. *What if I'm last and lose my way?* My friend said that he had no doubt that I could run the distance; it was just a matter of how long it would take. I felt I had to at least be able to jog 6 miles just so I would know for sure that I could run that far. I built up to 6 miles in plenty of time to do the race, although it was only at a 9-minute pace. When race day came I put myself right in the front of the line. Being ignorant of running etiquette, I didn't know that you were supposed to line up according to your running pace. I started out at a pace that was way too fast for me, mostly so I wouldn't get mowed down by those people who rightly belonged in front, and I was quickly passed by the "real runners." I did finish though, in about an hour, give or take a few minutes, but at least I didn't get lost and I wasn't last. It was an inspiring event, running along the beautiful Chicago lakefront on an early Sunday morning, and I knew I'd race again.

Eventually I got my husband, Mike, involved in running so we could run together. We never cared that much about doing speed work; we were okay with just being penguins. Our running was for the health benefits not for the glory of winning or placing in our age groups. We ran a few 5K races and then I suggested a 10K race called Lake County Races. It started in Waukegan, Illinois and also included a marathon and half marathon. It was a point-to-point race so we parked in the parking lot of an outdoor musical theater called Ravinia. There was also a commuter train stop there. Our entry fee included the train fare from the parking lot to the starting line in Waukegan. In this race all racers started at the same starting line and ended their respective race at the appropriate distance, paralleling the railroad track. The marathon ended back at Ravinia. At each finish line there was also a train station so those of us not doing the marathon could just get back on the train and ride back to our cars. It was a neat setup. Before dawn we boarded the train, grateful to get seats so we could get a little snooze on the way. We didn't know anything about sports nutrition, sports drinks, or even runner's lube. Near the starting line I wondered why people were rubbing their various body parts with Vaseline. We didn't even have our own water bottles. There was plenty of water on the course and it never occurred to us that having our own water bottles might be a good thing.

Because it was April, the day started out crisp and dewy but was sunny and not too warm—just right, actually. We didn't worry about splits or our pace—we only had one pace; the pace that was comfortable for us to run and not get too out of breath. When we did get to the finish line we were a little dismayed that most of the food was gone, giving us a little education that the faster runners could be little piggies, taking more than they really needed (this was also an observation at other races we ran in). All that was left for us slow-pokes was a few bagel crumbs and pawed-over, mushy bananas. I wondered what would be left for those who were still behind us. *Oh well, incentive to get faster,* I decided.

I suggested to my husband that we do the half marathon the following year. He asked if I really knew how far a half marathon was. "Of course," I said, "twice as long as a 10K!" But he agreed to run it with me. We began training for the next year's race. This past race, being a mere 10K, I didn't feel that was a sufficient distance to have to worry about recovery. I had often run 6 miles in the weeks before the race. This race had been just another 6 miles to me. Mike, thinking that I would give up this silly notion, didn't take the training as seriously as I did. Until then he would meet me at the track at school after he got home from work and we would do our run for about 6 miles, not really knowing anything about training for a long race. After that distance, he balked a bit about going farther because he always was too busy to put in the time and I don't think he really wanted to do it. He also didn't want me to tell anyone about our attempt for fear that we would be jinxed and then doomed to failure. My running had become therapeutic and I wouldn't quit. The more he pooh-poohed me, the more stubborn I became. So on Saturdays I'd get up early and run outside in the park or on the track. My distances got longer and longer and one day I actually ran 12 miles. The following week I did it again, a half hour faster than before. Suddenly Mike noticed that I really *was* serious and he began to run the longer runs with me. Of course, by now there wasn't much time and he hadn't trained enough to finish without being totally done in. We finished in about 2 hours 40 minutes or so; I had barely broken a sweat and Mike was really tired and looked like he was ready to collapse. Again, most of the food was gone except for a few orange slices. After grumbling about that a little, we got on the train to be transported back to our car.

While we were en route to our car I suggested that we train for a marathon. Mike gasped in horror at my comment, again asking if I knew how far a marathon really was. "Yes," I responded, "twice as long as a half marathon." I also said that if he didn't want to do it he didn't have to. I did-n't mind, but I wanted to try it. I'm sure he thought that his wife had become deranged.

During the next year I began training for the Chicago Marathon. Being true to my nature, I did what most newbies did: too much too soon. My injury began as "shin splints" (they tell me), except I had read that with shin splints the shin pain occurs after the run when you've cooled off and goes away when you warm up. In my case, my shins didn't hurt at all except when I ran, and the pain (and tingliness) increased the longer I ran until my motor control of my foot was affected. The pain went away in minutes as soon as I stopped running. Clearly, my goal to run the marathon had to be put on hold until my foot problems were resolved, much to my chagrin.

I went from one podiatrist to another, each one fitting me with their own style of orthotics. Some of them watched me walk quickly in their waiting room; some didn't watch me do anything but sit on a table. None of them watched me run. Eventually my shin pain left and heel pain began. New orthotics were made but my podiatrist quite suddenly left the face of the earth, for reasons unknown to me, before he could fine-tune them, so I never really wore them. Eventually the heel pain resolved; one day I woke up and it was just gone, with no warning or fanfare. Then I had some down time while I helped take care of my dying mother and then again while I was recuperating from major surgery. My heel pain came back while I was recuperating from surgery, but now in the other foot. I was advised to stay off my feet, as if my pain were caused by overuse. Except I had already been off my feet for the previous six weeks when the pain started. I decided that my pain was probably due to my inactivity, not overuse, because I hadn't been doing any stretching or exercising during my convalescence. Sadly, I had also gained 30 pounds during two years of inactivity. I started to do light aerobic exercises, began walking and then running, without any orthotics. *How can these doctors fit me properly for orthotics when they've never seen me run?* I thought. *My running gait is different than my walking gait.* But gradually the heel pain became bad enough that I was forced to see yet another podiatrist. This time my running gait was observed on a treadmill and I was fitted for, you guessed it, another pair of orthotics. Part of my problem was plantar fasciitis and part of it was an irritable nerve in my foot. The new orthotics and the correct pair of shoes helped. Only now I experienced one thing I never had all the time I was running: blisters! A couple of adjustments helped and they got better, but my heel pain never quite went away. It was always there, my nasty companion, making itself known at each step. I could still run, but I *had* to stretch and I *had* to ice my heel every day to keep my pain down to a low roar.

My husband and I discovered a race that we both really enjoyed and have run in for several years. There is an 8-mile race around Mackinac Island every September. We eagerly put in the miles to do that race. It's flat, the weather is usually cool, and the scenery is always beautiful, although the island does have a definite horse smell to it, horses and bicycles being the only transportation allowed on the island. And although my heel was somewhat painful along the entire course, it was manageable.

Now, I felt, was the time to start thinking about my goal of running the

Chicago Marathon. Mike rolled his eyes at the suggestion, citing my age, weight, foot pain, time commitment, and a host of other reasons why I/we couldn't or shouldn't attempt it. That of course fueled my resolve and made me even more stubborn. I explained again that he didn't have to run it; I didn't want him feel obligated to do it just because I wanted to do this crazy thing. But he just said, "Of course I'll run it with you."

We began training for the October race in May, thinking that would be enough time to work up to a 20-miler a few weeks before the big day. That would be true if we had a better running base than we actually did. Being avid skiers, we don't run much in the winter; we ski. And just coming off the ski season we had to start at the beginning again.

To seal my commitment, I joined the "marathon team" to raise money for Children's Memorial Hospital, where I worked. I was probably the oldest, slowest, and heaviest team member, but they didn't care. I never attended any of their fun runs because I knew I'd probably be the slowest one of them and I'd be embarrassed about getting left behind; I'd rather run alone, or with Mike, because at least I'd be running with someone with the same pace. We finally began training for real. We experimented with running clothes and socks, selecting those that chafed the least. We experimented with runner's lube, even Tegaderm in an effort to find a system that worked for us in keeping chafing and blisters down to a minimum. Chafing of our thighs was not a problem because we run in midthigh-length stretch shorts, but our arms were vulnerable. I also had a problem with chafing from my jog bra, so I started wearing them inside out so the seams were not against my skin, although it looked kind of weird when I wore tank tops. I used Tegaderm to cover tender areas where my jog bra rubbed, which worked great until I got excessively sweaty.

Mike didn't have any foot problems per se, but he tended to get blisters in the oddest locations, like on the balls of his feet or between his toes. Part of our training included learning to identify "hot spots" on our feet before they became blisters. In spite of all our foot woes, we felt we'd be ready on race day.

We experimented with the various energy drinks and gels and found a brand of energy gel that caused the least amount of gastrointestinal discomfort. We only used half of a gel packet because consuming a full one made us feel a little queasy. We developed a system where we'd run 15 minutes and walk 5, and every third walking break we'd split an energy gel pack. I got to be pretty good at ripping the gel pack open with my teeth a few seconds before our walking break started so I could quickly suck out half of the packet and give the rest to my husband. The idea was to swallow the stuff and water as soon as possible so that we'd have a full five minutes for it to be absorbed before we started running again. The system worked for us and although we hadn't done a 20-miler before the race, we felt confident that we could finish in the allotted time needed to get the finisher's medal.

Slowly but surely we increased our mileage, trying to increase it as fast as possible yet still not overdo it. We hit a plateau when we got to 13 miles for our long run and a bunch of piddly things kept us from progressing. We were stuck at 13 miles for the long run for three or four weeks. For one thing, I had nasal surgery so I was down for a couple of weeks. Then I still had my nagging heel pain. Some days it was sorer than others, and the intensity really didn't seem to be related to my running intensity. The pain's intensity could change several times during the day for no apparent reason. I iced, stretched, took oral NSAIDs for weeks, then steroid injections followed by oral steroids. Each thing made my heel feel better for a little while but it never went away. I realized I'd just have to grunt it out. By the time we progressed to our first 18-miler the marathon was just weeks away.

As race day approached, we had our system ready and working. Then we made our first big mistake: listening to the advice of our running friends who had done the Chicago Marathon in previous years. They advised us to leave our water bottles at home since there are so many water stops along the way and that we didn't want any more weight to drag around with us than absolutely necessary. Being naive, we took their advice and left them at home, although I didn't feel good about that. The second mistake was to heed the advice of the Chicago Marathon registration guide, the part where they told you where to park your car. They told where to exit Lake Shore Drive to get to the underground garage in Grant Park, where the race would start. They also said that the best place to park was one and a half miles away at historic Soldier Field, home of the Chicago Bears. There would be shuttle buses to take runners to and from the race start/finish.

Race day finally arrived! My heel pain, while still present, was behaving itself. We ate our predetermined race-day breakfast, which we had previously experimented on. The weather promised to be good. No rain or snow, just cool, crisp, and sunny. We were ready. I was psyched; I think my husband just wanted it to be over.

We drove to the race on Lake Shore Drive, preparing to get off before downtown so we could get into the underground garage, as the race information packet had instructed, except that the exit was closed down because of the race! So we couldn't get off. *Well,* I thought, *we'll park at Soldier Field— no problem.* We followed the directions to Soldier Field as described by the race information packet, except that from the direction we were coming from, the exit we were supposed to take was (again) blocked in preparation for the race. Well, I knew of a way to get off farther down the road, turned around and finally made it to the parking lot. The instructions also said there'd be shuttle buses to take us to the start, but they didn't say where they'd be. We never saw any shuttle buses and were afraid to stand there and wait for fear that we'd miss the start. So we walked the mile and a half through the park to the starting area. Of course at that time of year it was still dark with limited lighting in the park, but we made it okay, glad that we hadn't gotten mugged along the way. It was a nice warm up walk, except that the race wasn't starting for another hour or so, *and* now my heel pain was exquisite. No way was I going to tell this to my husband after all we'd been through training for this race. So I kept quiet about my pain. I had spent months learning to focus my thoughts and I knew I could focus my pain into oblivion. Yeah, right.

Because we didn't bring our water bottles with us I brought a fanny pack with lots of energy gel packets, extra Tegaderm, blister block, moleskin, and a tiny pair of scissors. I thought about the irony of leaving our water bottles at home partly to get rid of excess weight only to bring all this other stuff. I also brought a disposable camera. My husband just shook his head when I pulled it out but I wanted to document my first marathon. I took pictures of the sunrise over Lake Michigan and at various other places along the way. I took them on the fly rather than stop and compose a good picture, because of our time constraint. Oh well, the camera didn't have a flash on it anyway so most of the photos were kind of dark.

We finally lined up for the race. This time we were way in the back with the other penguins. In fact, we were so far back that we didn't even hear the starting gun go off. We just sort of noticed that the crowd started to move forward and we just followed the person in front of us, like lemmings to the sea. It took us 15 minutes to even get to the starting line. God bless those timing chips! We would have liked to have waved to the photographers perched above us at the starting line but by the time we got there, there was so much debris from the runners ahead of us who threw off their jackets, hats, gloves, and other stuff, we would have tripped and fallen over all this stuff. The first mile was more like an obstacle course than a racecourse. I pitied any poor soul who may have trained relentlessly for months to be in this race, only to trip crossing the starting line over someone's jacket.

We finally got out of the downtown area and the multitudinous runners spread out a little more. We began to enjoy the path along the lakefront and got into our stride. Uh-oh, only 5 miles into the race and already my husband was developing a blister. At least it was just a hot spot at this point so I could just cover it with a blister blocker. It was on the bottom of his foot, of all places, and his foot was sweaty so the blister blocker wouldn't stick. I had no choice but to dry his sweaty foot with my T-shirt (this must be love) so I could reapply the tape. This time it held in place. Farther down the road there were bands playing and people all dressed up in costumes on the side cheering us on. I took out my camera to get a picture. I discovered that it was hard to take pictures while running; you have to keep both eyes open. I hadn't practiced this while training for this race. I didn't want to tell my husband that I was taking pictures as a diversion from my heel pain, my companion from hell. And we hadn't even gotten to the halfway point yet. Well, at least it wasn't getting worse. How could it? It was already maxed out. But I could still focus on putting one foot in front of the other, and that was good.

We soon realized that leaving our water bottles at home was a *big* mistake. Although there was water stop every one and a half miles along the way, those stops did *not* correspond to our fifteen-minute run / five-minute walk routine. When we were supposed to be walking and taking in an energy packet, there was no water to drink with it. When we got to a water stop it would be just after a walking break and we were in our running period. We got totally out of sync. So we occasionally ran right after taking our energy packet, which didn't agree with our tummies, or we just didn't take our energy gel at all— another mistake.

By the time we got to mile 13, my heel was really sore although I didn't think it was possible for it to hurt worse than before. Also, I was getting really tired, since our routine of taking carbs in every so many minutes had been disrupted. Apparently my training hadn't been enough after all, and I was feeling disheartened. I still refused to say anything to my husband; I kept hearing *I told you so* in my head and decided it would be more painful to hear him say that to me than to just keep going. We started drinking the energy drinks offered at the water stops, but since we were in the last third of the runners, they had occasionally run out of it by the time we got there. We still had energy gel packs, but didn't use them as often as we should have and when we did, we started running too soon afterward so our tummies began be unhappy.

The neighborhoods we ran through were interesting and varied and included New Town, where the more colorfully flamboyant citizens lived, Greek Town, Pilsen, the Gold Coast (where the upper-crust wannabes live), Little Village (a Hispanic neighborhood), and Chinatown to name a few. It was interesting to see the different architecture, ethnic smells, and people who had come out to cheer us on. It was like one big festival. It was a beautiful autumn day, sunny and cool, so I didn't have to be concerned about the weather, just focus on the task at hand. But I was getting really tired, and was in pain. All the merriment, bands playing (too loud), along the way and all the revelry were now becoming distracting. The worst part was when we were going through Chinatown, which came around mile 18. The various smells of the Chinese restaurants, which normally made my mouth water, now made me gag. As we progressed under a railroad bridge, someone thought it would be helpful to cheer us on by banging on a large gong over and over again. I had visions of where I wanted to stick that gong and I wanted to say, *Shut up! I'm trying to focus here!* But I didn't; I just plodded on, my self-controlling side once again conquering my darker, primordial side. Our regimen of run fifteen/walk five degraded into a run ten/walk ten regimen. The mistimed consumption of our energy gels and Gatorade (when we could get any) was making my husband, and myself to a lesser extent, nauseous and after a while, he was unable to drink even water for fear of upchucking.

We finally passed by White Sox Park and began the final leg of the race, heading back to Lake Shore Drive. They were passing out small bananas now but I couldn't even imagine eating anything; I'd never get it down. I was also developing a blister, but at this point I doubted if I'd even be able to bend over to put a bandage on it, so I ignored it. As we headed down Lake Shore Drive to McCormick Place we fell behind a group of racers who were running with a race pacer. They were singing! *How can they be singing,* I thought incredulously? *Shut up, shut up! There's no singing at mile 23 in a marathon!* I thought. I was wiped, thirsty, I was getting a blister, my heel was killing me, and my poor husband was approaching pukedom. Our run/walk routine was now run five/walk fifteen so we were way behind our projected finishing time. And time was also running out before they stopped giving out the finisher's medal (so they said). We had to finish and get that darned medal. Then we got to McCormick Place and I knew the end was near. My spirits picked up a little as we went down the ramp onto Lake Shore Drive. *Only a couple of miles to go now; I can do this.* Then I saw the 26-mile marker! We just had to go up the ramp off Lake Shore Drive, cross the street, and we're done! Woo woo! The exit ramp we took to get off the drive was uphill (of course). *Walking is good* was my mantra that I kept saying to myself over and over; just to keep moving, knowing the end was in sight. Suddenly, my husband stopped, saying that he couldn't run another step. "What!" I said. "You can't quit now, the finish is less than a block away! *Aarrggh!*" He assured me that he would finish; he just couldn't run any more. Whew! We walked up the hill and saw the finish line. There's something about actually seeing the finish line that gives you a little energy boost. As tired as we were, we actually jogged (slowly) across that blessed line, holding hands. They should pass out tissues along with those little silver wraps they give you when you cross the finish line, for I suddenly burst into tears as soon as I crossed it. We did it! We took on the challenge of this 26.2-mile monster, we were mightily tested, and yet we prevailed!

My husband suddenly declared that he had to sit down—now! I don't know how, but I found him a chair, sat him down, and got him some Gatorade, which he drank though a straw. Very quickly, he seemed much better and we got up and got our precious finisher's medals, had our finisher's photo taken, and walked to the food tables, where there was actually some food left. It was really good. I don't even remember what kind of food there was; I just ate it. It took us nearly six hours to finish a race we had projected would take five hours (later, our "official" time showed that my husband had beaten me by one second). But that's okay. We were done and it was worth it. We hobbled away to find a patch of lawn to sit on. I'm sure we looked comical to passersby in our effort to help each other, two middle-aged, sweaty, smelly penguins, to the ground. When we finally got on the ground I spied someone holding what looked to be a pint of beer in his hand. I (slowly) got up and asked him where he'd gotten it. I couldn't believe it: We had walked right past a big beer truck. I figured that we'd earned it so I got us a couple of frosty cold ones, being very careful not to spill a drop as I hobbled back to where my husband was lying on the ground.

After we rested, stretched, and quaffed our beverage, we sort of leaned on each other like two drunken sailors as we attempted to feebly get back on our feet. Then we looked for the shuttle buses that our race packet assured us would be waiting to whisk us back to our car one and a half miles away. There weren't any. So we slowly walked back, me with my wretchedly sore heel, retracing our steps from this morning. In the daylight, we could now see where we were walking and actually enjoyed the lakefront scenery. It was our turn to cheer on the runners who were still chugging toward the finish line, now running on the sidewalk because the streets had been reopened to traffic. I could feel their pain, since they had been hoofing it for two hours longer than us (and for them, there probably wasn't any food left). Still, we were stunned by our achievement. "Well," I said, "now that we know what our mistakes were, we can correct them for our next marathon." My husband turned to look at me as if I were insane, his jaw agape and his eyes bugged out. He just shook his head and we continued our walk to the car—in silence.

# SINGING THE MARATHON BLUES

**STEVEN COUSINS**

**D.O.B.:** 1-17-57
**RESIDENCE:** STONE MOUNTAIN, GA
**OCCUPATION:** ENGINEER, COCA-COLA
   CORP.
**FIRST MARATHON:** 2001 COUNTRY
   MUSIC MARATHON, NASHVILLE
**AGE AT FIRST MARATHON:** 44

*A cyclist first and foremost, Steven thought his endurance and training as a biker would see him through his first marathon. Wrong! He did train but made the mistake of thinking that long rides would compensate for long runs. When he finished his first marathon, I asked him how he felt and he replied, "It hurts!" Despite his initial feeling Steven is planning on doing another—only next time he intends to train better.*

On Saturday, April 28, 2001, I ran my first marathon—the second annual Country Music Marathon in Nashville, Tennessee. I am not entirely happy with the experience or about my performance. Before this marathon I participated in a number of recent organized athletic events. Biking is my main focus, and I've participated in 40 organized running and cycling events over the past four years. This was my first time running a marathon and I expected more out of it.

For most people it seems that their first marathon experience leaves them feeling that they could do almost anything. It is one of the highlights in their lives and they describe their experiences with exhilaration. For me, after this first marathon I'm thinking that maybe I'm not in as good physical shape as the average runner. And maybe I'm not in good physical condition at all. I thought being in great shape for biking meant being in great shape for running. As a result of running this marathon, I think less of myself as an athlete.

My finishing time in the 2001 Country Music Marathon in Nashville, Tennessee, was 5:07:32. I placed 3,043rd out of 6,000 runners. My half-marathon split time was 2:22:09. My 20-mile time was 3:43:29. Yep, that's right, it took me 84 minutes to do the last 10K. But even more disturbing to me is how I felt after the marathon, which is the worst that I've ever felt after physical activity. By the time I finished, my thighs were in extreme pain and my lungs were burning. I was dizzy and felt like I was going to pass out. I was nauseous and weak. It was hard to support my weight. For days later, my thighs were weak and in pain and I could barely lift them. I had to walk up and down stairs backward.

Let me start at the beginning. Since deciding in mid-September 2000 that I wanted to run a marathon, I put in 370.5 training miles in 69 days of running. My average run was about 5.4 miles. I did five runs that were over 12 miles, with my longest run being 15 miles. Time is a rare commodity for me and since I refuse to significantly cut into my biking miles, running took a backseat. During that same time period I put in over 2,000 miles on the bicycle in 106 days of cycling so I thought I was in good shape and that the biking would compensate for the running. Was I ever wrong!

Despite possible inadequate training, I decided to go ahead and run the marathon. I'd been running on and off over the past three years and competed in a few 5K and 10K races, even completed the Atlanta Half-Marathon in a pretty good time. My plan was to take it easy and run a steady 11-minute-per-mile pace, and finish in under 4:50. I planned to follow the recommendations of the "experts" and take in fluids at 2-mile intervals and drink 1 to 2 cups of water. The weather was a negative factor that day as it was 65 degrees at 7 A.M. when the race started and by the end of the race it was up to 83 degrees. The race marshal called it a hot day for a marathon. Several who ran the same course the year before said this time it took them longer to finish, even though they trained more. In the aftermath, 19 runners were taken by ambulance to local hospitals, suffering from dehydration and muscle cramps. Dozens of others were unable to finish.

I spent the night before the marathon at a hotel near the Nashville Airport. The next day I went to the marathon expo at the Nashville Convention Center to get my race number and time chip and then walked about 3 miles of the marathon course, at the point of the longest hills. When I returned to the hotel I wanted to get into the pool but I did not want to risk contracting a virus (common to community pools) on the day before a marathon. I didn't do any carboloading the night before. My dinner consisted of two bananas and a 6-inch veggie sub from Subway. I watched the local news on television as I ate in my hotel room. Later, as I lay in bed, my mind drifted through concerns. Would my body hold up through 26.2 miles of punishment? Would the swelling of my right knee—which was bothering me—hold off and be pain free? I was concerned about my lack of training, and how it would manifest itself.

I set the alarm clock for 4:00 A.M. but woke up at 3:30 A.M. I put on my favorite pair of running shorts and shoes and a mesh singlet that's actually a biking shirt with rear pockets to hold bananas or a water bottle but I threw in a sweatband and a running hat to safeguard against the heat and sun. I was pretty relaxed at the start of the race and didn't put too much pressure on myself as my objective was the easy and seemingly simple and achievable goal of completing the marathon in less than five hours.

I arrived at the start of the marathon, Adelphia Stadium, at 5:00 A.M. Runners were herded to the starting chutes in the order of their bib numbers. I intentionally went to the back where the higher bib numbers and slower runners were staged. Despite the fact that I was behind thousands of runners, it didn't take long to reach the starting line once the race started—less than a minute. I was surprised at how fast the runners were going out. I was at the back in the slowest group and yet everyone was passing me. Numerous runners contorted their bodies to squeeze their way around me as they ran faster. Tens of dozens of people passed me within the first half mile.

As I approached the first water station, a huge mass of runners had engulfed the tables like ants covering a crumb. I didn't even realize that it was a water stop because so many runners had surrounded the tables and volunteers. I made my way to the center of the road to avoid the crowd and kept running. According to plan, I stopped at the next water station. It wasn't easy drinking the water as it was warm and tasted horrible, as if it had come from a bad water hose. Even the Ultima (the Gatorade-type beverage) had a bad taste, as if it had been mixed with bad water. I'd like to take a moment here to state my irritation with some of the volunteers manning the refreshment stations. I believe that it should be the runner's option and decision as to which water stop to take advantage of but at several of the stations, volunteers would take their cups of water and move into the middle of the roadway in futile attempts to force their water onto runners. Other runners and myself had to dodge and weave around these volunteers to avoid them or get through the refreshment area. I even saw runners bump into volunteers who would dart out into their path trying to force a cup of water onto someone. I think volunteers shouldn't interfere with the race; just fill empty water cups at the tables.

One of the selling points to the Country Music Marathon was the 27 bands along the course playing live music. I was inspired by the idea of running from band to band, listening to the music as I ran. It should have been energizing, but as luck would have it nearly half the bands were on a break as I ran past. I wish they had plugged in canned music during the break for inspiration but they didn't.

The course was packed with large crowds of spectators. The largest crowds were at the start, the 20-mile point, and the finish, which is the same point on the course because the last 6 miles loop out and back to the finish. The crowds were loudest at this point with their excited cheers. For about a quarter mile, all of the spectators on my side of the street laughed and jeered as I ran by, hysterically pointing in my direction. I wondered, *Could I be that ugly a runner?* I turned to look behind me and noticed three or four guys dressed like Dolly Parton. The only other costumed runner was a man in his late 50s dressed like Uncle Sam, in a star-spangled shirt and the American top hat.

After a while, I found the cheering to be downright annoying; it got old real quick. Much of the course was through residential areas of Nashville, and the locals made a party of it all with lawn chairs and tables in their yards or along the sidewalks. They had coolers and barbecue grills, beers and mixed drinks. They were loud and boisterous and I found the yelling and verbal barrage to be intimidating and deflating. What made it annoying was that some of the encouraging cheers were too unrealistic. People were yelling things like, "You look great," when you knew you looked like crap. Or, "Keep it up, it's all downhill from here," when you know that the worst hills are yet to come. Or, "Keep going, there's not much left," when you know there's over 10 miles left. I guess I'm used to running alone. All of my training runs were done solo, at hours of the day when no one is around. As I ran the marathon, I was wishing that all of the spectators would just go away and let me run in solitude.

The course winds through the Hillsboro-Belmont-Waverly area of Nashville, an older, heavily shaded part of town. Plenty of residents were spending their morning enjoying the runners go by. But what else was there to do? Their street was closed to vehicular traffic, and so many other city roads were closed that you couldn't easily go anywhere anyway. I saw chairs in front yards, chairs on heavily populated porches, chairs on roofs, people hanging out of windows—getting into the race festivities any way they could by engaging dialogue with the runners. I heard comments like, "We closed these streets off just for you," or "We planted these trees to give you shade for the race."

I passed a group of guys sitting in lawn chairs on the sidewalk with an open ice cooler of beer. Everyone had a beer and it looked like they had already consumed several others and it was not even nine in the morning yet. I yelled for a beer as I approached them, and one of the fellows reached into his cooler and handed me a bottle as I ran by but I didn't grab it, just laughed and kept going.

The course was mostly rolling hills as I ran back into the downtown area. At mile 9 a volunteer stood in the middle of the roadway with a box of energy gel packets. It was some brand of energy gel that I had never heard of called Carbboom. I took one and downed it on my way to the tenth mile. It wasn't exactly appetizing, but what gel is? And it didn't seem as if the gel packs were too popular as I saw what looked like unopened gel packets discarded by runners and scattered throughout the street. The same was true at the 17-mile point where gel packets were again being distributed. There seemed to be the most disdain for the Gatorade energy bars. They, too, were being distributed along the course at two points. As I ran beyond those distribution points, I would pass a sea of unopened or once bitten Gatorade bars discarded and strewn throughout the course over the half mile past the distribution point.

As I passed through the downtown area between miles 10 and 12, I engaged several runners in conversation or I listened in on the conversations of other runners. I spoke briefly to a runner from Newark, Delaware, who lived only a few miles from my old neighborhood in Pike Creek Valley, Delaware. She told me that there were runners from my old neighborhood running in that same marathon. I chatted with a fellow who ran in the Chicago Marathon six months earlier. I spoke with a woman who completed the New York City Marathon at the end of last year. I shared words with a three-generation family running the marathon together. Lots of runners had their names on their shirts or singlets. Spectators would call out encouragement to the runners by name as they passed through the streets. Once I realized this was going on, I was pleased that my name wasn't on my singlet. I ran close to a woman wearing running shorts that were in the pattern of the Texas state flag. Spectators referred to her as "Texas," yelling out things like, "Go, Texas, go." Or, "Hey, Texas, lookin' good."

The course headed north via a major city thoroughfare onto Metrocenter Boulevard into the Metrocenter business park. I considered this to be the dog-days section of the course, between miles 13 and 18. The scenery wasn't too pleasant, it was hot, the roads seemed to be sloped uphill, the bands weren't playing, and the cheering teams looked irritated. I took note of the cheerleaders through this section of the course. They looked too young to be high school cheerleaders, more like youth league cheerleaders. They looked like they were tired of cheering and just wanted to go home. Plus it felt like the temperature was over 80 degrees and there wasn't any shade, so I know it was tough on them as well as us.

I actually passed runners on this stretch of the course, as they ran out of gas and were at a standstill. Many were now walking. I continued to run and passed the greatest number of runners during that period of the day.

At mile 17 I was still doing 10.5-minute miles but my thighs began to get weary and a staple stitch developed but then disappeared by mile 20. By then I was running at an 11-minute-per-mile pace but even at that pace it was becoming burdensome to lift my thighs in a running motion. Consequently, my running pace sagged to 13.5 minutes per mile. I stopped to use a Porta-Potti. I wanted to stop earlier, but the lines were too long at all of the Porta-Pottis along the course. And I refused to run into the bushes and relieve myself (as I saw several of the runners doing). I can't believe it! What is it about a marathon that makes grown men and women urinate practically in the open public? I saw runners just pause against a tree, bush, or building and go—while in full view of observers. I had to wait for two others ahead of me in the Porta-Potti line, so I lost a little time. I also stopped twice to stretch so lost a little time there, too.

A nice downhill between miles 18 and 19 brought us back toward the downtown area. Once again, most of the participants along this section of the course were walking and I passed them all. These were probably runners who went out fast and had no more steam beyond 15 miles. I noticed that I was passing some of the same runners that passed me at the start of the race. I rounded James Robertson Parkway past the State Capitol Building and Municipal Auditorium. Running was getting increasingly difficult, and I was glad that the Victory Memorial Bridge crossing the Cumberland River was downhill. There were lots of spectators from the State Capitol Building to Main Street on the other side of the river. Running was hard and I was in pain. The cheers of the crowd, encouragement, and chatter seemed to be more like ridiculing taunts to me. I know that they were not meant to be. But my pain and attitude created that impression in me.

At mile 20, I ran by Adelphia Stadium and knew that this meant I had about another 6 miles before looping back to finish at the stadium. The crowds were thick here but I wanted them to all shut-up and leave me alone. I wanted to be ignored along the course but they would call out my number and say, "Hey, 6272, you look strong. Keep going, the race is almost over," but I knew I had some hard miles ahead of me. The course enters Shelby Park at mile 22, a peaceful pretty place to be on any other day but today. The 24th band played at the entrance to the park and the next band was at the exit, with less than 2 miles to go to the finish. As other runners picked up their pace to make a strong finish, I was unable to do so and kept to my 13-minute-mile pace.

Is it possible to run at a pace that is barely faster than a walk? I was having problems raising my thighs at all so my steps were protracted. My pace was less than that of a fast walk. Despite my pain, I chuckled at the Nashville Hash House Harriers banner, A DRINKING CLUB WITH A RUNNING PROBLEM.

This next comment will seem insignificant, but I began to notice marathon runners wearing their finisher's medals around their necks running in the opposite direction toward me as if they hadn't gotten enough running in so they were running more of the course in the opposite direction. I've seen this in organized bike rides. Actually, I've been guilty of doing the same thing in some of my organized century bike rides. Among the first finishers, I hadn't gotten enough so I rode the course backward to get in more miles. I never realized that people did the same thing in marathons. I guess I now know how some of those weary slower cyclists felt.

Finally, with less than a mile to go, I swung my arms wildly trying to get momentum and move faster—to no avail. The distance between the 25-mile point to the 26-mile point seemed to take a very long time. Once I hit 26 miles, I entered into what was the best imitation of a sprint that I could muster. It must've looked dumb because it was only a 12-minute mile pace. I saw the photographer's bridge ahead with the cameramen taking pictures of the marathoners as they crossed the finish line and thought, *Boy, if they photograph me it will sure make an ugly picture of a very forgettable moment.* The course was deeply lined with spectators from about 150 yards from the finish line, and they were noisy. They were yelling encouragement at everyone. I ran through to the finishing chute alone in painful isolation. I felt like crap, nauseous and weak. I just wanted to lie down.

My strained walk through the finish area was very much unsupportive. There were stations where the runners could get water, a Mylar blanket, fruit, their finisher's medal, and have the timer chip removed from their running shoe but no one seemed to want to give anything to me. I staggered through in an uncomfortable daze, not entirely cognizant of what was going on around me. A pack of volunteers had the water table blocked and I had to rip a bottle of water from a person's hand. I wrestled a mylar blanket away from a volunteer who seemed much more interested in playing around with her fellow volunteer friends. And I had to wait for someone to drape the finisher's medal around my neck—should've just picked one up off the table and kept going. It wasn't because the finisher's area was crowded—it wasn't. My theory is that since there weren't too many finishers coming into the area, and since the volunteers had been doing their duty for the past four hours, they had become restless and were more absorbed with entertaining each other than to be bothered with slower marathon runners like myself staggering in late.

I felt very weak and looked for some place to sit down, but the only tent provided was designated as a VIP area or exclusive to the charity fund-raiser participants. I dropped onto the ground at a small grassy point, drank the water, and didn't move for another 25 minutes. I felt weak, sick, and dizzy. I decided that I needed to move on, so as I soon as I had enough strength I walked to my truck and lay down in the back for another 15 minutes. Next, I drove to a convenience store a few blocks away and drank a 20-ounce Coke, a 20-ounce Sprite, a 20-ounce cranberry juice, and three 12-ounce bottles of V8 juice. I retreated to my truck and rested for another half hour, but still felt nauseous and dizzy so I decided to get something to eat. I went to a McDonald's and got a Big Mac. That Big Mac was magical. Within moments of eating it I felt stronger, the dizziness went away, and my nausea vanished. I shoved off and drove home to Atlanta.

As I mentioned earlier, I don't rate this first marathon experience as highly as most other organized athletic events that I've participated in. If I plan another marathon anytime soon, it will be a much smaller and cozier event.

# IN A MARATHON STATE OF MIND

**MICHAEL DOVE**

**D.O.B.: 2-11-47**
**RESIDENCE: MONTEREY, CA**
**OCCUPATION: DEFENSE DEPARTMENT**
 **MANAGER**
**FIRST MARATHON: 1989 BIG SUR**
 **INTERNATIONAL MARATHON,**
 **CARMEL, CA**
**AGE AT FIRST MARATHON: 42**

*Mike is the type of guy who believes in giving back to the running community, so every year he teaches a new group of first-timers how to tackle the Big Sur Marathon. His students love him and seem to come back for more, repeating the experience of running Big Sur time and again. He is a true believer in owning your running and not quitting after accomplishing the marathon goal. Mike has a gift of infusing his spirit for the marathon in all his students.*

I am a third-generation San Franciscan. Grew up in the Bay Area where my father was a championship tennis player. As a kid, I did just about every sport from baseball to golf. In high school I was on the basketball and golf team. In fact, golf was my favorite sport. I did run for one year in high school because the cross-country coach was also my English teacher and he practically guaranteed a good grade if you ran on his team. The fastest I ran was the 2-mile at 11:35 at age 16. Ironically, I run faster than that now at age 55.

I attended the University of California at Berkeley, as did my father and mother and oldest son, and continued with my golf on the university team. I was a pretty good competitive golfer. As for running, I never ran again from that one year in high school until I was 38 years old. Running was definitely not my thing. I loved golf, won a few tournaments, and it was easy to stay in shape for the game—just walk and drink beer. No conditioning whatsoever.

Ironically, it was golf that got me into running. My friend and I had planned a golf outing in Scotland, a once-in-a-lifetime trip, and I started running to get in shape for the hills of Scotland. After we returned, I picked up running because I had really enjoyed it and gradually gave up golf. What appealed to me about running was the competitive nature of the sport, and the camaraderie. Running is also more fair than golf. With golf, you can be perfect in practice and then enter a tournament and act like you don't know what the heck you are supposed to be doing out there. With running, if I put in the training for a 5K or 10K usually it paid off with a win. I had a lot of buddies who ran but in the beginning they wouldn't run with me because I was too slow. Gradually I got up some speed and with a bit of encouragement entered my first race at age 40, an 8K, and placed second in my age group, bringing home a medal. In all the years I played golf, I rarely brought home a medal!

At the race, I didn't know what to expect as I didn't know much about training. I just went out fast and stayed at that pace for as long as I could. Actually, I was amazed at how fast I ran. I flew through the first mile, so excited and on a high. Miles 4 and 5 were painful but satisfying and of course I died at the end. But it was all worth it and I got hooked. Did I mention how great it felt passing other runners? I guess that's my competitive spirit showing through.

After the race I started to get serious and bought Galloway's book on running. My buddies also gave me some tips but more than anything, I just seemed to have a sense of what to do. Maybe that came from all the sports I played in high school and years of being dedicated to golf. I started speed training on my own before I read the book and found I was doing everything correctly. I had good instincts when it came to training. I also watched the good runners and tried to imitate what they did.

I ran with a great bunch of friends. We were an informal group, not a club, although we evolved into our own informal club called the Monterey Bay Wednesday Night Laundry Runners. The story behind that is a bunch of people in Pacific Grove did their laundry on Wednesday and went for a run while the clothes were being washed and dried. Other people started to show up just to run and eventually we formed the club. We've got some excellent Laundry veterans with impressive credentials. There are a lot of good role models in the Bay Area and they always welcome the newcomers. Sometimes newcomers are afraid to run with the better runners but you learn so much from them; it's a great way to pick up valuable tips and training methods. Now that I am a volunteer coach of first-time Big Sur marathoners, I always tell my newcomers not to be afraid to get out and run with people who are better or faster than they are.

Before I get into my marathon story, I have to stipulate that I was one of those people who adamantly stated I would never run more than a 10K. My friends talked me into it. The inaugural Big Sur Marathon was in 1986 and my friends were running but it took me four years to decide to join them. I didn't even watch the marathon before that—and I live close to the finish line.

What got me to finally sign up was a combination of peer pressure and wanting to test myself, but truly, it was more the pressure from my pals that got me out there. And by then I viewed myself as a serious runner, no longer a tentative newcomer. Also I have to admit that subconsciously I think I held off the marathon until I knew I would do well.

To prepare for the marathon, I followed Galloway's book to the letter. I gave myself six months to train, and did it with my friends. Galloway comes out to Big Sur every year and I made a point of meeting him. He is the man! Back then, his regimen was a bit different, and his schedule called for a 22, 24, 26, and even a 30-miler. The reason I trained so hard was first, Galloway said to, and second, Big Sur is a very difficult and hilly course with the wind always in your face from north to south. Also, I did pick a finishing time of 2:50 for my first marathon. That may sound lofty, but in the book Galloway said I could do it if I trained for it. And if Galloway said I could, I knew I would.

The first thing I did when I made the commitment to run the marathon is to swear off alcohol and sweets from January through marathon day in late April. I should add that Galloway did not suggest this; I just thought it would help my training. I have a very compulsive personality, and although it wasn't easy I kept my vow. I happen to enjoy beer and wine and candy so this was a real test. My family got involved with my marathon and encouraged me along the way. All three of my kids are competitive swimmers so they had always known the rigors of training and competition; it was almost a bit of role reversal for me to finally experience what they go though with their sport.

I have a good friend, Mark, who is my age and broke three hours at Big Sur. There is a prize for the local runner with the best time and Mark usually won or was near the top. I could keep up with Mark on our training runs so there was a part of me that felt if everything went right, I would make my 2:50 time. And just maybe, I would beat Mark and bring home the prize.

The night before the marathon I was ready, but had absolutely no idea what to expect. I was still somewhat concerned and nervous, which is the beauty and challenge of a first marathon. It's a onetime, lifetime opportunity that you will never forget. To some degree, no matter how many marathons you run you will never experience the thrill of your first one.

Even though I had run 30 miles, it wasn't in a marathon so I was still unsure of what to expect when I was out there running the real thing. I can't say I slept much between a good case of the nerves and drinking water all night. In all honesty, I don't think anyone could have trained better for a marathon than I did. I was so dedicated to my training routine, coupled with the abstinence from alcohol and sweets, and my natural competitiveness, there was nothing I could look back on and wish I had done differently to prepare. I was as ready as I would ever be.

This may come as a surprise for people who don't know the Big Sur Marathon, but the runners get bused to the start between 4 and 4:30 A.M., as it takes about an hour to travel the 26.2 miles down Route 1. It is a very circuitous road and the runners take this in with a shudder as they view the course from the bus. I was up at 3 in the morning, ready to go and face the race, which starts at 7 A.M. Some other facts about the Big Sur Marathon that separate it from the norm are that the average finish is around 5 hours and only a small percentage break three hours, about 30 runners each year. The course is unmerciful but the views make up for it.

I started up front with my buddies. It was cool out and very windy. I ran conservatively and decided to run this as my "discovery" marathon; I wanted to enjoy it as well as do my best. There were about 2,000 runners and it was the fourth year of the run. It had grown in numbers each year as word of mouth from the running community trickled through the marathon media. I felt very comfortable up till 22 miles. There was never a time I felt awful or thought it was tough through that point. I thoroughly enjoyed every mile.

The course is uphill and downhill the entire way. Miles 10 through 12 is Hurricane Point, a 500-foot elevation gain, and the biggest on the course. The entire course is actually a net downhill but when I say that, most people don't believe me.

I spoke with a lot of people on the course and just had fun. It is definitely not a spectator marathon and there are large stretches with no cheering fans at all. Most runners are by themselves most of the time. But that's the beauty of Big Sur. It really is a state of mind and you find yourself in your own world. Sometimes I'd catch myself drifting off and not focusing and I'd think to myself, *Hey, there's nobody here!*

I passed my friend Mark at mile 17 and that gave me some added confidence. I kept the same pace throughout the race and just stayed steady. However, by mile 22 I was getting tired. I won't say I hit a wall, but my legs were achy and my quads and ankles were doing a lot of complaining. But by that point I knew I was going to make it.

There is a slight hill at mile 25. The marathon has a musical theme and the hill is called D Minor Hill at D Major Time. Once you get over that hill you can see the finish line a mile ahead and people start to line the road so there is actually some cheering going on—which is a good thing because I needed that. I got a nice boost just from seeing and hearing the spectators and knowing my family was waiting for me at the finish line. The finish was great. I raised my hands high and got very emotional. It still makes me emotional to think about it. You never really know until you cross the finish line that you can do it. The six-month commitment of training and hard work paid off and I finished in 2:56:35.

It was an amazing challenge, the best thing I ever did. Way better than all the golf games I played. And even though I hurt the next day, it was a rewarding hurt. The soreness is like a badge of courage.

My family was waiting for me and there were hugs all around. I wore my medal, which again is somewhat different than most marathon medals. They are all handmade out of ceramic by a local artist. And even though I didn't win the local prize that year I have won it in other years and those medals are even more different. One of them is a cow sitting on a bench playing the cello and another is a cow standing on a wooden base playing another instrument. If you haven't figured it out yet, the cow is the official mascot of the Big Sur Marathon.

Many runners describe Big Sur in spiritual nuances. The difficult course is easy on the eyes and has plenty of musical highlights along the way. There is the blind piano player in a tuxedo at the halfway mark playing a baby grand piano. There is the skeleton dressed in running clothes at mile 25.5 aptly named Decomposer. There is the heifer mascot named Tchaicowsky. The Robert Louis Stevens Orchestra performs at Hurricane Point. At mile 22, a local farmer hands out fresh strawberries. The runners themselves and the musical guests stationed along the way make up for the lack of crowd support. It's like one big moving party. Runners who are attracted to Big Sur are not looking for fast times or PRs (personal records). They are looking for a different experience and they truly get it.

In 1998, ten Big Sur Marathons later, Wally Kastner, the race director of Big Sur, asked if I would teach a training clinic for local first-timers who wanted to run the marathon. I was thrilled with the opportunity as I enjoy teaching and love running. We start the clinic in November and hold sessions every other week for 20 weeks. My marathon philosophy is that you have to enjoy the process of training for the marathon. You have to enjoy the pure act of running, so I make sure everyone tries to become a dedicated runner. I also tell them that no training program is foolproof and that they should do what works best for them. I teach them about visualization and that you have to want it to succeed. I stress the importance of the long runs, try to instill confidence, and let them try the walk-run approach that Galloway stresses now if that will help get them through. And of course I recommend that they read Galloway. And as for diet, I certainly don't recommend that they abstain from alcohol and sweets as I did. Basically I tell them to eat sensibly and as a touch of humor, I tell them to eat what the guy who beat them in the last race ate. The bottom line I try to stress is that in a marathon, 99 percent of the race is confidence and positive thinking based on consistent training. The object of the clinic is to get them through their first Big Sur and then to teach them to train themselves so that they will continue to enjoy running and do more marathons.

The last session is the week after the marathon and we all sit around with pizzas and soda and everyone shares their story. Some get emotional and there is lots of crying. Others get spiritual. The stories all share the same theme of overcoming obstacles, having a more positive attitude about life in general, and how the marathon changed their lives for the better. One older man told us he had polio as a kid and was hooked up to an iron lung. The doctors told him he would never walk again. And here he was, completing his first marathon at 65. There wasn't a dry eye in the place. A grandmother who completed Big Sur has 26 grandchildren and dedicated each mile to one of them. It is a great time and reinforces why I love to give these clinics. It makes up for all the late-night phone calls I get at home from my runners who are having anxiety attacks or a case of the nerves during training.

After the marathon tribute tales, I leave them with the "What's Next?" speech where I reinforce that they are now runners and must keep it up. By now, most of them love running and have become committed to their sport; they just need some direction as to what they can do with it.

Running is an integral part of my life and my family's. My wife has run a 3:11 marathon, my daughter-in-law has completed one, and my middle son has completed a half and was on his way to a full marathon when he got injured. (I should mention I was *not* his coach!) My daughter and her husband run every day as well. My first wife died from brain cancer, and running and my running friends got me through some very tough times. I met my current wife at the Big Sur Marathon when a group of us who were at the top of our age divisions, all 39 or 44 or 49 or 54, decided to run it as a centipede tied together by bungee cords and wearing antennas. Julie was the lone woman in the 13-person pod.

Running has definitely left its mark on my life and I can still recall the sensation of my first marathon. It taught me a lot about myself and gave me a more positive attitude, a feeling that I could do anything I set my sights on. Training for a marathon teaches you to overcome obstacles. And as a coach it is very rewarding to see these people who couldn't run a step complete a marathon and gain the same empowering feelings. My life is full and I wouldn't trade places with anyone.

# WHAT WAS I THINKING?

**JOHN EBERLE**

**D.O.B.: 4-13-61**
**RESIDENCE: PORTLAND, OR**
**OCCUPATION: MARKETING OF**
    **SPORTSWEAR MERCHANDISE**
**FIRST MARATHON: 1985 TWIN**
    **CITIES MARATHON**
**AGE AT FIRST MARATHON: 25**

*When I spoke to John, he said I wouldn't be interested in him as he made too many mistakes. What was he thinking? I love people who make mistakes because we all do, even the elites. And John was a collegiate elite, making a living from his running after graduating from Georgetown University. However, his distance was definitely not the marathon. When his training buddy got injured, John took his spot at a marathon thinking that since he could beat marathoners at the 5K and 10K distance, it should be a breeze. John learned firsthand that the marathon is a race to be respected, not taken for granted. Even though his first time was a humiliating DNF experience, John's sense of humor enabled him to look back and analyze his adventure with wit and wisdom.*

I grew up in New Jersey in a neighborhood filled with kids. My two older brothers and I were always outside playing a sport with the guys. Hockey, baseball, football—you name it, we played it. In junior high school my older brother Steve ran on the track team and tried to recruit me, but like most guys in high school I wanted to play football. I could run fast and had good hands so I thought I was a natural. Unfortunately, I wasn't that good at it and got sacked in the first preseason game. As I lay on my back on the field I decided this wasn't the game for me if I wanted a nice long life. That evening, nursing my concussion, my mother suggested I run track with my brother. A few days later I joined the team.

In high school I really came into my own with track thanks to our team captain. He encouraged me and told me I had talent, so I decided to take it seriously and see what I could do. He later went on to be an incredible track coach. I had immediate success on the team. When you are looking for identity during those teenage years, you grab it and go with it. Running did that for me. I was second in the state at the 2-mile and basically won everything. Running also enabled me to get a scholarship to run at Georgetown University, a school my mom could not have afforded.

Moving up to the collegiate level was a real eye-opener, a tentative transition. I went from being the star to one of many stars. It was also made clear to me that I was on scholarship and had to do well. My first year there I almost flunked out. Georgetown is a school that does not suffer athletes who don't make the grade, and it was tough! I started out pre-med but quickly changed to economics. That switch and the camaraderie and support of the team got me through some tough times. Back in focus, my running and my grades improved. I made all-league and went to the nationals but the team was so good that I was mainly a contributor, not one of the incredible talents or standouts on the team. I ran three seasons. When you get a full scholarship, the school expects you to give them your best, all the time. That meant running cross-country in the fall, indoor track in winter, and spring track. During summers the real elite runners, like my wife, Suzanne, ran in Europe. The European track scene was—and still is—huge. Track and field in Europe is what baseball is in our country. You really had to be good to compete over there.

After graduation in the spring of 1984, I wanted to continue running. It had been my identity and I wanted to keep that. My girlfriend/now wife Suzanne was a top runner at Georgetown and competed well in Europe. We thought we could make it financially if we both ran and won. Staying in the D.C. area, we spent the summer competing at road races and were fairly successful; we could make a living off our running, excelling at the 5Ks and 10Ks and 10-milers. It paid the rent and kept butter on the bread. We stayed away from the marathon, although that's where the big money was. A winner could take home $10,000 or more from a marathon where we were making anywhere from $500 to $1,000 even $2,000 from our races. At this point of my career I was running every day, sometimes twice a day, racing every weekend. The money was good but it was a grueling existence and physically tough on the body. And it was becoming more competitive as the Kenyans and Mexicans started appearing at the road races. I decided to take a job and found one very suitable to my running, managing a Nike store. They actually told me to run and encouraged my athleticism. It was a nice combination. I had finally made the switch from being an athlete/student in high school, a student/athlete in college, to an athlete/worker postcollege.

My life was very simple but pleasant. Work, run, hang out with Suzanne. The main event was planning the weekend race. It was a very narrow existence but I felt my potential was wide open. I was only 25. Then I made the mistake of running a marathon.

During the spring of 1984 I trained with a Kenyan runner, Joseph

Kipsang, a great marathoner with a PR of 2:11. He was contracted to run in the elite field for the upcoming Twin Cities Marathon so we would do long runs together in the hills of Maryland. We were up to 19 miles and I was handling the distance really well. As he spoke of the marathon I though to myself, *How cool is that? You go for a long run and come home with $10,000.* Heck, I was beating these same marathoners at the 10K distance so I thought I could most likely beat them at 26.2 miles as well. Then Joseph got sick.

Since I had put in most of the hard training with Joseph, he suggested that I take his place at the marathon. It was four weeks off and I thought, *Why not? How hard can this be?* The race director accepted me as a substitute although he wasn't willing to pay me appearance money since I was an unknown. But I did get the travel expense and the elite status so I was on my way to my first marathon through a serendipitous route. Little did I know how over my head I was going to be. I went into this blind, and paid the price.

Not only did I not ever plan to run a marathon, I didn't know how to run a marathon. I didn't study it, I didn't practice drinking on the course, which I never do in a 10K, and I didn't think about carboloading. When I received the elite-runner water kit, which explained how the elite runners keep their own water bottles at separate tables, I literally had to go out and buy a couple of water bottles. I thought I would just show up, run, and go home. Big deal. Was I ever wrong.

Upon arrival, the elite-team coordinators met me and they gave the elites a tour of the course. Even this didn't begin to prepare me. Instead of being intimidated by the distance and paying attention to the course, I was caught up with the beautiful scenery. It was crisp and cool, the sun was out, we passed beautiful lakes, and I was like a deer in the headlights, completely oblivious to what was about to whack me on the head. Even when some of the elites got off the bus to run the last 4 miles, I just sat there thinking, *Wow this is so cool.* I first started to realize maybe I was a bit out of my league at the pre-race pasta dinner.

I had read about carboloading and since it was the night of the race I thought I better start loading and ate a whole pizza. That kept me on the bowl all night and also dehydrated me at a point when I was supposed to hydrate. Then I filled my water bottle with a powdered mix and water, but I put extra powder in thinking it would give me more energy. Wrong! What was I thinking! Also, I had never tested the powdered mix before, a dangerous omission for any runner. I had never taken a drink on a run and here I was complicating the issue with a bad mix. But as fate would have it, I never got to my water bottles anyway. Every time I went to grab one I either knocked it over or couldn't find it so I never drank. And I wasn't savvy enough to think ahead and take the regular water from the open stations. I was clueless about hydrating, which eventually did me in.

Marathon morning it finally hit me. As I stood on the start line with the other elites a wave of nerves suddenly hit me and I thought, *What am I doing here?* Strategy? A plan? Technique? I had none. Everyone went out fast so I followed. I did whatever the other runners did. Then I heard a coach yell from the side for his guy to slow down so I slowed down, too. When I race a 10K I usually go out at a 4:30 pace so it didn't feel that fast to me, but then again I was never on the starting line of a marathon before. I never had to run slow and controlled.

I stayed with the lead pack but kept my eye on Frank Shorter. I knew of Frank and knew he was an excellent runner and a great technical runner so I decided to run like him. When I passed 10 miles and my time was under an hour I thought I was so slow. I wasn't sweating, not tired, just thinking this was so easy. I wasn't even hot and didn't get it when I saw the other runners drinking all the time and pouring water over their heads to cool off. Finally at mile 20 I started to get thirsty and took some water but by then it was too late.

By mile 23 I was dizzy and fatigued and had trouble focusing but still ran strong. I knew I was bonked but kept going. I was running by sheer determination, the "mind over body" method. As I got to mile 24, I felt a sharp pain, as if someone hit me in the back of the leg with a baseball bat. I turned around in pain, but no one was there. What had really happened was a popped hamstring. It popped so quickly I was stunned. I couldn't walk and had to get picked up by the sag wagon, which was a real drag.

Prior to the hamstring injury, I was among the top seven runners with 2 miles to go. I was even in front of Frank Shorter who finished in 2:14. The way I figure it, I was on the page to run a possible 2:12.

I could have been a contender. But that's the nature of a marathon. I couldn't run for a year after that. On the flight back to D.C. my hamstring hurt so much I couldn't even think about my performance. My first attempt at 26.2 miles ended abruptly and I put the experience out of my mind.

Later on, my wife's coach told me he would train me correctly so I worked with him and eventually made the Olympic marathon trials in 1988. Although my hamstring was healed, the injury left it shorter and threw off my entire biomechanics so I never got back to the shape I was in prior to the marathon.

The irony of the marathon is that it made my middle-distance running much better. Competitive runners tend to be selfish; selfish with their energy and their focus. They have to be in order to stay on top. It takes a tremendous amount of drive and inner focus to be one of the best. When I went through the humiliating experience of the marathon, my focus changed. I decided to run for other reasons, to be less introspective and more giving. I spent more time volunteering with kids' programs and helping Suzanne with her career. And realizing that the injury would hamper my ability to get back on top, I stopped competing and went back to school for my master's degree. For me, it was time to move on. You take what life deals you. Looking back 15 years later, I sometimes think, *What if I had seriously trained and done things right?* But then I straighten up and realize life is too short to play the "what if" game. Maybe I would have had a bad day anyway. Maybe I would have overtrained and gotten injured. The marathon is always an unknown no matter what.

I learned a valuable lesson that day that stays with me. Prepare yourself when you go anywhere, whether it is a business meeting, a new job, or a social gathering. Just prepare. There are so many things in life that you can't control—make sure you control the things you can. And running has brought me so many wonderful things in life. It got me into a great college I could not have afforded otherwise. I met my wife through running. Even the best man at our wedding was a running buddy and still is. I can't allow one bad day to take away all that.

I did run another marathon. In 1996, I ran the 100th Boston Marathon with my boss. He wanted me to pace him so we ran it together and it was a great experience. What a difference it made to run for fun versus running for the dream—and pressure—of winning. I did everything correct and had a ball. And yes, I did drink.

I continue to run 50 miles a week at a nice pace. I never set foot on a track and definitely do not incorporate any speed work. The mountains are my new destination. I've run Mount Fuji and Mount Kilimanjaro. I love climbing and the running gets me in shape for the climbs.

I used to live to run; now I run to live. It is something I enjoy and my life wouldn't be complete without it.

# THEY DON'T CALL IT BIG SUR FOR NOTHING

**CAROLYN ECKERT**

**D.O.B.: 6-4-53**
**RESIDENCE: FELTON, CA**
**OCCUPATION: HOMEMAKER,**
   **AIDE TO JUNIOR HIGH SCHOOL**
   **RUNNING COACH**
**FIRST MARATHON: 2001 BIG SUR**
   **INTERNATIONAL MARATHON**
**AGE AT FIRST MARATHON: 47**

*Even though Carolyn was a runner, she wasn't quite sure what a marathon was. She had heard of them but without realizing what she was getting herself and her unknowing her husband into, she signed up to run the Big Sur Marathon, one of the toughest marathon courses out there. Only through sheer determination did she finish her first marathon, but later on she realized she had actually inspired the woman who was struggling through her own first marathon behind her to finish as well.*

I was born in Japan and adopted at the age of three. My new parents were American and my dad was in the military. He was a preacher so I had the double whammy of being an army brat and a preacher's kid. Every three years we moved so my home was all over the world.

I got interested in physical activity because of my family. Dad was big into sports, an avid walker and hiker. He was also the boxing coach, a bit unusual for someone in a religious position. My younger brother was very athletic, also. I took up swimming, which is something I could do wherever we were stationed. I knew I could always find a pool whether we were living in Germany or California, where my dad retired when I was in high school. I was a good swimmer and went to the Junior Olympics.

It was hard living a life of constant travel with no roots, but looking back I realize what a wonderful opportunity it was to see and witness the world firsthand. My kids will never have those same experiences. My family drove across the United States countless times, and each time my dad made a point of stopping at a different national park or monument so we could walk or hike the place thoroughly. I can tell you that Utah has seven national parks because I walked them all. There was always something fun and exciting to do outdoors and I am thankful to my family for providing this type of lifestyle.

I got married right out of high school. My future husband was our youth group leader, and my dad was the one who introduced us. We were engaged at 15, married at 19, and I had my first child at 23. I attended college at Humboldt State for a few years but having a family was our first priority. I stayed active, but not to the extent that I was prior to marriage. My husband and I both love the outdoors so we hiked, walked, camped, hunted, fished and enjoyed exploring new areas. As our family grew, we took the kids along.

Even though I didn't start running till later in life, being active was always important to me. For 12 years I ran a day-care facility out of my house. Every afternoon I took the kids across the street to a park for lunch and then walked through the park. The kids loved it and it gave us a chance to be active and run around like kids like to do. My kids played a variety of sports and after dinner we'd head over to the local school to burn off steam and play pick-up games. We'd take the dog along and run for hours. Just as my family had, I wanted my kids to enjoy the freedom of the outdoors, the rewards of physical exercise, and develop a love of this beautiful land around us.

Later on I became a physical education teacher for the local elementary school and took over a running program involving Nike, geared toward introducing running to kids.

The program was for grades four through six and involved all sorts of ways to get the kids active and running. I also encouraged the parents to partici-pate, as I did. The concept was to get the kids interested in running by hav-ing them log their miles and finding creative ways to utilized the numbers, like marking their miles on a world map, as if they were traveling across the world. One summer my group theoretically trekked across Africa. Nike donated prizes like hats and T-shirts and other stuff. It was a great program but unfortunately Nike discontinued it.

Subsequently, I moved up to the junior high and coached track and cross-country, on a volunteer basis. Running was becoming a daily activity for me. I enjoyed working with and encouraging our local youth. I've done fund-rais-ers to provide uniforms for female sports teams in our high school and have been a spokeswoman on a variety of concerns to our school and sports boards. I truly believe that sports are an important part of a child's development and I don't think enough is done to get kids active or support their participation.

I officially started running because I needed a stress relief. Having teenage kids does that. At this stage of my life, running was the easy choice, not swim-ming. It was convenient (anytime was good), accessible (right out the door), I was getting outdoors to enjoy the air and scenery. My husband joined me and it became something we shared together. He was also looking to lose some weight and knew that running would help his cause.

My first race was the 10K Wharf-to-Wharf Race in Santa Cruz. I got involved on a fund-raising level for the schoolkids and ended up running it. I loved the excitement and the challenge. I was coming off a back surgery so I wasn't ready to run just yet. I walked the entire way but to me it still counts as my first race. After that, I jogged a little, walked a little, and slowly morphed into a real runner. I was looking for a running partner and joined my friend, Kim, a physical education teacher as well who was also looking for company.

On one of our runs, Kim suggested we do a marathon. I didn't know anything about them but Kim assured me it was easy and that I could do it. She knew I enjoyed setting goals—but I didn't know just how big a goal this was.

Not quite ready to commit to this huge undertaking, we decided we needed more information as to just what a marathon was. We also thought it would be good information to pass on to our kids, another way of involving them in sports. Kim went online and found out that the nearby Big Sur Marathon offered clinics so we attended one just for information purposes only.

At the meeting, we listened to Mike Dove, who was running the clinic. When he said, "Anyone can run a marathon," that was our hook. If anyone can, we certainly could, and ended up signing our names to the newcomers' list. He brought out great motivational speakers, including a 70-something man who ran his first Big Sur recently.

After we officially registered we started a nine-month training program. There were three levels of training routines starting with elite, then intermediate and beginner. We decided to go with the intermediate level because we had so much confidence in ourselves and already had a base of 20 miles a week. We thought we were advanced!

The clinics were very helpful but it also reinforced how little we knew. I was shocked to find out I didn't even know how to buy a pair of running shoes. Obviously, price was not the way to go and said good-bye to my $19.95 on-sale sneakers forever. Things like socks, clothing, everything was an eye-opener. I thought I knew how to tie a pair of sneakers until Mike showed us the proper way.

Words like *pronator, hydration,* and *goo* entered our vocabulary. We started to enter all the local races and moved up to the half-marathon distance, 13.1 miles. I kept to the program, monitoring my miles so I wouldn't get hurt. When my knees started to bother me I wore a Cho-pak band. I also bought some orthotics but didn't realize I had to take out the inner sole of the shoe first. My arches were killing me for a while until I figured that one out!

I trained for nine months but looking back, it wasn't enough. I got sick a lot during the training and ended up with bronchitis. I also never trained in the cold or the rain. In retrospect it wasn't the best year to take on a marathon. There was too much going on in my life with all the training, my son's graduation from high school and my job, and going back to school myself. Too much stress to also take on a marathon, but I'd committed to it and was going to see it through regardless.

The night before the marathon we stayed in Carmel. We watched old movies on television but sleep never came. I wasn't worried about completing the marathon because I knew if I had to I would walk it, I would. But still, I was very nervous.

We met the bus at 4:30 in the morning. I tend to get carsick so I thought I would get nauseous on the bus but managed to hold it together. It was pitch black and very windy. When we got to the start there was still lots of time to kill so I kept going to the bathroom over and over again and tried to stay warm.

The race started at 7 A.M.; we were off and excited. The first 5 miles are lined with trees so I didn't feel the effects of the wind or the spray from the surf. But as soon as the trees ended I got hit with a 40 mile-an-hour wind and instantly froze. My attitude went from *This is going to be a breeze* to *Oh my God what am I doing* in a matter of minutes.

The first 10 miles I was fine, especially since the first 5 are downhill. The course is incredibly beautiful and I can relate to every inch of the route as I have driven it so often. It was sunny, but still windy and cold. I ran with Kim and we maintained a 10-minute-mile pace, which was the game plan. Everything was going according to plan, at least for now.

The toughest part of the course was still ahead of me, a 2-mile climb up to Hurricane Point. I managed to get through that but by the halfway point, the Bixby Bridge, my quads started to cramp. This is the point of the race where a piano player in a tuxedo greets the runners with a few inspirational tunes. My husband, who started with us but soon ran ahead, waited for me at this point because we wanted our picture taken together at this scenic spot.

My quads continued to get worse and I had to slow down. I told Kim to run ahead because I knew I was holding her back. By mile 14 I couldn't run anymore and stopped at a first-aid station. I rubbed some pain cream on them but by now I was in such pain I was crying. My labor pains were easier than this!

The pain, and the fact that I knew I was in big trouble, had me totally freaking out. My husband stayed with me because he was frightened for me, but I wanted him to run his own marathon so pleaded with him to leave me and finish his race, which he reluctantly did.

I managed to get to mile 16, but my quads were shaking and hurting so badly I stopped at another first-aid station for a massage. The woman who attended me thought I should drop out and call an ambulance. "No way!" I cried. She called the paramedics over but I refused to drop out, saying I could make it another 10 miles even if I had to crawl.

I walked the remainder of the marathon in excruciating pain. I promised the paramedics that I would stop at every aid station, which I did, and everyone knew my name and made sure to check on me before I continued.

I wanted that medal more than anything, and it was only through sheer determination that I made it through. It took me 6 hours and 10 minutes. During the last mile I could see the finish line through the trees, and as I headed around a curve I saw a member of our training group. He gave me a high five and said, "You can make it. In fact, I bet you can run it in if you really try." That was all the support I needed and I mustered up all my resilience and ran the last half mile to cross the finish line in style.

I was in tears as I crossed the finish line, both from the pain and the realization that I had accomplished my goal. My husband was waiting for me and after the hugs and tears and congratulations, I realized how hungry I was and made a dash for the food table. After getting my medal, that is.

At our postmarathon training meeting the next week we all got a chance to talk about our experiences. A woman in our group stood up, looked right at me, and announced that I inspired her to finish because she was behind me and in bad shape as well. But when she saw me struggling to finish, she did too. I never realized I was actually someone's inspiration. It was a touching moment for both of us.

Crossing the finish line of my first marathon was a major accomplishment, especially under my painful circumstances. To stay focused for so long, to run so many miles, to finish against all odds, was a huge challenge. The only negative aspect was that our kids were not at the finish line for Tom and me. We were both disappointed because we were always there for them at all their events and now, at the most challenging event of our lives, they were absent. They just weren't thinking, and afterward when they realized what a tremendous accomplishment this was, they apologized.

After my amazing 26.2-mile journey, I didn't think I would ever run another. But six months later I ran the Sacramento Marathon and bettered my time by 40 minutes, finishing in 5:30. It was an easier course and I trained better. My quads acted up again at mile 13 and I considered only doing a half marathon but thought, *What the heck, I've done this before!*

Believe it or not, Tom and I are actually planning on doing Big Sur next year. I know that must sound crazy after everything I went through at my first marathon but I absolutely love running the marathon and getting that feeling over and over again. I also want to improve my times. And I have a new goal: to do Big Sur pain-free and actually run the whole distance.

I also keep running marathons for health reasons. After I hit 40 I noticed that my body shifted in ways I never thought possible. Running helps to keep me fit and keeps my body looking the way I want instead of the way it wants! I also have more energy now and have turned into a health nut. I just went for my first bone scan, as I am reaching that age when menopause and the concern for osteoporosis are right around the corner, and the results came back great. I have the bones of a healthy teenager! I keep telling my kids that at this rate I'll make 100 so they'd better get used to having us old folks around for a long time.

When I turn 50 I want to hike the Swiss Alps, something I never could have dreamed of prior to running. Now I know my lungs and legs will hold up. It's wonderful to be able to set goals that I never thought possible a decade ago. And the best part of taking up marathons at my age is that I can now look forward to winning my age division when I really get good at this!

# GREETINGS FROM ARLINGTON, TEXAS

**WANDA ESTES**

**D.O.B.: 4-16-37**
**RESIDENCE: ARLINGTON, TX**
**OCCUPATION: RETIRED TEACHER**
**FIRST MARATHON: 2002 NEW**
    **YORK CITY MARATHON**
**AGE AT FIRST MARATHON: 65**

*Wanda describes herself as a new old runner. After her debut at the New York City Marathon, she wants to spread the word that running is a gift to our minds and our bodies; she is on a personal quest to instill the love of running in others. Deeply spiritual and religious, Wanda believes that God had a hand in her plans to run a marathon. God, and her 11-year-old granddaughter, Cate, brought her to the start and saw her to the finish. Wanda is not only a decent runner, as proven by her ability to finish her first marathon with only three months of training, but she's a real class act as well.*

I grew up out west on the range. Nothing but ranches and farmland as far as you could see. We were always outside playing but my only form of organized sports was physical education in high school. I played basketball but wasn't that good. In college I fulfilled my gym requirements with badminton and bowling. That was the extent of my athletic life.

After my freshman year of college I quit school to get married. I was a stay-at-home mom, but always regretted not finishing my college education. At the age of 44 I went back to school. By that time I had three kids and we'd all do our homework together. It wasn't easy for me but once I set a goal I go after it until it is finished. I'm not a quitter.

While I was going to school, my youngest was in junior high. When I dropped him off at school in the morning I'd see the teenagers smoking across the street from the school, and they seemed so misdirected. Right then and there I decided to become a teacher because I felt I could teach them a thing or two and straighten them out. I got a teaching degree along with my college English and business degree—and wouldn't you know it, when I applied for a teaching position I was assigned to the very same high school where our youngest son would attend.

That was one of the first times I knew God interacted on my behalf. This was a God thing; He showed me what I was supposed to do. You see, I made a pact with God years before when my youngest son was diagnosed with infant meningitis. He went into a coma and we didn't think he would live. I prayed to God to spare his life and if He did I would do whatever He asked of me. So every once in a while God asks me to do something and I follow His will. I knew this teaching thing was God's way of asking me to help encourage students who were struggling with life and learning.

For seven years I taught sophomore English and also remedial and advanced reading. One of the most fulfilling classes I taught was ESL (English as a second language), which was a challenge not only for the foreign students but me as well. I thought if I could just teach these students to read, then anything would be possible for them in life. It was extremely rewarding and I cherish some of the thank-you notes they sent me. One student wrote, "Thank you for teaching me to read. This is the first book I have ever read all the way through." I think this is what God intended for me when He asked me to teach.

When my husband retired in 1992 he asked me to retire also so we could do things together. With our free time we wanted to do something charitable, so we volunteered at Mission Arlington and our church and did various projects. In June and July 1995 we went to Poland and helped at a camp for orphans and abused children. My teaching background really came in handy.

We went back to Poland at least once a year from 1995 until after September 11, 2001. We didn't think travel was safe anymore and the world seemed at such unrest. We still send supplies and monetary funds and some day we hope to go back.

Up to this point, I was not active with any fitness or exercise routine. There was one brief point when my doctor suggested I take up exercise to help reduce my cholesterol levels. He suggested walking or running so I started running around the block, about a quarter of a mile. A few days later one of my girlfriends said, "Oh Wanda, that is so bad for women. You can ruin your body," so I quit.

In February 2000 my granddaughter, Cate, asked me to run in her school's 5K race. She was in third grade and needed a parent to accompany her in the race and she chose me. She said, "Grandma, you can walk it if you want."

I started training and picked up running around the block again, but I knew 3 miles was much farther than that. I did a run-walk pattern, but mostly it was walking. That got real boring so I lengthened the run a bit every week. By the start of the race, I was running maybe a mile. But I wasn't nervous or scared. I figured this was another thing God had put in my path and I had to go with it until I figured out the big picture.

I ran most of the race and felt pretty good at the finish, even though it took me the better part of an hour. The next day at church the director of our class made a big deal about my race in front of the whole group. Everyone hooted and hollered and congratulated me.

The next year I ran the race again and in February 2002 I graduated to the 10K. To my surprise I finished fourth in my age division. By now I was getting real excited about these races. I felt like a real runner. And the best part was, I could eat whatever I wanted and stay slim and trim. I liked this!

God's plan for my running was beginning to form and the terrorist attack of September 11 played a part. Our son Kevin is the musical director for a church in New York City not far from the World Trade towers. After the terrorist attack, I followed the news on the Internet and learned that one of the firehouses that lost so many men was nearby my son's church. I read the biographies of the men and one in particular stuck in my head. His biography said he had run the New York City Marathon and I vowed that one day I would run that marathon for him and for all those who lost their lives that day.

Kevin's church had become an aid station during the weeks following the attack. Wanting to help, my husband Neal and I immediately drove our truck cross-country and positioned ourselves at the church to do whatever we could. One day I was out walking doing errands and passed what looked to be a florist shop. On closer inspection, it was that fire station I read about on the Internet. The flowers had been placed in memoriam.

I couldn't get those men out of my mind. Back in Texas, I decided to start fulfilling my pledge to run a marathon and joined the New York Road Runners club. I knew my chances of making it into the lottery system were iffy so I decided to apply every year; if in three years I still didn't get in, by rule, I would automatically get a number. So in January 2002, I made my first application to the New York City Marathon thinking I had three years to train for the marathon.

Well, God must have decided that three years was too long because on July 9, 2002, on my first try, I made it into the New York City Marathon. Oh my Lord, I cried. I was shakin' in my boots. And to show you how God's hand was in the picture, as I scrolled down to the E's, there were three Estes. I was the middle one and the only one that got in. Even my kids said, "That's God again, Mom. He wants you to run!"

Well by gosh, now I had three and a half months to train with a base of zero miles! There is no way my body should have been physically able to handle this, but I was confident because I knew it was God's will. I never even questioned that I would finish the marathon. Before I started training I went for a physical checkup just to make sure all the parts were intact. When I told the doctor I was running a marathon, he looked shocked and said, "You have no business running a marathon at your age."

I started running in earnest. Then I learned through the New York Road Runners website about a fund-raiser, the Foundation Team for Kids. The money raised helps to establish youth running programs in schools and community centers for New York City kids who have no access to physical education. The foundation provides coaches and buses and race entry fees to teach them how to run and embrace it as a healthy lifestyle. Even though I lived in Texas, the thought of New York City kids not being able to run and learn to love running was overwhelming. The teacher in me came out in full support of these kids. I became a Foundation Team for Kids member and raised $1,000.

The benefits of being a team member may have seemed lost on someone in Texas but my team members back in New York City talked to me on the Internet almost every day about their training routines. One member, Carl, told me about a website by Hal Higdon that was dedicated to seniors running a marathon. I logged on and found a great training schedule that was perfect for me.

My longest training run was 20 miles. That came back to haunt me because I hit the wall at mile 20. In my next marathon, I will run longer mileage in training.

The entire family, including Cate, who got me into this running thing in the first place, all came to New York City. Kevin and his fiancée were also there with my husband, Neal. We mapped out the route and plotted intersections where we could meet.

It was wonderful meeting my Foundation Team training teammates for the first time when we boarded the special team bus to the start of the marathon. I wore lime-green shorts, Cate's favorite color, despite the chill in the air.

Part of God's message that I think He forgot to tell me about regarding this marathon was the pain. God wanted me to make a sacrifice, and I did. I was doing well until mile 20. I was actually ahead of schedule, which caused me to miss my family at some of the earlier locations we planned.

After mile 20 I needed to walk. My quads were cramping and I was so tired. It was also getting dark out and colder. Unfortunately, the walking felt terrible; it made me cold so I started to shiver so I immediately started running again. The only thing that kept me going was knowing I'd see my family at mile 24. The biggest problem I faced after mile 20 was the lack of Gatorade. I relied on it to keep my energy up but by now I had been running over five hours and the water stations were depleted of Gatorade; some were actually closing down. I was one of the last runners still on the course. The only person I passed was a man in a wheelchair.

Finally at mile 24 I saw Cate and Neal with a bottle of Gatorade. I was never so happy to see them or the Gatorade. Cate, my daughter Carol, and good friend Donna ran with me for the next mile and then I felt revived enough to finish the marathon on my own and in fine form. I even passed at least 30 people and was able to gently jog over the finish line, relieved to have it over. The volunteer who placed my marathon medal around my neck commented on how nice my hair still looked. That was the least of my concerns at the moment; all I wanted was a warm shower. My time was 6:40. I plan to beat that in my next marathon.

My son Kevin and his fiancée Jenny were at the finish line with lime green posters (to match my shorts). Neal took pictures of all of us rejoicing. We couldn't get a taxi so I had to walk more than 2 miles back to the hotel and then climb five flights of stairs. After a well-deserved shower we all went out to celebrate in style—Texas style!

Everywhere I go people refer to me as the Grandma who ran a marathon. It was an incredible day, and compares to my graduation from college. It probably is the greatest physical accomplishment in my life.

I went to a sports medicine doctor afterward to have my foot looked at and he did surgery to remove a neuroma. That's why I had so much pain during the marathon. I go to physical therapy three times a week now in Fort Worth. It's where all the professional athletes go. Turns out the owner of the practice taught at the same high school I did 10 years ago. He was the trainer and I had actually spoken with him a few times. That's another sign that God was with me all the way. He brought everything full circle. And He added a bit of fun for me. Some of the professional players came over to me and ask for my autograph. Can you beat that?

Running has allowed me to experience myself as the individual person God created me to be. Running helps keep me physically, mentally, and emotionally healthy. Running allows me to excel without competing with anyone else but myself. Running this marathon was one of the greatest joys in my life because it allowed me to sense in my heart what God wanted me to do and I did it.

One of my favorite quotes from the Bible talks about running and sums up what I feel. God says it better than I can. "…Those who hope in the Lord will renew their strength. They will soar on wings of eagles; they will run and not grow weary, they will walk and not be faint." (Isaiah 40:31, NIV)

In my next marathon I will train harder so as not to be faint and grow weary at mile 20.

# LIFE BEGINS AT 50

**RICHARD FRIEDRICHSEN**

**D.O.B.: 7-29-42**
**RESIDENCE: CLARKS, NEBRASKA**
**OCCUPATION: CATTLE FARMER**
**FIRST MARATHON: 1996 LINCOLN**
**MARATHON, LINCOLN NEBRASKA**
**AGE AT FIRST MARATHON: 53**

*I met Richard at the 16-mile marker of the Mystic Places Marathon in Connecticut. He was having a ball, chatting it up with everyone and sporting a big smile. He was exactly what I needed at that point: someone to keep me on pace and entertained. He was 59 years old and had flown in from Nebraska to run the race as part of his 50+DC Club requirements. "Don't you just love it darlin'?" he asked as we ran. "We can enjoy the scenery and the company and not have to kill ourselves." Richard's marathon philosophy should be shared by all. He turns the marathon into a social event and loves every minute of it. Every first-time marathoner should be so lucky as to find a someone like Richard on the course.*

I was born and raised on a farm. That's where I first started running, but not for fun. Getting up early, I had to run around the farm to get all my chores done before school. I'd run to get the cattle, run to the milk the cows, and run to feed the chickens. Then it was off to school. I got a ride to the one-room schoolhouse I attended in rural Nebraska, but after school I had to run 1 ½ miles along a gravel road to get home. When I got home the same set of chores had to be done again.

In addition to learning the three R's at my country school I learned football, baseball and track. All 25 students, grades K through 8, participated. I also ran track in high school but didn't get on with the coach so I never ran to my fullest potential. I wanted to run the mile but he only let me run the half. I guess I could be ornery and bullheaded that way. In the end, we both lost out to my stubbornness; the coach lost out because I didn't give him the times he wanted and I lost out because I never developed to my fullest potential.

My father died when I was in high school so I had to run even harder to get the chores done. I wanted to go to college so my mom sold all the animals and machinery to get money for my schooling. But college wasn't for me so I enlisted in the army in 1962. Never saw any action but I did train the soldiers who were being shipped out to Vietnam. I tried to stay in shape and managed to win my company's physical fitness, which afforded me a three-day pass. Everyone was surprised that I could run so fast. Two years into my service I married Marlene and by the time I left the army we had two daughters.

We went back to Nebraska and I worked my father-in-law's farm. After 10 years I bought my own farm, 80 acres. Today that same farm has 2,000 acres. I raise mostly cattle and corn. I didn't much like milking cows so I got rid of them and started raising cattle. Growing corn is still hard manual labor. There's no shortcut there. I am still up with the sun and in bed early, a 12- to 15- hour day. Being my own boss, I am pretty hard on myself. I do make time for other interests such as hunting and fishing. I've always declared that I farm to make a living, I don't live to farm.

My favorite pastime is archery hunting for elk. Believe it or not, this is how I get the most physical exercise and was probably the initial training for my marathon-to-come. Every year I take 10 days off and go up in the Colorado Rockies with my best friend to shoot elk with a bow and arrow. We spend the days running up and down the mountain for elk sightings and then if we see one we chase it up and down the mountain. To get in shape for this yearly event I run in boots a couple of miles a day. After I build up to that, I then add the next dimension, which is running and shooting. I'll run 2 miles to a target, shoot 100 arrows, then run back another 2 miles. I repeat this a few times every day till I feel confident I have the endurance and stamina to do it at high altitude, up in the Rockies. Over the 10 years I've been doing this I have only killed two elk! That shows you how much I enjoy just being out in the wilderness with my buddy acting like young kids. It was more the camping and camaraderie than it was the hunting.

Since I was in such good shape from all that running I decided to enter a local 5K. It didn't draw a whole bunch of people, only 30, and I placed second overall. There wasn't much competition but it was thrilling to win nonetheless. Actually, I found it difficult, as I have never run that fast for that distance. But I got the bug and decided I needed more competition. I was 53 years old and didn't have a clue what I was getting myself into. I went to the big city of Lincoln and entered another 5K and came in just about last! That was a rude awakening. I went home with my head hanging and went right out and bought Jeff Galloway's book on running and started to read up on my new sport.

I started training the right way and felt confident enough to enter more races. I started to get a few wins, with times of 19 and 20 minutes for 5Ks. I enjoyed the competitiveness; that appealed to me. I was on a winning streak and wanted to keep on winning. I always approached a race as if I was going to win. It was great to come home with a medal to show off for Marlene and the kids. I always play to win, even at cards. I love a challenge.

Meanwhile, I followed everything Galloway said to do in his book. If he said run 5 miles, I ran 5 miles. I was very dedicated to his routine. I raced every weekend and got hooked. In the beginning of the week I would scan the racing section of the *Omaha World Herald* for an upcoming race and go. Twice a month I'd make the 100-mile trip to Omaha to get better competition and was able to hold my own. Slowly I moved my distance from a 5K to the 10K and finally ran my first half marathon and won my age division.

After that half marathon, people started talking to me about doing a marathon. Very few people around here run marathons so I wasn't really sure what it was all about. I ran another half marathon and then decided to run a full marathon the next year. I heard that the Lincoln Marathon was a good one so that became my target.

I followed Galloway's plan for a first-time marathon. I was comfortable doing 10Ks but when I ran my first 10-miler I ran out of gas and got nervous. I kept doing the long runs and soon could break 10 miles but had a real hard time with the longer distances. In fact, I had to cut back on Galloway's schedule for the first time since I followed his book. When he said to do 20, I did 18. When he said to do 24, I did 20. I really struggled with the distance. I finally did do a 20-miler but only once and no longer distance than that.

Marlene and I drove up to Lincoln the night before the race. I admit I was nervous because I knew there would be unfamiliar faces and steep competition whereas I was used to the same old faces and being the winner. When I went to the pasta diner the night before the marathon I was in complete awe; there were thousands of people milling around, exchanging stories and talking about the race. I couldn't believe a marathon would draw so many people. I'd never met people like this before and my excitement continued to grow. Someone was preaching the benefits of keeping hydrated, which I had never done before, so I started drinking lots of fluids, but that only made me have to get up all night to go to the bathroom. This was all so new to me. My goal was to run an 8-minute-mile pace. At least that's what one of those pace charts said I could do based on my best 10K pace.

I couldn't sleep that night for two reasons: one, I was going to the bathroom every hour; and two, I was so excited I almost fell ill from the excitement and mystery of it all. After managing maybe four hours' sleep, I got ready for the 7 A.M. start. A misty rain fell on the runners at the start of the marathon. Everything was so new to me including the 2,000 participants, the crowds of spectators along the route; even the potty lines were different. I felt very calm the first 5 miles and fell into a comfortable pace but when I passed a time clock I realized I was doing a 7:45 pace. The course was a double loop, shaped like a heart. The first loop was easy, nice and flat, and I ran effortlessly. In the second loop, runners began to feel the toll of the distance and spread out more, some slowing down. At the halfway mark I was still maintaining a 7:45 pace—too fast, I thought, but it felt good at the same time. This was all so new to me I didn't know what to expect. Should I slow down? Stay the course?

I kept the pace and felt great up to mile 17 and then I began to get tired and had trouble making it up the slight incline into mile 18. Blisters were beginning to develop on the bottoms of my feet but I decided to ignore them. I was determined to finish even if it meant walking. Pain settled in for the long run. This was a new sensation for me and I wasn't sure what it meant but I kept on going. By 20 miles, my muscles were tight as a stretched bowstring and my calves were screaming. Mile 21 was a downhill but then turned into an uphill. I sure was noticing those inclines now. I wasn't talking anymore, just tried to relax and concentrate on my running. Someone in the crowd said the 3:30 marathoners would qualify for Boston and that stuck in my mind. I wondered whether I could do that. Here I was, not even finished with my first marathon and wondering if I could qualify for Boston. That's competitive!

When I approached mile 25, I panicked because I couldn't remember if a marathon was 26 miles or 26.2. I knew the 0.2 would do me in if I didn't start running faster. Thinking I wouldn't qualify for Boston, I picked up my pace and ran with a vengeance, despite the fact that I was tired as hell. The course finished on a track and as I rounded the track I could see the finisher's clock and sprinted for all I was worth and crossed the finish line at 3:28:20. I was so excited. Marlene gave me a big hug and took lots of pictures. I looked at her and said, "We're going to Boston!" Meanwhile, I couldn't even walk another step. I never felt so hurt and in such pain in my whole life. I could barely walk over to the awards table to get my medal.

I crippled on over to the fieldhouse to collect my belongings and sat there complaining about my pain with a bunch of other guys and Marlene walks over and says to us, "Let me get this straight. You do this for fun?" It truly was the most difficult thing I have ever done in my life.

After a while I forgot the pain and started planning for Boston. Our neighbors acted impressed but would follow up their congratulations by saying, "So, what's a marathon?"

Besides the pain, I didn't have any serious injuries. Now I know why Galloway insists on the long runs of over 20 miles. The following April I ran Boston after training slightly better and getting in a few more longer runs.

After the thrill of running my first marathon, followed up by Boston, I needed a new challenge and found it in the 50+DC club. I turned the farm over to some friends to manage, which gives me the time to travel around the country running marathons. To date, I've run 41 marathons in five years and have 28 states credited to the 50+DC club.

Every marathon is a new adventure. It's like climbing a mountain and not knowing what's on the other side. Marlene comes with me to every one; she is my support crew. After I ran my first Boston, she was waiting at the finish with a rose. That's the type of gal she is.

I never stop training and run 12 months a year so I am always prepared. I visit friends on my travels and am having the time of my life. Marlene and I put together a marathon calendar by region. In the fall we drive east to Virginia and stay with my daughter and get in all the New England fall marathons. It's a treat for us to see the seasons in different parts of the country. I do love autumn in New England; nothing beats their fall foliage.

Every race is totally different and that's what keeps it interesting. Over the years I've had to teach myself not to go out too fast and try for a win, although I usually place in my age division. Nowadays when I run I love to talk with the other runners. Maybe I talk too much because sometimes I'll be running with someone who stops answering me and says very politely, "I like listening to you but I can't keep talking any longer." I guess I am having way too much fun at these marathons. I think my next goal after I do all 50 states plus D.C. will be an ultramarathon. That is, if the cattle and the farm and Marlene agree.

# A SOUND RUNNER

**INGRID GAMM**

D.O.B.: 7-19-46
RESIDENCE: HAMDEN, CT
OCCUPATION: STORE MANAGER,
   HAMDEN HALL COUNTRY DAY SCHOOL,
   SALES ASSOCIATE, SOUND RUNNER
   RUNNING STORE
FIRST MARATHON: 1999 LASALLE BANKS
   CHICAGO MARATHON
AGE AT FIRST MARATHON: 53

*Ingrid is petite in stature but has a very powerful voice when it comes to running. She believes anyone can run a marathon if they have the determination, stamina, and desire to complete 26.2 miles. And time is not important. She advises everyone in her running groups and at the running store where she works to do it for their own good and reap the positive mental and health rewards that the running life will bring. She is an inspiration to all who know her and truly believes in the spirit of the marathon. After all, her father's spirit accompanied her on her first marathon.*

I was always a recreational jogger but felt intimidated to even think of running a marathon. I thought that was something reserved only for serious runners, although the idea intrigued me. To actually complete a marathon seemed so remote and unattainable.

I started running in my late 20s for general exercise. I didn't have any foundation in sports as I attended high school in the era when girls were not encouraged to sweat. I was a late bloomer when it came to anything physical but took to running immediately. It is such an easy sport to ease into; all you need is a pair of shoes, some time, the desire, and the determination.

I was happy with my 5 miles a day, never pushed beyond my comfort level. Then I heard about Leukemia Team-in-Training approach to running a marathon and decided that was how I would run my marathon. With that major decision made, I immediately knew to whom I would dedicate my first marathon: my dad, Louis. He died 21 years ago from multiple myeloma, a form of leukemia.

Now that my marathon plans were becoming a reality, I was scared of running that distance. But the memory of my dad sent a charge of excitement through my whole body. He was very important to me and as soon as I decided to run a marathon, it just felt right to dedicate it to him.

Part of my marathon preparation was to start racing. I started with a local 5-miler, which was very difficult, but the reward and accomplishment of doing it outweighed the difficulty. Never having been to a race before, I looked around and took in the colorful racing culture. There were lots of running club banners, and one was for Warren Street. I chose that group randomly and went over and talked with the runners, who were friendly and helpful and suggested I join them. A Leukemia Team-in-Training representative was the head of the club, so it fit perfectly into my plan.

I still remember the first time I drove to the workout session with Warren Street. I was so nervous I had knots in my stomach and felt nauseous. And just as I predicted, I finished at the end of the pack in all the drills but I loved it anyway. Being a member of this club opened my eyes to the running community and it became my new way of life. Quickly, running became my passion. I couldn't imagine my life without it. It felt great; an aura of friendship, love, and caring I have never before experienced. It felt as if it was meant to be; I was accepted unconditionally. Tuesday was workout day and it was permanently marked my calendar for all to see.

Despite the fact that I loved being a member of the club, it wasn't easy for me to accept the fact that I was now a real runner. I was plagued by a voice in my head telling me that I really didn't belong there, that I was just fooling myself to think I could run a marathon. In order to combat this negative force, my running became visionary and I imagined myself a strong, solid runner. I wouldn't allow myself to visit that place in my head where the little demon kept telling me I was not a runner, that I didn't belong. As long as I focused on my goal I could keep the demon away. It took a while, but as the weekly workouts became part of my life and my friendships with the club members solidified, the nagging voices stopped.

Team-in-Training gave me a schedule with four months' lead time to prepare for the marathon. I chose the Chicago Marathon because some of my club members were also running that one and we could travel together. I did my long runs with my club. It made it so much easier to do the long ones with friends. I also had to raise $2,000 for Leukemia Team-in-Training and ended up with $2,600. My cousin donated $25 a mile as he also loved my dad and wanted to honor his memory.

The months seemed to fly by and before I knew it, I was at the start of my first marathon. Although I was excited, I was also nervous and realized I didn't know anything about the logistics of running a marathon. My club members spoke about pacing, but the only pace I knew was slow. Thank goodness

I didn't give myself the added pressure of finishing in a certain time. Whatever it took was fine with me. I wanted to run my first marathon not for time but for my dad.

I was blown away by the size of the crowds and the valuable support they provided. That was an added benefit I hadn't counted on. I was on such a high that I was yelling back at them. I told everyone I passed that I was from Connecticut and running for my dad, Louis. I had his name written on the palm of my hand and every time I needed inspiration I looked at my palm and continued forward. It was a glorious day.

I ran the entire 26.2 miles by myself. Although I traveled to Chicago with members of my club, I had no family members present; just my dad at my side. I felt his presence the entire marathon. I didn't care about my finishing time of 4:46. All I cared about was how wonderful it felt to get my medal and how proud I was of my accomplishment. The memory of my dad helped me not to give up, and got me through the last 6 miles. And honestly, I wore my medal every day for a month.

Despite my euphoria, I ached all over. I took an Epsom salt bath when I got home and had to hobble around for a week. But even with the pain, I knew I wanted to run another marathon. I was hooked. Now that I had completed one, I wanted to run another and see if I could better my time. And honestly, it wasn't that difficult.

With that plan in mind, I met someone who changed my life. Julie Francis and her husband, Bob, are runners who own a running store in Branford, Connecticut. I kept bumping into them at the local races and then one time Julie and I both placed in a 5K. Finally, we formally met. She told me she had seen me run and felt that I had untapped potential. She offered to teach me to develop my hidden talent. I was shocked and surprised. With those words of encouragement, she planted a seed and I let it grow.

Julie became my coach and she introduced me to running in a way I never knew. All of a sudden I wanted to know everything about training and running marathons. I spent hours at the bookstore reading about stretching, training, and healthy eating. I wanted to learn all the lingo, like *negative splits*. I was like in a kid in a candy store. For the first time, I saw running for what it is supposed to be: a lifetime sport.

We trained together, running a minimum of 8 miles four days a week. I became a faster runner due to my increased distances. The short-term goal was to improve as a runner and the long-term goal was to tackle my next marathon. Julie wanted me to build up a positive attitude and believe that I had the ability she saw in me. She became like a sister to me and through our training and personal relationship she erased any doubts I had about being a better runner and, more importantly, a runner for life.

I had so much fun becoming a real runner! She trained me like a professional. I learned all sorts of things, like just what the heck is lactic acid, anaerobic versus aerobic exercise, and what a 4x400 is at the track. It was the best summer I ever had. I was 54 years old and having the time of my life. It was like being at running camp.

We selected my second marathon, the Mystic Places Marathon, which was close by in East Lyme, Connecticut. The best way to describe the difference between my first and second marathon is that I ran my first as a jogger and the second as an athlete. I now had knowledge, power, and the desire to do better. As I stood at the start of my second marathon, I felt entitled to be there. I had earned my spot. I think that is the biggest difference between the two.

I was just as nervous at Mystic Places as I was at Chicago, but I also felt better prepared. I knew what lay ahead of me. I had my splits written on a card so I could follow along and know where I was at every mile, or at least where I should be.

As I approached the 13th mile marker, I was feeling great. When I reached mile 18, I started to feel fatigued and my quads tightened. To stay inspired and not think of the pain, I focused on my accomplishments, and that seemed to keep me in a positive zone. As I reached mile 25, I gave it all I had and finished in 4:04. I couldn't believe I took almost an hour off my first marathon finish time.

The feeling of crossing the finish line at Mystic Places was very different than in Chicago. This time, the feeling of accomplishment was not that I finished but that I did such an amazing job. The pride that I felt was greater than anything I had ever felt. Every part of my life after my second marathon changed for the better. I saw myself for the first time as a strong, determined woman.

The final difference between my first and second marathon is the way I felt physically. This time around I felt fine. I was back running in three days.

When I finished Mystic, I was so thrilled with the time that I didn't notice I had actually qualified for the Boston Marathon. Only the best runners get into Boston. Along with placing second in my age division, I was going to Boston. That was the icing on the cake.

Once I knew I'd qualified, I had to focus on Boston. This was going to be different because I had to train in the winter, whereas all my other marathon training had been in the summer and early fall. I started January 1 and found my groove again. I had never run such a populated marathon before and that scared me. I felt like cattle being put into a corral. But it turned out well and even Heartbreak Hill didn't faze me. It was a super day.

I've become an advocate for running. I assist in running groups at both of my places of work. I want to share the knowledge that anyone can run a marathon with the proper training and realize that same feeling of accomplishment that changed my life for the better. The only person who doesn't believe me is my 90-year-old mother, who thinks I am going to hurt myself. I grew up with the old myth that women weren't supposed to do things like run marathons. I overcame the *you can't do that* attitude that followed me around most of my life and still does when I speak with my mother. I'll never get her to change but I can try and get other women to see it's a different world out there and women can indeed do anything they set their minds and hearts to do.

People tell me that I am an inspiration to them because I've run three marathons in my 50s. But I tell them that they can also be inspirations to others if they just believe in themselves. Running a marathon is 90 percent mental and 10 percent physical. All the rewards and accomplishments and kudos and self-esteem are there for the taking if you just believe.

# EVERYBODY STRUGGLES

**SAM GROTEWOLD**

**D.O.B.: 4-6-78**
**RESIDENCE: AMES, IOWA**
**OCCUPATION: WEB DESIGNER**
**FIRST MARATHON: 2000 CHICAGO**
**    MARATHON**
**AGE AT FIRST MARATHON: 22**

*When I first spoke with Sam as a potential interview, I politely dismissed him because he was too fast; I was more interested in the stories of struggling midpackers. But Sam is also smart and taught me a lesson. He was gracious with my decline and just before he hung up, he said, "You know, just because I can run faster than most doesn't mean I don't hurt and struggle in the marathon. Everyone struggles in the marathon." At those well-chosen words, I decided Sam had a story to tell after all. Besides that, he is the only runner I know who landed a job through the marathon.*

I never really considered running as an option in high school. Never gave it a thought. I played basketball and tennis and ran only for conditioning. Although I realized that I could run for a long time, I never liked to run, even when I had to do it.

I spent some time in the summer before my senior year in high school in Mexico City and met a runner, also from the United States. I remember listening to her speak about running and the joy that it brought to her life. That made a big impression on me, and when I returned to the states I thought often about her enthusiasm for the sport. Later in the summer my family was on vacation, and I entered a 5K road race where we were visiting, mostly because of what my friend in Mexico had told me. To my surprise, I came in 12th place with almost no training.

Based on my performance in that 5K, I almost immediately decided to join the cross-country and track teams for my senior year. My school had a large and very successful track program, many times over state champions. My high school coach, John Sletten, is a legend in the state of Iowa; until recently he had won more Iowa state titles in track and field than any other coach in history. We all joked about Mr. Sletten being a "slave driver," but now that I'm more experienced (and hopefully wiser) I see that he wants one thing: to see his athletes get better. Though I don't always agree with his training philosophy, I credit Mr. Sletten with teaching me that improvement comes through hard work, and that is something I remind myself of nearly every day.

Knowing next to nothing about the competitiveness of the Ames High School cross-country team, I figured that my 12th-place finish in a small-town road race would almost surely mean success on my high school team.

I found out quickly that I wasn't a very good runner. Not used to the daily running and heretofore unheard-of speed work, I suffered injury upon injury that season, and they never got better, just progressively worse. I tried to run through my injuries, because I didn't know that I wasn't supposed to. I was naive about this whole running thing. The desire to run when my body should probably be resting is something I struggle with to this day.

After high school, I thought I was done with competitive running but through the summer I continued to train on my own and started to see improvement, I even picked up my first road race win a few months after graduation. I contacted the cross-country and track coach of the college I would be attending in the fall and asked if he would be willing to let me on the team. He had never heard my name, but he knew my high school program and said yes.

The first year on the cross-country and track teams at Simpson College was frustrating for me; my inexperience showed. There were times I finished the race very embarrassed. I always felt like I was playing catch-up with the rest of the team members who had more years of running under their belts. But instead of being intimidated, I studied them and tried to learn from them. My coach, Keith Ellingson, was very supportive. Maybe he saw something in me, and maybe it had nothing to do with running, I don't know. But he is one of the few people who really encouraged me to keep going that first year, when I felt like most others were wishing I would give it up.

I kept going, and I kept getting better. I enjoyed (and continue to enjoy) the feeling that I'm always improving. Particularly my junior and senior years, I felt that the sky was the limit if I continued to work hard. By the end of my four years at Simpson I was a vastly different runner. Without the support of Coach Ellingson I would not have accomplished what I have accomplished in this sport, and I have doubts as to whether or not I'd even still be running. I owe him a huge and heartfelt thank-you.

After my senior year of track I took a week or two off from running. It had been a very long season, I was running the 10,000 meters nearly every weekend, and on a few occasions I was asked to run the 5,000 and 10,000 in the same meet. Shortly after my break, in early June, I ran a half marathon and felt very good about my performance. But the next morning I woke up in a terrible funk. My mind and body would not work together. It was a terrible feeling, and what was worse was that there was absolutely nothing I could do to get out of it. Though I ran nearly every day during that time, there were many occasions where I would give up halfway through and walk home, confused and disappointed about what was happening. Now that I have some distance between that period and now, I chalk it up to the postcollege blues. I was living at home, did not yet have a full-time job, and it was very much an adjustment period. There was no, "what's next?" lined up.

This difficult and confusing period lasted nearly six weeks. In July some of my college teammates and I got together and ran one of the larger local road races, something we had done for several years. Though I didn't feel I ran especially well that day, I somehow ran the funk out of me. I had lost a lot of fitness while in my rut, but at least it got me excited about training again. The next morning I went running and felt better than I had in weeks.

The marathon was something that I had begun to consider during my senior season, but with cross-country and track meets nearly every weekend, it was something I couldn't spend much time thinking about. Now, for the first time in five years, there would be no "next season" to look forward to. I needed something to motivate myself. I decided it was time for me to put my focus on running a marathon.

The decision to make the Chicago Marathon my debut was an easy one. It was only a five-hour drive from my home, I've always liked the city, and I had some friends living there. The Chicago course was getting quite a bit of favorable press after Khalid Khannouchi's 1999 world record there, and although that wasn't a necessarily important consideration, it didn't hurt my decision to run there, either. If I was going to run a marathon, I wanted to run it as fast as I possibly could.

I really had no idea of what I was getting myself into. I talked to Coach Ellingson, who had run several very good marathons, but I didn't want to bother him too much; he was busy with the men's and women's teams for both cross-country and track and field. I read several books on training to run fast in the marathon, and decided on a goal time of 2:40 to 2:45. I had gotten pretty comfortable running a 5:20-per-mile pace for 10,000 meters on the track, so I thought running 6:20s for the marathon would be manageable.

I've always considered myself a high-mileage runner, and while the long run is probably the most important component of training for a marathon, it does not entirely sum up my preparation for the race in Chicago. Though I completed four runs of 19 to 22 miles during my buildup to Chicago, I saw one of the most important aspects of my training being my midlength runs at my anticipated marathon pace. Training at race pace is something I picked up in college. The idea was that we could train our bodies and minds to run at a particular pace so that when it came time to race, we could run almost automatically. This particular philosophy has worked very well for me, and rarely is my quality training faster than the anticipated pace for my peak race.

Race weekend came and I felt ready. On Friday evening I left for Chicago with my parents, brother, and girlfriend. One of the things I had overlooked in my marathon preparation was booking a hotel room. By the time I got around to doing that, about three weeks before the marathon, there really wasn't much left. I considered myself lucky to get a hotel near O'Hare Airport, a 45-minute drive to the start line.

The night before the race we ate dinner and then returned to the hotel and watched (appropriately, I guess) *Forrest Gump* on television. I slept better than I anticipated and got up at 3:30 A.M. to grab a bite to eat. The Chicago Marathon has an early 7:00 A.M. start, so I just stayed awake from that time on. Saying good-bye to my family near the start was very emotional for me, but I tried to hide that from them. They are my biggest fans, and although they don't always understand why I run, they have always been very supportive.

Using the posted pace signs at the start, I lined up with the 6:20 pace runners but as soon as the barricades were moved with 10 minutes to go, everyone started pushing forward and mayhem broke loose. It became one huge swell of people all pushing to get up front. I picked my way forward and was able to cross the start line within 10 or 15 seconds of the gun.

Despite my knowing better, I went out too fast. I couldn't help it. For the first 6 miles I was running at 5:45 pace, driven by pure adrenaline. I was so caught up in the excitement of running my first marathon, I vividly remember running through downtown Chicago at the 4-mile mark and crying. It was such a release of tension. I was very caught up in it and also very nervous about the journey ahead.

Up to 16 miles everything was going well even though I knew I was running too fast. At that point I had to make a decision to either slow down or risk having the wheels come off later on. I decided to gamble and keep going at that pace. It was a gutsy move and I have no regrets, even though it almost killed me. I had no idea what lay ahead.

The one aspect of Chicago that I didn't like is that after 16 miles there are very few spectators on the course. Much of the course parallels a freeway and the neighborhoods get pretty dicey. With no crowd support and my faster pace taking its toll, I started to falter around mile 18, and I began to realize that my anticipated blowup was going to happen sooner than later. Like a light switch going off, I melted. One second I was fine and the next I was not. I truly didn't think I would survive—as in *live*.

With 8 miles to go, I was feeling horrible. I know that poor form is one of the biggest drainers of energy, so even though I slowed down significantly I made a very conscious effort to maintain good form. I may have looked okay, but I was not feeling good. There was, however, never, ever a question in my mind that I was not going to make it. I've never dropped out of a race, and this was not going to be my first. I was so determined to finish that I would have crawled all the way on bloody stumps if that is what it took. I knew a friend was planning on waiting for me at Comiskey Field, near the 21-mile mark, and that helped pull me through to that point. But when I got there he was nowhere to be seen. I would find out later he hadn't planned on me getting there that fast! With 5 miles to go and few spectators, I knew I was in for a long journey.

The only thing left to do was go to another place—mentally. This is something that I taught myself to do in collegiate track when I was running the 10,000 meters, often with few other competitors to focus on. As I navigated the streets of Chicago, I tried to think about anything and everything not directly related to how desperate I was. I promised myself a bottle of Nestea iced tea at the finish; that helped keep my mind off things for a while. I would have tried to talk to someone, but at that point the few runners around were passing me pretty quickly. At mile 23, word filtered back that Khannouchi had just won again in an American record time, so I did get in with a group and chat with some of the runners about that for a little while, but most of the time I was alone and hurting.

Even though Chicago is known as a flat course, it is not without inclines. Shortly before the finish, the course heads up an entrance ramp into Lincoln Park, site of the start and finish lines. Though I'm not sure how steep this grade actually is, it felt like a significant hill. I was able to pick off a few people who were also struggling, and that helped a little bit. After cresting the incline, it's a flat final quarter mile to the finish line. By now the spectators were back along the course in full swing, which really helped, and as an added incentive I saw my brother out of the corner of my eye in the middle of the crowd. I picked up the pace—at least it felt like I did—and crossed the finish line. I wanted to raise my arms or do something in celebration, but I was too tired. Some people beat themselves up after a race because they didn't make their predicted time or some other reason, but I was glad just to get through it. I didn't need to beat myself up because physically I already was beat.

Five hours later and somewhat rested, I was already planning my next marathon. Physically, I knew I had to take time to recover, but mentally I had learned so much running this marathon that I was excited to try it again. Every single mile was a learning experience for me and I couldn't wait to correct my mistakes. As the days passed, though, I realized that I wanted to take a longer-term approach to the sequel, which is scheduled for the upcoming Boston Marathon.

Before the race, I made plans to go to the postmarathon party on Sunday evening. Not really thinking about it, I decided to wear some nicer dress shoes that I had just bought and really hadn't had a chance to break in yet. Looking at the map, it didn't look like the party was especially far from the el train, so I decided to go that route as opposed to taking a cab.

It ended up being a 45-minute walk from the el stop to the party, in these new shoes, 10 hours after I had finished a marathon; it was not especially pleasant. If I have one lesson to pass on, it would probably be that one. Save the feet!

I didn't get back to running for three weeks. It was a good time to take a break, and I was very sore. It hurt to go up and down the stairs, but what was really tough was having to make a seven-hour drive to a job interview in Kansas four days after the marathon. I had to crawl out of the car I was so cramped.

My first marathon was a tremendous experience for me, even more so because I landed a job at the marathon. In early October, I saw a job posting for an opening at New York Road Runners and sent in my résumé. They gave me a phone call and wanted to somehow set up a meeting. In passing I mentioned I was running the Chicago Marathon the next weekend; it turned out they were also going to be at the marathon expo. So I had my job interview at the NYRR booth at the Chicago marathon expo. It was so noisy inside the convention center that I barely heard what was being said, but I must have made a good impression because when I returned home after the marathon, I had a job offer waiting.

Training here in New York for the upcoming Boston Marathon is a very different experience. In Iowa I could run 20 miles in any direction and not see a single person or car or cross the same street twice. Here in New York, everyone expects to stop at every stoplight; everyone accepts that they have to run loops to get their miles in. I also have had to schedule my training around my job, something I didn't have to do before, but somehow I have been able consistently run higher mileage. Having a structured day seems to be working to my advantage.

In the six years I've been running, I've gone from someone who routinely finished toward the back of the pack to someone who has won nearly twenty races on the road and track. There aren't many people out there who believe I was born with a great deal of talent, but everybody will agree that I work as hard as anybody else out there, and that's something I take a great deal of pride in. That said, I've learned a few things about running and racing. I think it's applicable for a race of any distance, but it especially rings true for the marathon. I know it certainly applied when I was in Chicago. Someone can go into a race or run with the best-laid plans or goals to simply finish the distance, to run a particular time, or to flat-out win—but things are never that easy. No race has ever been perfect, and nearly every runner will find that out at one time or another.

I guess what I've learned over my career is that's okay; maybe it's even what makes something like the marathon so exciting. When it became apparent to me that I was not going to meet my "goal" of running 2:45 in my first marathon, I readjusted my thinking to a different goal. When I finished, although I was 10 minutes off where I had initially hoped to be, I was still happy and excited because I had taken a gamble, and though I paid for it dearly, I emerged years wiser.

If someone wants to take something away from my experience to help them in their own marathon, I hope it would be that they should be prepared to make adjustments, and to be okay with that. To realize that what they are doing is still a tremendous accomplishment.

# THE MARATHON TO THE MILE

**SID HOWARD**

**D.O.B.: 2-6-39**
**RESIDENCE: PLAINFIELD, NJ**
**OCCUPATION: OWNER,**
**    SUPER-FAST DELIVERIES, INC.**
**FIRST MARATHON: 1978 NEW**
**    YORK CITY MARATHON**
**AGE AT FIRST MARATHON: 39**

*Photo courtesy New York Road Runners*

*A high school dropout, married and a father at 18, life was hard for this former track star. But Sid persevered, stayed married, and raised six kids. He also received his college degree at age 59 to prove to his grandchildren that anything in life is possible. After he picked up running again at 39 to convince his kids that he wasn't old, the exercise turned out to be the catalyst that changed his life and kick-started his dormant love for running. But with nine marathons under his belt and a personal record of 2:46, Sid abruptly quit the marathon and picked up the mile. He currently holds the world record in his age division for the indoor 800 meters. There is only one thing that will get Sid to run another marathon.*

There were 10 kids in my family, 5 boys and 5 girls. It was a crowded house. I never slept in bed alone until I joined the air force at 17. My younger sister was the only one of us to graduate high school. My parents migrated from Georgia looking for work and brought their southern roots with them. I don't think either of my parents ever attended school. We were very poor, but no matter how little we ate during the week, Sunday morning was a down-home southern feast: grits, biscuits, corn bread, chicken, collard greens, enough food to stuff us for the day.

My parents worked long hours in the factories so we had to look after one another. It was understood that the older ones looked after the younger ones. When my parents were home, they were strict disciplinarians. No one dared cross them or disobey. The beatings weren't worth it. We soon learned not to repeat something that displeased my dad.

I was the typical class clown in high school, never taking school seriously. A star on the cross-country team, I thought the coach would pull rank for his top-flight runner. But when I failed math and wood shop, I was thrown off the team. All I had to do was go to summer school to graduate, but I didn't. Instead, I quit school. Looking back, it was the worst decision I ever made. I entered the air force at 17 and came out at 21. I grew up fast during those four years, becoming a husband and father along the way after managing to get my girlfriend pregnant before I left for the air force. We didn't plan on this, as she was only 16. It was the very first time we had intimate relations and three months later she announced she was pregnant. But I did the right thing by her; we got married and she had a healthy baby boy. Then we went on to have five more babies. We were babies having babies. I wasn't even shaving yet and had a son. But I have to believe that the Lord looks after fools and babies, and we qualified in both categories. Most stories that begin this way don't have happy endings, but ours did. We stayed married for 39 years until she passed away four years ago.

While in the air force, I received my high school equivalency degree. By the time I got out of the Air Force at 21, we had four kids. Landing a job as a copy machine operator for $100 a week, we were able to move into the projects paying $60 a month rent. For 10 years we worked hard, trying to save money and raise the kids the best way we knew how. There was no time or money to do anything recreational. I hadn't run since high school, didn't even think about it. For four years I never took a day off, never had a sick day. It was work, work, and more work. In 1970, when I was 31 years old, I got a new job as a delivery man, making an astounding $125 a week. My boss trusted me and allowed me to take the truck home on weekends and moonlight my own delivery jobs. After a month, I went into business for myself. Over the years the business grew, and now 33 years later I'm still in my own business employing 28 people.

When I was 39 years old, my son mentioned a mile race that was being sponsored in town. He said, "Dad, there's a race for old guys like you at the high school." I hadn't run in 23 years, never even gave it a thought. But something triggered my glory days on the track and my love of running poured out and I became determined to run that race. I trained hard for three weeks and won the race. My kids were shocked, couldn't believe their old man could run so fast. I didn't even own a pair of running shoes, ran in a pair of old track shoes.

Running came back to my life like an old friend. Someone mentioned the New York City Marathon and being macho, I thought I could do it. Besides, running a marathon was the ultimate challenge for runners and I wanted to go straight to the top with my newfound running.

In July I applied to the 1978 New York City Marathon and signed up for marathon training classes with the New York Road Runners. Every Wednesday night we met in Central Park and ran 18 miles. I didn't know any better; I thought everyone ran distance and this was a typical run. Even though I never ran that long or hard in my life, my ego wouldn't let me quit. I kept up with the guys and they gave me confidence. I also ran 9 miles every morning. I never took a break, never took a day off. Recovery? Never heard of the word. Taper? Never heard of it. Stretch? Never.

These guys were serious runners. The goal on the Wednesday-night runs was to drop someone, leave them in the dust. I loved it; it appealed to my machismo and I never got dropped.

Three months later I was at the start of my first marathon. I boasted to everyone how I would break three hours. I was so cocky. Even though my friends encouraged me to just run it to enjoy the experience, I pooh-poohed them and thought this would be a piece of cake.

I started out fast and tried to pass anyone in my way. I zigzagged across the Verrazzano Narrows Bridge for the first 2 miles, wasting precious energy going around everyone. I was so inexperienced. I was also caught up in the thrill of running a marathon. There was a buzz in the air that filled me with excitement. The helicopters, the big boom from the cannon, ladies and men urinating on the bridge—this was a place I never knew existed and now I was a part of it.

I flew for 20 miles, unaware of anything except that I was having the time of my life. Then, bam—I lost it. My body just stopped and I had nothing to do with that decision. I wasn't consulted; my body just revolted and quit. I was totally depleted. Part of my inexperience and naiveté was not eating anything that morning. I thought marathoners were supposed to be lean and mean so I didn't eat.

By mile 22 I was walking through Central Park in a daze, tired and starving. I started stealing food from the spectators that held out oranges and bananas for their friends. I didn't even care, I just snatched whatever I could get my hands on, like a crazed madman.

The food helped to energize me enough to start running again and I was able to run across the finish line in 3:02. I couldn't believe it. I almost made my goal but I suffered too much along the way. As I walked ahead to meet my family, I was already determined to run faster next year.

After the marathon, my body was shot for weeks. I couldn't walk downstairs or upstairs. I could feel the aches and pains in every bone of my body. I felt like a walking skeleton. Despite the pain, I fell in love with the marathon.

I ran the Jersey Shore Marathon a month later. The temperature was below freezing and I knew nothing about how to dress for the conditions. To keep my legs warm, I wore ladies' panty hose and put an old pair of socks on my hands to keep them warm. But nothing worked; I stayed cold the entire race.

This time around I did eat and made it to mile 23 before hitting the wall. I walked a few miles then ran across the finish in 3:03.

By now I thought I had this marathon stuff down. I thought I was experienced and just needed some fine-tuning. I spoke to as many marathoners as I could and picked their brains. I learned about training, stretching, tapering, and fueling my body. My third marathon was the 1979 New York City Marathon and I finally broke three hours, with a time of 2:51.

I went on to run a total of nine marathons in five years, with a personal best of 2:46. However, by 1983 my love affair with the marathon was waning. I couldn't answer the question, "Sid, why do you run marathons?' Although I was fast, it never felt right with my body. Even my friends and coach were telling me to quit, that I would make a better sprinter.

Marathons were just too hard on my body and I suffered too much after every one. When I crossed the finish line of the 1983 New York City Marathon, I said, "That's it. It's over." The training takes too much time and during my brief marathon career I was juggling the kids, my wife's early stages of heart disease, working all day, and attending school at night. Although I gave up the marathon, running continued to be the catalyst for everything I did. Running gives me the energy to get through the day, which starts at 5:30 in the morning with a run before going to work. I tried to get my kids to run by bribing them, but even money couldn't get them out the door. They'd come up with imaginary aches and pains in their ankles and knees and feign a few limps. They taught me a valuable lesson: If you don't want to do it for yourself, you won't do it at all.

After giving up marathons I switched to shorter distances. I joined the Central Park Track Club, and that opened up a new world. When New York Road Runners held the Fifth Avenue Mile in 1981—a very prestigious run that attracts top talent—I entered. It's my favorite race and I believe I am the only masters runner who has run that event every year. In 1999, at age 60, I won my division in 5:12. I never thought I could run that fast. And the funny thing is I keep getting faster! My times are actually improving and I won again in 2001. That may sound crazy, but runners are not normal people. We have to be nuts to do what we do.

I owe my success in track and field to my years as a marathoner. It gave me a base for everything else I have accomplished. I was able to parlay the training to shorter distances and had incredible success. There is a fine line between building up and tearing down and I got out in time. Most of the people I ran marathons with back in the 1980s aren't running anymore. They're done; I benefited from my mistakes.

Turning 60 was the best year of my life. Not only did I get to enter a new age division in racing, my accomplishments were even better than I ever wished for. On my birthday, I set an age-group world record of 2:14:75 for the 800 meters indoor. I also hold the American masters record for the outdoor 800 meters.

You know, I'm just a simple boring guy. I eat, run, work, sleep, in that order. When my wife was sick, I took care of her the best way I could. It was time consuming, an act of love and devotion, but in a way it left me with little time to think about the suffering and devastation it placed on us. Now I live alone and really miss her. The kids are out of the house and have busy lives of their own. My days are still filled with morning runs, out the door to work till late in the evening and sometimes weekend work as well. When I want to relax and have fun, I go dancing. My six kids, 17 grandchildren, and one great grandchild are a big part of my life because I know how important family ties are. As a kid, I visited my grandfather every weekend. He lived to be 100 and was still sharp as a tack. My own father died before my grandfather. Even though Jackie Robinson was my first hero, my dad was my second. And after he died, my grandfather took his place. He was a gift to me and I returned that gift by spending my weekends with him. I've always believed that you have to be a giver in order to receive.

At 62, I don't consider myself old. It's mind over matter: If you don't mind, it doesn't matter. Exercise has helped me formulate my thoughts on aging, and I have come to the conclusion that most of the ailments associated with aging can be prevented with proper diet and exercise. I used to be a smoker. Started smoking when I saw all the baseball players puffing away on their Lucky Strikes. That was my brand because I saw it advertised at the Dodgers games. And when I was in the air force, you could always get free time by asking for a cigarette break. I smoked for twelve years and then quit when I decided to get healthy. It was a very hard thing to do, but I never picked up a cigarette since. It all goes along with my theory that you can do anything you want if you have the discipline and the desire. You can be healthy at any age if you make the effort. Of course it's easier if you have a good foundation, but healthy habits can start at any age and still show benefits. And you don't have to run marathons to be fit.

I consider myself very fit. I don't eat any animal protein, sugars or wheat. I stretch and take care of my body instead of beating it up. After a race, I recover with an ice bath. It's not easy to do the first couple of times but you get used to it. I fill the tub halfway with cold water and then put in four 10-pound bags of ice. Then I submerge my body in the water for 20 minutes. At first I could only stay in for three minutes but after a while the body gets numb and you don't really feel the cold. I take the opportunity to return all my phone calls while I am taking my ice bath. It's my quiet time.

My biggest accomplishment in life was finally getting my college degree in 1998, at age 59. It was a shock to me how much I enjoyed learning. I loved the class dynamics and it never bothered me that I was by far the oldest in the class. In fact, it made me realize that I did have something to offer, that my life had been rich with opportunities in many ways. I also wanted to show my grandchildren that anything is possible if you want it badly enough. And on commencement day, nothing in my life to date compared with graduating from college. All the races in the world, all the medals I've won could never equal the accomplishment of my college degree.

My goal is not only to reach 100, but to still break records for running the mile, 3-mile, and maybe even the 5-mile. I also plan to be self-sufficient, still drive my own car, dress myself, and cook for myself. I don't want to be a burden on anyone.

And the one thing that will get me to run another marathon is my neighbor. She is 35, the mother of two kids, and is thinking about running a marathon. I told her if she does one, I'll run it with her. That should be interesting.

# HAD TO DO IT AGAIN TO GET IT RIGHT

**CM JENKINS**

**D.O.B.: 6-5-59**
**RESIDENCE: DOUGLAS, GEORGIA**
**OCCUPATION: TEACHER; MIDDLE**
   **SCHOOL COACH OF FOOTBALL,**
   **WRESTLING, AND SWIMMING**
**FIRST MARATHON: 2001 COUNTRY**
   **MUSIC MARATHON, NASHVILLE**
**AGE AT FIRST MARATHON: 41**

*CM is a triathlete turned marathoner and after his two marathon experiences, he prefers the triathlons. Not that the marathon wasn't a great adventure; he tells an exciting tale and went back for more. As a school football coach, he knows what it is like to go after a goal, suffer along the way, and feel the spark of competitiveness at the end. He is a great role model for his young players as he isn't afraid to face a challenge and have some fun along the way.*

Down south, the big sport is football. Everyone wants to be a football player. In high school I played football just like every one else, as well as basketball and baseball. No one ran. Some kids went out for the track team but they weren't considered athletes.

In college I majored in physical education. This was the late '70s and Jim Fixx and Dr. Cooper had caught the nation's attention with fitness and running. I wasn't good enough to play college-level sports but running was something everyone could do so I convinced a buddy to run with me. He was a tennis player and joined me so he could build up his endurance for tennis.

By junior year running became my sport. I think I made the transition to a real runner when I started running on my own without a partner and missed the days I didn't get to run. Running didn't replace the sports I grew up with like football and baseball, but it was new and I liked that. I read all the sports and fitness journals and just couldn't get enough information on anything to do with exercise and fitness. Besides, exercise physiology was my chosen field and running is a very scientific study of the body's interplay with oxygen. I learned about fast-twitch and slow-twitch fibers and all sorts of interesting stuff. Truth be told, these days I'd rather sit around discussing $VO_2$ max than who is playing in the super bowl.

After leaving college, I didn't run for three years. I was too busy with a new coaching position and starting a family and getting caught up with my career and life. There was no free time for anything. I also gained 30 pounds during those three years.

In 1984 I decided it was time to start losing the extra weight I was carrying around and started running again. I picked up where I left off and fell in love with it all over again. I started entering races, 5Ks and some 10Ks, and did this for the next 15 years. I was a maintenance runner and happy with that. Any idea of running a marathon was beyond comprehension. I had no desire to jump my miles up and take on something like a marathon.

Then two things happened. I turned 40 and changed my coaching job from high school football to middle school. Coaching high school football was an intense, busy lifestyle for so long that I needed a break. I never had a weekend off, nor afternoons or evenings. Although it was my decision to change, I was very passionate about my coaching and now I needed a new passion.

The first thing I did was take up triathlons. A friend of mine called and asked me to join him for a triathlon event. I was turning 40 that weekend so I thought, *Why not? this is something new and interesting.* Taking up swimming and cycling was just the fix I was looking for. I developed a new passion for sports I never realized I had before.

After the triathlon season came to a close, I decided to increase my miles to make up for the loss of the swimming and cycling during the winters. I met someone who liked to do long runs so I joined him. When I reached 15 miles I decided I could do a marathon. With my triathlon experience and some long runs under my belt, I thought I was ready. It had become a realistic goal, no longer beyond comprehension.

I made a commitment to run the 2001 Country Music Marathon. I started training in October 2000 for the April marathon. In selecting my first marathon, I had two main criteria: make it big and make it close, at least a drivable distance.

I ran my first half marathon Thanksgiving Day. It felt great and I maintained a nine-minute pace. The competitive juices were flowing. I continued building my mileage and was on track but a last-minute scheduling conflict created a problem. I wanted to do my last long run of 22 miles three weeks before the marathon and then taper down but I had to go out of town on a conference. I weighed the difference of running it early with four weeks to go or running it late with two weeks to go and I decided to run my last long run four weeks out.

That was a major mistake. I had too much time on my hands to taper down. But I didn't realize that until it was too late.

The next mistake I made was the night before the marathon. My wife and two kids drove to Nashville with me and we decided to see the sights and walked all over Nashville. By the time I went to bed that night I must have walked 5 miles, up and down hills, and man, I was tired!

The third mistake was not realizing that Nashville would be a weather change for me. I'm eight hours south of Nashville and all my long runs were on cool days in the early spring. Now it's late spring and hot in Nashville, which is stuck in a valley between two mountain ranges. The locals kept telling me it's always hot in Nashville! Who knew? I didn't prepare for running in the heat. By 7 A.M. the morning of the race it was already 78 degrees.

I didn't sleep the night before, mainly because I was nervous, but I was also plagued with a nasty cramp in my calf from walking all those hills.

The morning of the marathon I had plenty of time on my hands to roam around and take in all the surroundings. I strolled by the elite runners' tent and decided to go find out just what an elite runner was. Since there was very little security around their tent, I just popped in and started talking to the folks. I saw some Kenyans and Ethiopians and just hung around talking with them, but most of them couldn't speak English. They kept staring at me, probably trying to figure out what a 6-foot-2, 240-pound guy was doing in the elite tent standing next to a bunch of 5-foot-4, 100-pound runners. I think I scared them.

Finally, we all lined up for the start. I started mid-to-back of the back, planning on finishing in 4:45. I was psyched and felt prepared and ready to go. There was no way of knowing just how bad a day I was about to have.

The first 10 miles went really well. I was having a grand old time, chatting it up with the other runners and truly enjoying myself. I maintained a 10-minute pace, slower than expected but comfortable. My plan was to run the first half at a 9-minute pace then toward the end slow down to a 10-minute pace but that plan was canceled. The course was hilly and it was hot but I was still feeling good.

The major attraction of the Country Music Marathon is that a band plays at every mile. That was a great diversion and I enjoyed the upbeat music. One band was playing a Steely Dan song, which happens to be one of my favorite groups, and I went over and high-fived the lead singer. I was having a ball. I tend to be a bit of a ham and I like fooling with the crowd. Heck, I wasn't doing this marathon to win it, just enjoy myself and experience it. But as the day—and the miles—progressed, it got hotter, up into the 80s, and I was starting to feel real tired. Looking forward to hearing the bands kept me going.

At mile 16, the course wanders through an industrial section with no spectators and no bands. Just when I needed somebody, anybody, there was nothing but the hot sun blazing down on me. It was murder. I started mumbling to myself, *How in the hell am I going to make it 10 more miles!*

The only thing that got me through that hell was seeing my family at mile 19. It is also where the cramps kicked in. Because of the intense heat, I tried to take in as much water as I could at the water stops but it was difficult to swallow anything in those little cups. I'm sure the cramps were due to the heat as much as the hills.

My wife Pam and the kids were waiting for me as planned at mile 19 so that was a nice bit of relief. My 10-year old son, Travis, decided to run a mile with me so off we went after drinking some more water. We ran together till the 20-mile marker and then I told him to find his mother, who was walking behind us. I could see her by a bridge as Travis left me. Little did I know this would be the last time I saw my son for hours to come.

I continued on at a very slow pace and my cramps got worse. I did a walk-run until mile 24 and then it was impossible to run at all. The cramps had moved into my quads. I walked to mile 25 and was in such pain I decided to stop and stretch. Suffice it to say this proved to be a tactical mistake. I sat down and couldn't get up. The cramps had spread through my entire body and I could not move at all. I flagged down a motorcycle cop and leaned on his bike to relax my legs. He called for an ambulance and I was ready to accept the ride and receive a Did Not Finish instead of a medal with no regrets. It was that bad.

But the ambulance never showed. After waiting five minutes I started to walk the last mile. I made it to the finish and jogged pitifully across the line, deeply disappointed in myself. The elation I had anticipated for months was not forthcoming. There was only a sense of relief, not exhilaration. It took me 5:15 and was not worth the toll on my body.

As soon as I crossed the finish line, Pam was at my side. But instead of comforting me she was panicked. Travis was lost. She'd never found him after he jogged mile 20 with me. Doing some calculations, I estimated he had been lost for over two hours. I was overcome with fear but at the same time I couldn't walk. I felt helpless. I went to the medical tent while Pam went looking for Travis.

While I was getting iced and the doctors were trying to bring my legs back to life, I heard an announcement for the parents of Travis Jenkins to come to a designated area. The medics had to hold me up as I went to find my son. We were all very relieved to find Travis, but as soon as I knew he was safe it was back to the medical tent for me.

The doctors kept me under surveillance for 30 minutes until they felt I could make it back to the shuttle bus for the 1-mile trip to the motel. My family and I got on the bus and then all hell broke out. It was like Gilligan's Island revisited. The 1-mile trip took 45 minutes as the bus driver kept getting lost. The bus was full with other runners and their families so I had to sit in the aisle next to the bus driver. Besides, with all the cramps, there was no way I could fold my 6-foot-2, 240-pound frame into a little yellow school bus seat.

After the fourth missed exit off the highway, I started throwing up in the driver's trash can. I couldn't take it anymore and we exited the bus with a block to go before the motel. I instructed my wife and the kids to get some Gatorade, sandwiches, and a six-pack of beer while I made my way to the room.

By the time I made it into the room I could hardly breathe and my legs were cramping again. One of the motel housekeepers rode in the elevator with me and noticed my troubles. I got off the elevator and as I walked into the room the pain was so intense I started hyperventilating. I sat on the bed trying to control my breathing when the door opened and the same house-keeper walked in. She was worried about me and wanted to check on my condition. I stretched out on the bed and she began massaging my latissimus area. Turns out she has a son with a bullet lodged in his spine and she has to give him daily massages so she knew just what to do. Her magic fingers made mincemeat of the cramps and they subsided.

When my wife finally made it back to the room, I had enough Gatorade, food, and beer plus a warm bath to keep the cramps at bay. Then I fell asleep till 5 in the afternoon.

The mistakes I made at my first marathon were not getting enough fluids before the race, walking too much the night before, not drinking enough during the race, and not taking into consideration the heat and hills. And in retrospect, doing my last long run with four weeks to go was too much of a lay-off.

The finish of my first marathon left a lot to be desired. I felt like I didn't deserve to say I ran a marathon. That's why I had to run another one! It took me one day to make the decision to run another. I needed the elation and sense of accomplishment and was willing to do it again to capture that.

My second marathon was seven months later in December, in Jacksonville, Florida. I made sure it would be a flat course and checked the weather to make sure it would be cool. My training was pretty much the same although I ran a 23-miler and did my last long run two weeks before the marathon instead of four. I felt confident at the start. I wasn't overwhelmed and still felt very excited. I also ran it with a friend, which made a big difference. It was nice to share the experience. I held on to a 10-minute pace till mile 23 and then gassed out. I took long walk breaks but always managed to pick up the running.

I finished in 4:40:41 and finally found that feeling of elation. It felt so good I almost cried. I finally proved to myself that I could run a marathon.

After two marathons, I honestly don't know if this is cut out for me. It's an exercise in human suffering and I don't think I want to go through that again. It's just too painful.

Having said that, I do like the challenge; it's like a drug. Maybe I have just one more in me.

# THE KENYAN WAY

**JACKSON KIPNGOK**

**D.O.B.:** 12-14-60
**RESIDENCE: BARINGO, KENYA**
**OCCUPATION: PROFESSIONAL
RUNNER**
**FIRST MARATHON: 1994 WALT
DISNEY WORLD MARATHON,
ORLANDO, FL**
**AGE AT FIRST MARATHON: 34**

*Jackson lives a life that is difficult for many American runners to imagine. Separated from his country and wife and children for long stretches of time, he exists only to run. Managed by an agent he hopes is trustworthy, he travels from city to city running races and bunking with fellow Kenyans doing the same thing. He sends his hard-earned winnings home to his wife to manage the farm and feed the kids. For Jackson, this is a good life. He is a hero in his village and dreams of retiring soon so he can return home and coach other Kenyans to follow their dreams of becoming great runners in America.*

My village is very beautiful. It is about three and a half hours from Nairobi, far out in the country. My parents were farmers but we didn't have a lot of money. We are seven children. I am the firstborn. No one in our village wears shoes. They are too expensive. That's just the way life is in our village. I got my first pair of shoes when I was in high school. I ran 3 miles to school and then 3 miles back home, barefoot. On weekends my job was to take care of the animals and I would chase them around the field. When they stopped to graze, I would run loops around them. It was fun, and the way I kept busy and entertained. Fetching our water was also far away, and sometimes that was my chore, too.

Everyone in my country wants to be a professional runner. Henry Rono was my hero, like Michael Jordan in America. All the kids look up to the professional runners who have made it big in America. In high school I played soccer (we call it football) and ran cross-country. But I loved running more than soccer. I won almost all my races and was champion runner of my school.

But still, I knew I wasn't good enough to go far in Kenya because everyone in Kenya is a good runner and you have to be the best to succeed. When I competed against other schools and villages I wasn't winning so I knew I had to get better if I wanted to make it as a runner. I wanted to run so good. It was my goal to be good enough to get sponsored and go to America so I could make money and take care of my family.

When I graduated from high school in 1986 I went into the military—the Kenyan air force. The military is a good place to get training as all the branches sponsor teams and have their own coaches. It is very competitive. We ran against other units like the navy and army. There was a running camp on the base and we trained two or three times a day. Actually, the military is a good route to becoming a professional runner. Running for the military is very prestigious. It is actually more important to be a good runner than a good soldier. The recruiters scout the high schools for the best runners and try to sign them up so they will have a good running team. The army has the best team.

I spent 10 years in the military. In 1991 I made the Kenyan national team and came in fifth in the 12K cross-country race. I didn't have enough experience to go to the world championships just yet and it took two more years before I was good enough to make the team. But still, I wasn't good enough to run outside Kenya. The Kenya Athletic Federation and their coaches make the decision what runners will leave Kenya to be sponsored. If you don't have their backing, you don't go anywhere.

I was one of the fortunate runners to meet a manager from London, and the federation agreed to have him sponsor me. He organized a trip to London for me with some other Kenyans. It was my first time out of the country and on a commercial plane. I did fly on planes with the air force but this was different. I was so excited. Here I was, 34 years old and just starting my professional running career. The manager pays my expenses and puts me in a house with other Kenyans. In return, I pay him 10 percent of the money I win. We stayed in London for four days and ran a race and then we flew to France for another race. I came in second in the first race and fifth in France. My manager was pleased and so was I. The manager gets us sponsorship with shoe companies; we were originally sponsored by Nike and then Reebok.

The first time I came to America was in 1993. I lived with other Kenyans and all we did was run. My normal routine was like this: Wake up at 6 A.M. and go out for an easy run, around one hour. Return for a breakfast of bread and tea. Then train at the track, with lots of repeats and intervals. Back home for lunch, corn cereal. In the afternoon we do another easy run for 50 minutes and return for dinner, usually rice or spaghetti. Then I go to bed. The next morning I start all over again. I drink lots of water and have very little fat or meat in my diet.

My first race in America was in South Carolina, the Cooper River 10K in Charleston. I took third place. Right after that I did the Cherry Blossom 10-miler in Washington, D.C., and placed fifth. Then I flew out to Spokane, Washington, for the Lilac Bloomsday Run and placed sixth. Although I was winning money, there is bigger prize money to be made in Europe.

Although my times and finishes were acceptable, I wasn't real happy with them and decided to step up the miles and do a marathon. I was 34, an age when younger runners were catching my heels and the marathon was to some extent an open field—not as competitive as the shorter distances. My manager did not want to hire a marathon coach for me as he felt I wasn't proven material yet so I went home to Kenya and trained on my own. I didn't know how to train for a marathon so I devised my own program.

I ran for two or three hours at a clip and just kept running longer and longer distances. It was tiring but I kept up with it. My manager promised that if I did well at my first marathon he would hire a coach for me so I had a reason to do well.

I carefully chose my first marathon and selected the Walt Disney Marathon in January 1994. Only three other Kenyans were running and I knew all of them and thought I had a good chance of beating them. I was nervous. My goal was to just finish but I also needed a good time. I wasn't sure I was ready, as I didn't know how to run a marathon. The race officials paid only for my lodging and entry fee so I had a lot riding on this. What I had most was courage. I really wanted this as it meant everything to my career and ability to make money.

I was very nervous at the start. I didn't run too fast at the beginning, just stayed with the pack of the top three Kenyans because they had run marathons before and I thought they knew what they were doing. But it was so far, just so far. I thought I was going to die. I didn't know anything about pacing myself. I was just so tired. We finished all in a row, and I took third place with a time of 2:16. With more experience, I think I could have taken first place.

Afterward, I felt the pain. I didn't feel it so much when I was running because I was focusing on what to do, but the next day the pain was terrible. I took a month off and started to run easy after three weeks and finally resumed total all-out training in four weeks. Back in London, my coach thought I did well enough to have my own coach. We trained in Colorado and he upped my mileage to 200 a week. I was running twice a day, sometimes three times a day.

He decided I was ready for another marathon so that April I entered the Boston Marathon and took third place with a time of 2:08. My countryman Cosmas Ndeti took first with a time of 2:07:15, which was a new course record, so I wasn't far off the mark for a winning time. I trained so hard for that and it paid off. Later that year I ran the Berlin Marathon in September and placed sixth with a time of 2:12. I learned to run smarter with each subsequent marathon.

It was crazy. In my first year of marathons I ran three in nine months. I did get injured after Berlin and went home to Kenya to rest. My manager just kept signing me up until I got that injury. I told him that was enough. He also had me run a 20K right before Berlin. It was too much. Too much. If I refuse he gets angry and then he may not let me run so I do what he says. But this was too much.

To date, I've run a total of 10 marathons with a PR of 2:08. I still feel strong although the younger marathoners are now coming up my heels. I think a good marathoner can still compete until 45 years of age. At least that is what I am planning to do. After that I will return to Kenya and become a coach. I am married with four kids so I still need to work. And I still support my mother. We always support our families. That is the Kenyan way and why we try so hard to win the prize money. If I hadn't become a runner I would have stayed home and managed the farm, which is not so profitable. This way I can support my mother and my own family in a nice way. I also took care of my brothers and sisters as well. I am the oldest; it is expected. I paid for their school, bought new land for the farm, and paid for anything they needed to keep the farm going. They are now on their own taking care of their own farms.

I go home every three or four months to visit with my family. There is no point in ever having my wife come visit me here. It is better for them this way. They get used to it. It's not such a bad life, especially when I am making money. I keep busy with running. That's all I do, train and race. I don't know how the Americans expect to be better runners when they don't put the time in. They train as individuals when they should be training with a group. It's too hard to train on your own. Maybe with the new training camps they will do better.

When I am a coach I will be honest with the Kenyans who want to go to Europe and America to run and make their fortunes. They must be careful and choose good managers. Some managers lie and don't tell the truth about what it means to be sponsored. Some of them sign the contract for the runners and don't even let them read it. I want to be a good coach and tell them about my experiences so they can avoid problems. Kenyans have a very strong desire to be the best. It is their ticket out of the country and a way to support their families. But sometimes we overdo it. The Ethiopians on the other hand are more selective. They only do a few races. But we have more runners so we can cover more races.

Right now I am taking a break to go home and visit with my wife and children. When I am home I will only run once a day. For me, that is taking a break.

# NEVER SAY NEVER

DAVID LAVALLE

D.O.B.: 4-10-74
RESIDENCE: STAMFORD, CT
OCCUPATION: TELECOMMUNICATIONS
  SALES
FIRST MARATHON: 1999 OCEAN STATE
  MARATHON, WARWICK, RI
AGE AT FIRST MARATHON: 25

*After running his first half marathon, David was convinced a full marathon couldn't be that much different and decided to go for the whole enchilada. He trained consistently and hard, a well-intentioned first-timer. But even with good intentions, a marathon can be full of surprises, and David was caught off guard by a number of things. He also learned a few valuable lessons to incorporate in his next marathon, such as not overdoing the hot mineral ice!*

I was your basic high school jock. Played soccer and lacrosse on the school teams. I was always team-oriented. The only sport I did on my own was skiing. What I enjoyed most about the teams was being part of something. I was always the captain and enjoyed the leadership role. It gave me confidence, and I liked teaching others and sharing that level of confidence with them. I was aiming for a college scholarship for lacrosse but blew my knee out senior year, which ended any thoughts I had on playing in the big leagues. My first operation was in June and the second was in August, right before I went to freshman orientation at University of Richmond. The doctor told me this was a crucial time for recovery and to take it easy, but heck, I was starting college. Things happen! By the time I enrolled in rehabilitation in Richmond, two to three weeks later, my knee was the size of a watermelon. Scar tissue had started to form over the anterior cruciate ligament. Ultimately I needed four operations and I spent my entire freshman year on crutches. Unfortunately I was plagued with the nickname Limpy, which stuck for most of my four years.

Not being able to participate in sports was unbearable; I was going nuts. The doctor gave me permission to lift weights so I took that up with a vengeance. I had a ton of hormones that needed a direction so I worked out really hard and it started to show. I got attention in the gym and that was refreshing. I could finally do something. I was lifting more than anyone else in the gym and that gave me a lift. It sparked me to continue lifting and keep it as part of my overall routine. Running was never part of the picture. I hated it. You couldn't pay me enough to run.

After my knee healed and I was back to lacrosse, I became captain of the lacrosse club. We had lofty goals and wanted to be the best club in the States. We made it to the finals and lost to the Naval Academy. It was the last game for us seniors but as captain, I played some freshmen instead of putting myself into the game. I rotated the squad so everyone would get the feeling of competitive play.

After college I headed to California and became a ski instructor for a season. It was fun but the money was lousy. I couldn't afford to join a gym so against all my sane rational thoughts I started running to stay in shape. I certainly wasn't dedicated to it and could only muster a mile but it was all I could afford to do. If nothing else, running is certainly the poor man's sport.

I came back to Connecticut and got my first real job. The first thing I did with my paycheck was join a gym. I was there at 6 in the morning ready to go. I was never a morning person but I soon discovered that it fit me to a T. It gave me a rush that lasted all day. I'd go to work so high and pumped up, my coworkers started to ask me what brand of coffee I drank. When I tried to explain it wasn't the coffee but how I felt after my workout, I was labeled as that "natural high guy."

At work I met a guy named Eddie who became my gym partner and mentor. He pushed me to do more than I could on my own. He was into individual sports, like running, the complete antithesis of me. He loved to run and I would listen to his stories and he actually got me to run with him a few times. Certainly not as a partner or anything resembling a commitment to running. It was more his personality and stories that got me interested in running, rather than running for its own sake.

Eddie organized the Chase Corporate Challenge for my firm, Greenwich Associates, and that was my first race, a 5K back in the spring of 1998. I didn't train, just thought it would be fun. When I saw the crowd I got psyched. I had never been part of an event with 3,000 participants and everything just seemed so exciting. I actually sprinted at the end to cross the finish line and I remember feeling so proud of myself and wanting to share that feeling with Eddie. When I looked for him, I just caught him crossing the finish line and couldn't believe I beat him. That was a real rush.

Then I met Wendy and running took on a new meaning. Wendy had also run the Corporate Challenge 5K, and we saw each other at the party afterward. We started running together as a social thing; at least that was what she thought. I was actually trying to get her to date me and thought she would be impressed with my running abilities, which I didn't even have at that time. I faked it. As an aside, after we dated for a few years Wendy confessed to me that on our first run she tried so hard to keep up with me that she injured her ankle. We were both guilty of trying to show off for the other. Either we are both too damn competitive or it was love at first run. But as our running together became more solid and part of a routine, I began to enjoy it. Soon it began to feel comfortable. When I could run 5 miles and still feel energetic afterward, I started identifying myself as a runner. That was a real turning point for me. I actually remember looking back to my high school years when I couldn't even run a mile, and realized how far I had come.

In the spring of 1999, Wendy and I ran the Cherry Blossom 10-miler in Washington, D.C. Wendy's sisters, Erin and Dana, went to school nearby and we all met. Erin ran with us and it was a great time. It was also cold and rainy but that didn't dampen our spirits. We all loved it. By now I was getting into a regimen, between running and still lifting weights. I did some serious training for that race and it brought back my college days of conditioning and team spirit. Wendy and I were a team and running began to define me.

Two months later I ran a half marathon. I wanted to take running to the next level. The day was hot and humid and the course was hilly. The amount of stress on my body was tremendous and I realized how tough running a marathon must be. I ran it with Wendy and her parents came to cheer us on. Her dad ran cross-country in high school so he knew the effort it took to run this distance. He met me at the finish and ran the last few yards with me up to the finish line. After the race he told me how amazed he was that I did that. He felt it was an incredible accomplishment and I was touched by his praise.

A week after the half marathon Wendy and I talked about the possibility of a marathon. I said to Wendy, "Heck, we've already run a half, let's go for the whole enchilada." She was hesitant and didn't think she had time to train as she just started a new job. I was annoyed at first because I wanted to do one with her and never imagined doing it without her.

Now that I was committed to running a marathon, I realized it was the first time I had set a tangible goal just for myself without a team backing me up. The focus to run a marathon would be totally on my shoulders. I started to plan my marathon, and it didn't matter where it was—just that I got to do it soon. The New York City marathon was coming up in the fall and I stood on line in Central Park to up my chances of getting in, but I didn't make it. Undeterred, I started training for my marathon even though I wasn't even in one as yet. A coworker and experienced runner gave me a training guide from *Runner's World* magazine for first-timers. My goal was to just finish and have a good time doing it; a predicted finish time was never an issue. I didn't want to get hurt or disappointed or frustrated. Just enjoy the experience.

I eventually entered the Ocean State Marathon, scheduled for the end of

October, giving me 18 weeks to get ready. I did most of my training at night after work and saved my long runs for the weekends. One memorable 15-miler was on a beautiful September Saturday, and my course took me through the old mansions and estates in Greenwich. To keep my mind occupied I reminisced back to my college days when I was known as the Good Time Guy, because I loved to party. As I ran, I saw a magnificent long driveway with the trees bordering the sides, leaning over and just beckoning me to come in. A wedding reception was in full swing on the lawn at the end of the drive and it looked so appealing and appetizing that, mesmerized, I just kept on running down the drive until I was in full view of the wedding party. A cluster of very cute bridesmaids were standing alongside a tent holding flutes of champagne and when they saw me, instead of calling the guards to haul away my sweaty body, they raised their glasses and tempted me to join them, like sirens from the mist. Well, I knew at that point I had to make a serious decision. I could either be the Good Time Guy all over again and join them or turn around and continue my long run. It was a tough decision but in the end the Good Time Guy turned around and went back down the driveway to continue pounding out the miles.

I didn't tell many people about my marathon plans. It was a personal decision and I didn't feel the need to shout it from the rooftops. It was a commitment to myself and I didn't feel the need to share that with others. It's like, *Don't tell people you are going to win the war until after you win it.*

My training went really well, with only one minor setback due to an injury. I hurt my neck and back because I always held my head down. After a few months of that my bad form ended up as an injury and I couldn't run for a while. As I didn't have the extra cash to buy a bike, I learned to swim. Wendy is an excellent swimmer and taught me. That saved me and eventually when the injury healed and I started running again I hadn't lost any of my endurance or pace. I also ate everything all the time. It actually bothered me how much I ate.

By October I was ready. My longest run, a 20-miler, was behind me and I was psyched. Wendy's sister Erin came with us and we all drove to Providence the morning of the race. Although I was nervous and had no idea what to expect, I felt quite mellow. I knew I would finish and that is all I wanted out of the experience. What really had an emotional effect on me was Erin's support. I knew Wendy would be there but having Erin was just really special.

Despite the fact that Wendy says I am chronically late, it really wasn't my fault that we were late getting to the start. We got lost, had to pick up Erin, and other little things that caused us to be late. I had bought a really ugly pair of shorts on sale that I trained in so I wore them for the race. They were on sale because they were really short. I mean short as barely covering what they are supposed to cover. And because it was cold, I wore a Jagermeister Liqueur

T-shirt over my singlet. A buddy of mine had told me his nipples bled during his marathon and that I should smear Vaseline on them. The thought of that was a bit disgusting.

On the way in the car, Erin read the race brochure to me for the first time. She started reading a paragraph about hitting the wall, a term I had never heard before. I turned to Wendy and asked, "What does that mean?" She thought it meant a point in the race where it gets really hard to run. I was so clueless. Ignorance was truly bliss.

Because we were late, I literally had to run to the start line. There was no time to reflect on what I was doing. My dad told me he was going to be there but I didn't see him anywhere before the race started.

What surprised me most of all in the beginning was the number of people running. I had never run in such a crowded arena before and I was amazed. For the first few miles it felt like I was just on a nice slow training run but then I thought, *Wow, I have a ways to go!* I saw my dad at mile 3 and that was very special. But what really got to me was the crowd support. No one had ever cheered for me before and I was overwhelmed by the encouragement and sincerity of the spectators. I truly don't think I could have made it through 26.2 miles without them.

One piece of advice I would give to future first-timers is to avoid too much mineral ointment. Because I was late I didn't get a chance to do my usual stretching. By mile 5 I was beginning to feel tight. I saw Wendy, Erin, and my Dad on the side and ran over and asked Wendy to rub my back with Hot Ice. They all got into the act and really lathered me up. The first minute back on the course it felt nice and warm but then it continued to get hotter and hotter until my back was on fire. I was practically crying from the pain. I overdosed on Hot Ice. There was no way I could get it off my back. I opened my shirt thinking the wind would wick some away but I really thought I would be done in by Hot Ice in my first marathon.

After that experience, I settled back into the pack and just soaked up the crowd. For the next 12 miles I enjoyed every minute of the crowd, talking with other runners and having people yell, "Go Jagermeister!" to me. Total strangers would call out, 'You can do it! Go!" just for me. Or so it seemed.

By mile 18 I was getting a bit tired. On top of that, this part of the course is flat and ugly, very industrial. An annoying girl started talking to me. She was mostly annoying because I couldn't talk and was trying to save my energy. I slowed down and she passed me. Then I ran with a bunch of guys who'd run Boston, so that was interesting. Then I caught up with that girl again and she started telling me the wall was coming. We were at mile 20 and she was really psyching me out, pulling me down with all this talk of the wall, like it was an inevitable obstacle we all had to face. I ditched her again and continued on.

I started to hurt everywhere. I don't actually know what it feels like to be hit by a train but I imagine this would have to come close. My knees, my back, even my mind hurt. At mile 21, there was a table with oranges and bananas and everyone seemed to be reaching for a banana, so what the heck, it was my first marathon so I did what everyone else did and grabbed a banana. Bad idea. My stomach started churning in a very uncomfortable way and I didn't know how I was going to survive. I went into a total meltdown and started bawling my eyes out.

I was so sad it was pathetic. And to make it worse, during miles 22 to 25, there were no spectators. Gone were my cheering fans, my rock, my foundation for getting through this journey. I felt abandoned and lost and miserable. The only thing that got me through was seeing Wendy and Erin at mile 22 and they jumped in and ran with me. It was a huge release for me; I needed them so badly they were like angels to me. I soaked up their energy and fed off it through to the finish.

With a half mile to go I could see the finish and hear the crowds, and that was a real lift. Something changed inside of me. I started getting energy from the crowd and despite the pain, the emotions, and the crying, I sprinted to the finish. It was like breaking through a high fever. Crossing the finish line was tumultuous. My dad was there waiting for me and gave me a big hug. Then Wendy and Erin were there and we all hugged. I've never been on a bigger high. I felt like I could do anything. But all I really wanted to do was eat.

Two weeks later I attended a cousin's wedding and told anyone who would listen about my marathon. Out of all my cousins I am the youngest and we always had a competitive thing going among us. We are all Eagle Scouts, too. My parents divorced when I was three and my dad raised me. During the marathon, my dad was always in the back of my mind so it made me proud to hear him boasting to everyone about my accomplishment.

On my desk at work I have three photographs: One is of Wendy, one is of my best friend, and the last is my marathon picture. I look at these pictures every day. When I look at Wendy's beautiful image I feel so lucky that I will be coming home to her every night, now that we are engaged to be married. When I look at my best friend, I think of the good times we've had and how lucky I am to have such good people in my life. Finally, I look at the marathon photo when I need to stay focused with my work. All three represent the balance in my life. When people come by my desk, they usually pick up the marathon picture first. It is such a major accomplishment in life, everyone feels inclined to comment on it.

I plan to run another marathon, but first I have to get through the wedding! Wendy and I have done a lot of the planning on our runs and it helps to keep us settled and focused as the big day approaches. I can only take on one challenge at a time so the next marathon will have to wait. Who knows, maybe this time Wendy will run with me!

# THE HEART OF A RUNNER

**MATTHEW LESHETZ**

**D.O.B.: 3-16-69**
**RESIDENCE: NEW YORK CITY**
**OCCUPATION: REAL ESTATE DEVELOPER**
**FIRST MARATHON: 2000 NYC MARATHON**
**AGE AT FIRST MARATHON: 31**

*Matthew's first marathon was one of the most important experiences of his life because it validated his very existence. Matthew had suffered for years with a debilitating heart disease known as Wolff-Parkinson-White syndrome. Plagued by the fact that he could never run without being terrified that an ambulance was his one-way ticket to the hospital, he spent years on medication longing to be normal and active. He would even renew his New York Road Runners membership every year thinking one day he would run a marathon. His positive thinking paid off and after a new operation for his condition was approved, he ran his marathon. When his heart rate goes up now he knows it is because he is enjoying his newfound life as a runner.*

Marathon morning. It was hard to believe that the day that had seemed so elusive and improbable for so many years was actually here. I woke up at 5:30 A.M. and began my usual rituals before a long training run including a hot shower and a few minutes of light stretching. I then headed out for a quick 5 or 6-block walk to loosen up and purchase a large bottled water and a protein bar. Outside my Manhattan apartment, located just a few hundred yards from Columbus Circle and the finish line of the New York City Marathon, it looked like any other cold, gray November morning, but something was definitely different today. I could feel it in the air and in my body. During my walk, I noticed a Swedish running team heading down Broadway to catch the marathon bus to Fort Wadsworth, Staten Island. As I continued, I noticed more and more runners emerging from buildings in every direction, each dressed in layers, carrying only their standard-issue UPS duffel bags. My excitement grew as I realized that up to this moment I had been just an individual with a dream, logging virtually every single training mile alone. I had learned to zone out and focus on the long runs and enjoyed that sense of isolation. But now I was part of 30,000 other people and their same dream to run the New York City Marathon. I was gripped by fear, anxiety, anticipation, and excitement all at once. I ran back to my apartment, gathered my gear and headed out for the bus.

While waiting for the bus near the public library, I bumped into an old friend, a college fraternity brother. We shared the 30-minute ride to the start catching up on news about mutual friends and trying to describe the incredibly positive energy we were absorbing surrounded by runners from all over the world. At Fort Wadsworth, facing a two-hour wait before the start, we hung out, stretched, ate bagels, drank water, and just waited in the nervous, excited throng of people. I remember looking at all of the runners—so many ages, shapes, and sizes—and wondering what their motivation was. What brought them to this point? Was this as important to any of them as it was to me? Before I knew it, I had just enough time for one more Porta-Potti visit before heading off to begin my marathon.

Standing on the Verrazzano Narrows Bridge and looking out over the river to the Twin Towers, which accentuated the ominously distant yet beckoning view of the Manhattan skyline, I knew I was about to embark on one of the most amazing journeys of my life. We were huddled like sardines, which wasn't necessarily a bad thing considering the windchill factor made it feel like 28 degrees. Finally, we all sang the national anthem, the cannon blasted, the song "New York, New York" started playing and the race was under way. The elite runners on the lower tier of the bridge started out and I could barely get a glimpse of them gliding effortlessly by. Within a few moments the masses started to slowly move, then shuffle, and then, finally, I was running—actually running the New York City Marathon! And as I ran I reflected on all the events of my life that brought me to that starting line and was convinced that anyone who decides to run a marathon, runs their first one more metaphorically than physically. Most first-timers have a compelling story or reason for choosing to put their mind and body through months of rigorous training and abuse, and I was no different; the miles of the marathon represent personal obstacles and challenges to overcome—and I had my share.

A few weeks prior to my high school graduation in June 1987, I broke my ankle during an American Legion baseball practice and was sidelined for the summer. . . . and that's when the fun began. A few days later, while still in a weakened state, I contracted the chicken pox from a 5-year-old boy in a doctor's office as I waited to take my required college physical. It took several weeks for the symptoms to emerge in full force but when they did, my condition became so severe that I became violently ill and actually missed my graduation. I remember throwing my graduation cap in the air about three weeks later in my parent's backyard—it sailed into the neighbor's yard and I think their two dogs ate it. That summer and through my first fall at Tufts, I suffered serious migraine headaches caused by a post-chicken-pox viral syndrome. By the spring, however, I bounced back and managed to pledge a fraternity, make the Tufts JV baseball team, and get my college life on track. But just when I thought my dreary days of illness were behind me, a new one emerged.

During the summer after freshman year, I was diagnosed with a heart condition called Wolff-Parkinson-White syndrome (WPW), a congenital heart disease that causes irregular and rapid heartbeats and can be fatal. I was terrified. As an active person, I couldn't bear just sitting out on life and missing the competitive activities I enjoyed. The general consensus among doctors was to perform open-heart surgery, but that seemed extreme so I went looking for alternatives. My cardiologist at Massachusetts General Hospital was experimenting with a new procedure to cure WPW, called radio-frequency ablation; however, it was only in the experimental stages with approximately a 60 percent success rate with varying degrees of complications. His advice was to wait, if I could live with it, until the technology improved. So for almost eight years I lived with this disease and a regular regimen of medication, a betablocker to reduce the effect of adrenaline on my heart. With the medication I was fine but if I went off it, I experienced very heavy and uncomfortable heartbeats. I wanted to be normal, to be active, so when I moved into New York City in 1991, I started running in Central Park but was always concerned that my heart wouldn't take the strain. Every time I ran by an ambulance I imagined that it was there for me. It was a very scary time.

After several years of being kept "in check" with medication, I thought my condition was improving so I upped my activities to a more rigorous level. It was 1993 and my roommate and close friend Steve had signed up to run the NYC Marathon and I decided to train with him. I had joined the New York Road Runners (NYRR) a few years back but never entered a race. I was never the type that jumps out of bed early on a weekend morning to go running. For years I held on to my membership, renewing it every year just in case I decided to run a marathon someday. It was a dream that I had from the moment I saw my first marathon in New York, but with my heart condition I was certain to drop dead somewhere during the 26.2-mile monster. When the club brochures appeared in the mail every month I would feel guilty that I never got involved and toss them. I ran with Steve but never on long runs. Watching him transform from a slightly overweight, mediocre runner into a focused, fit, and slightly obsessed marathoner was incredible. It was a thrilling experience to watch him cross the finish line of his first marathon, but also bittersweet since I knew I would never be able to achieve that level of fitness due to my heart. I wanted it badly, but not enough to die for it.

For the next several years I maintained a moderate running regimen, never going over 6.2 miles. During those runs I would fantasize about running the marathon. Watching the 1994 and 1995 marathons while stuffing my face with bagels at a friend's marathon party, I secretly craved to be a marathon-er. In 1996, against my better judgment, I finally decided to sign up for the NYC Marathon. I knew it wasn't the smartest thing to do and I didn't tell my family or close friends because I knew the response I would get: There aren't many positive or encouraging things a concerned friend or family member can say to a heart patient who plans to run a marathon. But I had to test myself to see if I could actually achieve such a goal. I wanted to show my family, my friends, and myself that my heart wasn't going to hold me back from enjoy-ing life the way I wanted to live it.

My friend Steve helped me train and, since my heart was feeling fine and my fitness was improving, I began to allow myself to go 6, 8, and ultimately 10 miles. When I completed those without incident, I began to get excited about the marathon. In early September, just eight weeks before the marathon, I tried my first half marathon. Afterward, my heart was beating extra heavy and not even an extra dose of my medication could calm it. I tried not to worry or think too much about it, and decided to take it easy over the next few days. I went to the Jersey shore for the weekend with some friends. But my heart was bothering me the entire time and I began to worry that I had gone too far. Dropping out started to enter my thoughts. Sunday morn-ing I began to feel extremely light-headed followed by serious difficulty in breathing. I started to panic and asked to be taken to the hospital. I remem-ber sitting in the car thinking that the sad reality was that I was going to die, that this was the end; I pushed too hard and now I would pay for it. Thankfully, my heart finally settled down after a few hours but the experience left me drained, slightly traumatized and depressed.

Since continuing to run would feel like living life on the edge of death, I decided to revisit my doctor at Mass General and found out the experimen-tal surgery we had discussed years ago had undergone vast improvements and now had a success rate of 95 percent. In fact, I found a cardiologist at NYU Medical who had performed thousands of ablations successfully and considered them almost routine. When he told me I was a good candidate—meaning the unwanted pathway was reasonably accessible—I decided to go forward.

The procedure involved the insertion of four catheters to map out my heart to locate the "bad" tissue and then another instrument that delivered a radio wave to destroy it. I was actually awake, albeit heavily sedated, and watched the whole procedure on a monitor—talk about reality TV. I went in at 8 A.M. and was out by 8 P.M.—cured of WPW. Or was I?

Even though the WPW didn't show up on any follow-up EKGs, it was still in my head and I had a long way to go to convince myself I wasn't in dan-ger any longer. Although my doctor gave me the go-ahead to run it took me a while to find the strength and courage to lace my sneaks and break a sweat. What if I wasn't really cured? What if I suffered an episode like I had at the shore? Doubts plagued my recovery and I made constant return visits to my cardiologist just to have him reassure me that I was okay. Even though he encouraged me to resume a regular exercise regimen, I had given up hope of ever fully enjoying physical activities—let alone running a marathon—and fell back into a sedentary lifestyle.

I was gaining weight, miserably afraid to exercise, and to make matters worse I ended a long-term relationship with my girlfriend who, at the time, was my greatest source of support to attempt a "comeback" from WPW. It was an incredibly painful breakup for me and I furthered my decline by drowning my sorrows in food which within a short time left me at my highest weight of my life—just over 235 pounds. In addition, I had recently moved out of my New York City apartment to New Jersey to be closer to my girlfriend. As a result, I was totally alone and rapidly approaching rock bottom. I struggled with depression for months until I couldn't take it any longer and my life narrowed down to a simple decision, best expressed by the character Andy Dufrane in *The Shawshank Redemption:* "Get busy living, or get busy dying." That was June 1999 and I knew I needed something to shock me back to life, something really big and positive to help me focus on a major personal comeback. For me, it was obvious that only one thing would do it: running the New York City Marathon. I sent in my application and waited on pins and needles until the entrant database was published on the NYRR website. I scrolled down the list and finally, thankfully, I saw the word ACCEPTED next to my name.

I attacked my training program and refused to give in to the fear that would occasionally surface regarding my heart. As the weeks and months passed and Marathon Sunday approached, my physical and mental fitness were dramatically improving. I couldn't believe I was actually going to accomplish this goal and felt certain something would obstruct my path. I didn't tell my family or friends that I was training for the marathon. I didn't want them to worry and I certainly didn't want to hear them express any fear or apprehension due to my former heart condition. It wasn't long before my sense of doom and gloom turned to reality and threatened my marathon hopes again.

As part of my training program, I signed up for the Manhattan Half Marathon in October (just weeks before the marathon). I was physically prepared for the race and mentally I simply tried not to think about my last 13-mile run, which had triggered the whole Jersey Shore nightmare and put me out of the running for the 1996 NYC Marathon. In my enthusiasm for a successful race I started up front with the 7:30 milers, a minute faster than my usual time. It must have been my day because I ran the entire race at that pace and never looked back. However, the combination of running faster than usual and the cold weather had a negative impact and I started experiencing chest pains and shortness of breath. Nervous that I was experiencing some sort of recurrence of my WPW, I went to a cardiologist, certain he would advise me not to continue training. Fortunately, my EKG was clear and my heart was sound. The doctor suggested that I had asthma and, after a visit to a pulmonologist, it turns out he was correct; it was exercise-induced asthma. Within a few days—and with the help of a prescription inhaler—I was back on my training program. I completed a few more long training runs, started the taper, enjoyed a week of massive carbo loading, and knew that—finally— nothing could stand in the way of achieving this goal.

On November 2000, Marathon Sunday, running across the Verrazzano Narrows Bridge has to rate as one of the most exciting and purely fun moments of my life. The enormity of the task ahead was clear as Manhattan loomed in the distance. I started passing people but the warnings about starting out too fast and the strong gusts of wind kept me in check and I settled into a comfortable stride as I approached Brooklyn. Spectators lined the streets cheering; it was all very exciting but also very strange. Running has always been such a personal thing for me. I train alone lost in my thoughts. For many years, even when lost in deep concentration, I would listen for warning signs from my heart. But here I was, running through five-deep crowds in neighborhood after neighborhood, drifting back and forth from midroad to the crowd slapping high-fives and straining to hear another "Go Matt" for encouragement.

Through mile 10, I was feeling great and making a conscious effort to stop for water and Gatorade at the aid stations, but during the next few miles minor aches and pains started to arrive. The cold temperatures and gusts of winds were beginning to take their toll and I began to get worried. At one point in Queens I was so weak and hungry I stopped for a handful of Chips Ahoy cookies for replenishment. The thought of running a marathon while holding on to a chocolate chip cookie for dear life caused me to laugh and relax a bit as I started the steep incline to the 59th Street Bridge. Running across the bridge was an incredible experience as so many different emotions swirled within me. My family was waiting for me at 70th and First Avenue and my friends were farther up at 74th. I wanted to be strong for them but I was already running out of steam and worried that I would be too drained by the time I got there to enjoy their enthusiasm. As the wind kept whipping me backward and the cars whizzed by on the bridge, Manhattan never seemed to get any closer.

Then finally it happened: I heard the roar of the spectators jammed onto First Avenue, and with that my pace picked up and runners all around me were getting psyched as well. I became so excited I could barely breathe—but this time I knew it was a good thing. The crowds were unbelievable; just a sea of people screaming and cheering us on. I was overwhelmed with emotion. It was the most incredible sight I had ever seen and I realized how fortunate I was just to be a part of it. It made me recall everything I had been through to get to this point: all the doctor appointments, the self-doubt, the lonely runs, the fear, the painful end to a relationship. And then my excitement grew when I realized my family was just 10 blocks away. It was the most emotionally intense, cathartic, and beautiful moment of my life and I will never forget it.

My family was relieved to see me run by in relatively good condition. At 74th Street friends of mine who have an apartment there hung a sign off the balcony reading, GO MATT! Some of the gang even streamed onto the street, giving me high fives, slipping me bagels and much-needed encouragement. At mile 18 my friend Steve, who had been such an inspiration to me, jumped into the race. I wasn't sure this was such a good thing as I wasn't used to talking while running, but his presence actually relaxed me and it felt as if I was on just another one of our runs in the park. At mile 20 I said to Steve, "I think this is where I am supposed to hit the wall but you know what I say? Fuck the wall." Instead of slowing down, we actually picked up the pace and coasted into Central Park running seven-minute miles. It was incredible and I couldn't stop. I had never run so fast before. As we sprinted down East Park Drive I was high-fiving the spectators and enjoying every minute of it. At mile 25 I saw my family again and that was the final boost I needed to pick the pace up even faster. This was against my better judgment and I actually had no interest in my finishing time but my pace had nothing to do with finishing time. It was a celebration of all my training runs through Central Park that helped me prepare for this moment and I enjoyed it to a degree I never anticipated. I had run that route so many times late at night, alone, in the rain, exhausted, depressed, feeling concerned about my health, and here I was, sprinting the final mile of the NYC Marathon with thousands of people watching and cheering at one of the biggest sporting events in the world.

As I ran toward the finish, I was again overcome with a rush of emotion. When I crossed the finish line, I threw my arms in the air triumphantly and then gave a Derek Jeter-like fist pump and thanked God and all of my doctors for this moment in my life. I proudly accepted my finisher's medal and sank into the silver Mylar wrap. As I walked toward the family reunion area on Central Park West, I reflected on my accomplishment and decided then and there to try and live the rest of my life with the same conviction and energy I put into the 2000 NYC Marathon.

But first, I had to stop at John's Pizzeria and throw down six slices, a calzone, and a chicken parmigiana hero that my brother-in-law dared me to eat. Hey, I was now a marathoner, up for any challenge.

# THE BEST-LAID PLANS GO AWRY

**SHARON LINSTEDT**

**D.O.B.: 5-13-56**
**RESIDENCE: BUFFALO, NY**
**OCCUPATION: JOURNALIST**
**FIRST MARATHON: 1987 MARINE CORPS**
**    MARATHON, WASHINGTON, D.C.**
**AGE AT FIRST MARATHON: 31**

*A high school track star, Sharon stopped competing during college but gave running a second chance when she met a guy who was a runner. When the relationship ended, her running stayed with her. As a news reporter in 1983, she covered the men's Olympic marathon trials and stood in awe of Bill Rodgers and Frank Shorter but never conceived of running that distance herself. That all changed when she met a neighbor who was a marathoner and convinced her it was a really cool thing to do. All through her train-ing she felt the shadow of impending doom as to whether she could run 26.2 miles; that was topped off by a bad dream the night before her marathon. But the U.S. Marines came to her aid and she finished her first marathon with honor, glory, and a sense of privileged pride.*

I don't remember a time when running wasn't part of my life. As a kid growing up on a Wisconsin farm we were always zipping around playing games, galloping down the road to a friend's house, or sprinting against sib-lings or friends in mock races across our sprawling yard.

While I could usually outpace my playmates in our casual contests, it was the President's Physical Fitness Tests that quantified my need for speed. Annually, I'd try to run faster than the year before in the youth fitness evalu-ations. Unfortunately, I rarely earned the coveted patch that signified superi-or physical ability because the tests also included a softball throwing skill test. I was off the charts with the running, jumping, and calisthenics portions, but had an extremely unimpressive ball toss.

My "big break" in running came in the spring of my freshman year when my tiny high school established its first-ever girls' track and field program. I ran the 800, high-jumped, long-jumped, and ran hurdles, even throwing the discus in a pinch.

The 800 meters, which back then was the 880-yard dash, was my event. I ran unbeaten in my conference through my junior year, eventually getting my time down to a 2:15 and setting a state record.

I loved hearing my name on the morning announcements and my mom put together a scrapbook of my ribbons, medals, and clippings from the local newspaper.

By my senior year, a combination of responsibilities at school, home and a part-time job made it impossible for me to continue running. It was no longer fun so I just stopped.

I attended a few track meets at the University of Wisconsin—Madison as a student, but didn't see myself as anything more than an interested spectator. It didn't occur to me that I could run just for fun or run a road race. In my head you had to be a committed track athlete or not run at all.

All that changed in the summer of 1979 when I gave running a second chance. Sparked in large part by my interest in an attractive neighbor who loped past my house every morning, I decided to lace up my shoes and hit the road. While my relationship with the guy never progressed beyond the casual dating stage, my relationship with running was the real thing. After a few months, I was entering races and taking home age-group awards.

My new identity as a runner also served me as a way to meet people. I moved around quite a bit in the late 1970s and early 1980s as a radio news anchor and reporter, and running helped me see more of my new hometowns and make new friends.

In November 1982 I moved to Buffalo on what I expected would be a one-year stint as a morning anchor at an all-news radio station. Despite its reputation for snow and horrible weather, it's a city with a great running community, long-standing running clubs, and a varied race calendar.

I tried my first 20K race. I ran races through snow and ice. I got a group of coworkers to enter a corporate team race, part of what is now the J.P. Morgan Chase Corporate Challenge series.

In 1983 Buffalo was the host city to the men's Olympic marathon trials. I got to cover the event and got a close-up view of Frank Shorter, Bill Rodgers and other top American marathoners. My new and rather slim understanding of marathon running had me glued to the TV to watch the Atlanta Olympic coverage, which included Joan Benoit Samuelson's amazing gold-medal performance.

While I didn't think of the marathon as a distance I would ever run, I was very curious about running 26.2 miles and made a point of reading newspaper and magazine articles about marathons and marathon training.

Meanwhile I met my future husband, Mark, a criminal defense lawyer who has yet to find a sport he doesn't excel in. I soon found myself joining him in triathlons (even though I am not much of a swimmer), cross-country ski racing, and whitewater kayaking. You know a guy is serious when he gives you a spray skirt and kayak paddle for your birthday.

Despite all that sporting activity, neither one of us had dared to run a marathon. In fact, in 1986 we went to watch the start of Buffalo's now defunct Skylon Marathon and shook our heads at friends who were crazy enough to attempt it.

Among those we deemed insane was our neighbor, Peter Ross. I'd seen him heading out to run with a small group of friends on weekend mornings, but I didn't realize that his training goal was the marathon.

I never would have forecast that I'd be part of that group the following year. After asking a boatload of questions and hearing his enthusiastic responses about how cool it was to run a marathon, I was headed to the Marine Corps Marathon in October 1987.

Even as our long run mileage increased and my entry confirmation arrived in the mail, I was still not convinced I could run 26.2 miles. Despite the support of the experienced marathoners in my training group, I almost didn't make it out of the driveway for a 20-mile practice run, the farthest I've ever run in my life. I couldn't sleep the night before as images of unimaginable pain and suffering filled my head. I was sure I couldn't run 20 miles. I was sure I could never, ever run a marathon.

My fears proved to be somewhat worse than the actual experience. I was slow and tired near the end, and walked the last couple of miles, but I came home alive.

Still, the fear of impending doom didn't go away. Peter, Mark, and I flew down to Washington, D.C., and I was positive my bad dreams were about to become a reality. It was a feeling that only got worse when I glanced around the race expo and saw too many people sporting Boston Marathon T-shirts and jackets. I was a lamb on the way to slaughter.

In a surprise development, Mark's brother Brian announced he was going to run as well. Never mind that his longest run was about 12 miles; he had previously run a few marathons and decided he couldn't resist joining us in his hometown race. He also felt it was his duty to play host and dragged us around D.C., to national landmarks and museums. That evening a pasta dinner was followed by visits to his favorite bars, with a few beers along the way and shots of bourbon as a nightcap.

This was not the way to spend the day and night before a marathon. My sense of dread had grown palpable. I was in way over my head.

The marathon plan was for Mark to follow the three of us on his bike, offering water and kind words as needed. Peter promised to stay with me for the first few miles and then run his own pace. Brian's plan was to start fast and see what he had left. I was immediately overwhelmed by the size of the field. I have never seen so many runners in my life. I also needed a bathroom and found myself standing in what seemed like a mile-long line for a Porta-Potti.

Sometime during the long wait we lost Brian. Then Peter and I got trapped behind a barricade as the starting gun went off and we had to sprint around the fencing to get in with the runners. As it turned out, the back half of the field was still moving at a crawl and we easily blended in. I turned around to wish Peter luck and he had disappeared, sucked into the sea of race numbers. I was all by myself.

As I started to panic, I also started running and my maiden marathon voyage had begun. The Pentagon went by, then the streetscapes of Georgetown. Spectators were smiling and shouting encouragement. A band played a John Philip Sousa march and the sun was shining. Maybe this would be okay.

I waved at the Marines and thanked them for the water and Gatorade they handed out. Their efficiency was astounding and I gained a new respect for the military.

I was oddly relaxed. I laughed out loud at a woman ahead of me whose running tights had started to foam as she heated up with sweat. I made a mental note to myself to always do a double rinse. I puzzled over the plywood boards covered with Vaseline that were offered at aid stations. Could chafing be that big a problem?

I moved on and eventually found myself running next to two cute girls who wore midriff T-shirts that showed off their bodies perfectly. Not a good choice of running buddies. Guys hooted and hollered and drooled over them for 8 miles. The more attention they got, the more annoyed I became. Why wasn't anyone calling out, "Hey you in the white T-shirt with the peace sign?" or, "Hey race number 14059!" I was really getting tired and cranky at this point.

I found myself at Haines Point trotting past the 18-mile marker and was astounded I was so far along. I also realized I'd consumed too much liquid and needed a bathroom. Not seeing one, I did what all real marathoners do and ducked behind a hedge to pee. As I jumped back on the course, there was Peter. He'd been behind me the whole way. I was feeling on top of the world. This was easy. I was actually feeling great. The dreaded 20-mile marker no longer scared me. I actually thought I would finish the marathon way ahead of schedule, and with dignity, crossing the finish line with my head held high in triumph.

As the 21st mile began, my legs felt a little heavy and I was a little light-headed, but I still had my game face on. As the 22-mile marker approached, my stomach was roiling and I began to wonder if runners ever threw up during a marathon.

I answered that question within the next 100 yards, as I stepped off the course and hurled the contents of my stomach onto the ground. Fellow runners paused; in fact they stood by as I vomited. I wanted them to go away but they were kind and courteous and wanted to help, and all I wanted is to just disappear and die.

In what seemed an instant, one of the extremely efficient marines was standing next to me holding a cup of water and a paper towel. He felt my forehead and pronounced me hydrated enough to soldier on. "You're fine ma'am. You're good to go." I apologized for throwing up on his course and felt totally confused, but I believed this guy, this angel in camouflage. The marine told me to keep going so I obeyed the command.

By the time I reach the 23-mile mark, I'm doing a trot-walk combination, but I'm moving closer to my goal. As I get nearer the sound of the finish line crowd gets progressively louder and runners wrapped in shiny Mylar blankets with finisher's medals around their necks pass in the other direction, assuring the soon-to-finish that we are almost there.

I crawl up the hill leading to the Iwo Jima statute and the cheers are deafening. In a blur, I see the finish line approaching and I cross it. A Marine shakes my hand and puts my finisher's medal over my head, telling me, "Good job, ma'am." Another marine appears out of nowhere and wraps me in a Mylar blanket, then escorts me to the family waiting area. I was overwhelmed by their dedication to the runners.

I feel a combination of shock and disbelief: 4:22:49. Overall, it wasn't as horrible as I imagined, although I think I swore I would never do that again. I was just happy I was done. Mark appears gushing about how proud he is of me, and with the news of Brian and Peter both finishing well under four hours.

I think my feet hurt but it is hard to tell because my quads are in spasm and I want to sit down. We shuffle slowly to the car, which is parked in a distant lot. I keep touching my medal in awe. I just ran 26.2 miles. Wow.

It would be five years until I would run another marathon, but with that one the floodgates would open. I've now run 18 with a personal best of 3:42:58.

Each one has brought its own rewards, overcoming a home and work schedule that now includes two daughters, tweaking my training, finding new running routes to keep things fresh, and running new marathons. You haven't really seen Chicago, New York, Boston, Buffalo, or whatever city, until you've traveled its marathon course.

And there is still that awesome thrill of stepping across the finish line and having someone put a finisher's medal around your neck. If running is an addiction, the marathon is my drug of choice.

I truly love the marathon. It is my forever thing.

# IT'S ALL ABOUT THE PICTURE

**JENNIFER LOU**

**D.O.B.: 4-11-78**
**RESIDENCE: MANHATTAN, NY**
**OCCUPATION: INTEGRATION**
**CONSULTANT, BLOOMBERG**
**FIRST MARATHON: 2001**
**LASALLE BANKS CHICAGO**
**MARATHON**
**AGE AT FIRST MARATHON: 23**

*Jen Lou breaks the profile of a typical marathoner. She's in shape and much too young to experience a midlife crisis. Her father and brother had run marathons but she wasn't interested. No way. Then when her mother assembled the family "Marathon Memorial Wall" in the family home, Jen wanted to be included. But the only way she would make it on the wall was to run a marathon. So she did, with her father at her side. The picture turned out great but something was missing. Her dad and brother had run two marathons and had two pictures on the wall to her one. Would she run another for the sake of a picture?*

I don't consider myself a runner. And after running two marathons I still don't like to run. I like sports, but not running. In high school I played tennis, softball, and basketball, none of which required miles of running.

I played a semester of rugby in college and spent one year with the crew team, where I ran 2 miles to the boathouse mainly just to stay in shape and because that is where we held practice each day. I guess I would describe myself as an athlete, but not a runner.

My dad and my brother Greg are the real runners in the family. My dad was the typical weekend warrior, getting in his 5 miles Saturday and Sunday morning. He would meet with his longtime running buddy, Jim Koster, religiously each weekend and run the county park. I would watch him leave to run and just thought of it as part of his routine.

He ran his first New York City Marathon in November 1993, and another in 1995. The whole family went to watch and I remember thinking it was awesome but never connected with it on a personal level. It was so out of my realm of thinking, not even a speck on the horizon. Why would I ever want to run a marathon and how could I ever fathom finishing it? The idea of running 26.2 miles was not appealing.

After his second marathon, my dad vowed it was his last and would only come out of retirement if one of his kids decided to run one with him. Still, this was not something I was willing to take on.

When November 1999 rolled around, Dad came out of retirement because the running bug bit one of his children. Guess who? Surprise surprise, not me. Greg was 18 at the time and unknown to us all, this event set the stage for a family tradition. He was in high school at the time and then proceeded to Northwestern University in Chicago. Even after the two of them ran a marathon together, the idea of me joining them never crossed my mind.

While a sophomore at Northwestern Greg became interested in running the Chicago Marathon, which just happened to fall on his birthday that year. He called my dad and enticed him into entering. It was to be Greg's second marathon and dad's fourth. My mom thought this would make a nice family outing so the two of us decided to go to Chicago and watch them run.

Out of the blue, Mom and Dad suggested that I run the marathon with them. My first reaction was, *What? No way! What are they thinking?*

By now, I had graduated from college and was working at my job with Bloomberg. At the time, I was living in Princeton, not far from my parents' home in Glen Rock, New Jersey. I only came home on weekends for a break and to do my laundry.

On one of my weekends home, I was wandering through the house and stopped in front of the "Marathon Memorial Wall" that we have in the living room. My mom has framed and hung all the marathon pictures of Dad and Greg along with their medals and certificates in a very prominent way for all to view when they visit our house. It was then that I realized how badly I wanted to be displayed on the wall. At the time my mom and dad proposed to me that I run the marathon in Chicago, they teased me, saying the only way I would be immortalized on the wall was to run a marathon.

I know this sounds like a silly reason to run 26.2 miles, but I did want to be up there on that wall, to be part of our family history. The pictures motivated me and I wanted to be included. So that was my one reason to run a marathon: to get on the wall. When I told my friends I was running a marathon and why, they teased me and said it would be much easier to just superimpose myself on a digital picture, but then I would know it wasn't real. I had to cross a marathon finish line to make it on the wall.

Once my decision was made, I knew I had to start training. Another reason I chose to run Chicago that year was because I knew I could train with my dad. There was no way I would ever do this alone and here I had a veteran marathoner to coach me every weekend. My attitude was easy; I'd follow whichever schedule my dad suggested.

My dad gave me a marathon schedule for beginners and I steadily crossed off the miles as I increased my mileage. I did my first 7-miler with my dad and Jim, his partner, and it wasn't so bad. The best part was getting home and crossing that day off the schedule.

I had good days and bad, no rhyme or reason as to how I felt. On a good day I'd run 12 miles and feel great and pumped and another day I'd run 6 and it would feel like forever. The day we ran 20 miles I was incredibly tired. I know that people say after you run that much, another 6 is nothing, but I was skeptical about that.

For reassurance, I looked at the schedule and realized I was following it day by day and most importantly, I could look back and see far I'd come since I started. I couldn't imagine running 7 and now I was up to 20. That was a big part of keeping mentally focused and positive. I had to keep reminding myself that I had come so far. But those last 6 miles still lurked in my mind. I just hoped the adrenaline rush that everyone talks about would be there when I needed it.

Training with my dad was really special. Sometimes we were able to chitchat and talk and get to know one another all over again. On other days we didn't talk at all, just ran together, step by step.

On the other hand, I felt like I was running my life away. My friends would joke and say, "Where is fun Jen? Where did she go?" Both they and I couldn't wait for the marathon to be over so I could go out and party with them again. During training I was home Friday night, up early on Saturday for a long run, and then I'd make an attempt to see my friends in the city Saturday night. Sometimes I could but other times, I was so tired I never made it.

When it came time for the marathon, I felt ready but had no idea what to expect. Finally, the months of training had come down to this one weekend. We all had a big pasta dinner the night before and the thought of, *What if I don't finish?* kept running through my head. I'd heard the stories of first-timers who didn't finish, those who hit the wall, who got severely dehydrated and sick, and I thought that could be me. It made me anxious.

On marathon day, we all hung out at the Chicago Hilton with the other runners staying warm and waiting for the start. Even though we weren't staying at the Hilton, they open their lobby for all the runners, which was really nice and convenient. My dad and brother commented on how Chicago is a much more relaxed marathon than New York City. Maybe it's a midwestern thing, but everyone was laid back and congenial.

We started toward the front with the eight-minute milers so we could be with Greg and all start together. I was taking it all in and feeling, *Wow, I'm here.* I couldn't believe it. Actually, seeing the huge crowd reassured me because I felt there had to be other first-timers in the pack, people like me who were there just for the experience and to see if they could actually run a marathon. It took the pressure off a bit.

We couldn't have asked for better weather, which was a real plus. Greg went out fast as expected and Dad and I began our journey through the streets of Chicago. The music was great, the crowds were fun, and in the first 5 miles I was having a ball, thinking I could do this all the time. This was fun. I was caught up in the excitement of the marathon theater and thinking it was a great way to tour the city.

I was still strong and feeling great miles 10 to 15. I was taking in all the sights. My dad and I didn't talk much because there was so much to see and take in all around us. Then we hit mile 18 and I hit the wall. Bam. I wanted to quit. I was so tired I didn't think I could go on. I was hurting, dragging, and empty. There was a water stop nearby with power gel goo along with the water and although I never tried them during training because I thought they were so nasty, I eagerly took them. Psychologically, I was hoping they would give me the instant boost I needed.

Unfortunately, they didn't work, didn't give me the magic I needed to keep going. Dad was great and encouraged me to keep going. We walked through some of the water stops, but I never wanted the water stop to end because that meant running again. I kept prolonging the end of the water stop, adding a few more feet. It wasn't until all the cups were gone from the street that I acknowledged the water stop was over.

Miles 20 to 26, I kept focusing on the finish and the fact that I would make it. It was around mile 23 that the crowds started going insane with their cheering, saying things like, "You're almost there. Keep going." I needed that and it really did help. Even the walkers started running.

In the last mile my adrenaline finally kicked in and I ran across the finish line in 4:37. Even though my legs were killing me and I didn't know how they kept moving, I forgot all about the pain the moment I saw the finish line. I tried to get into an open space and look pretty for the camera above. After all, this is the picture I had been working for and the one that was going to be on the wall.

Unfortunately, after I passed the camera it all ended. I didn't feel the euphoria or exhilaration I had heard about and expected when I finished. All I felt was pain. My dad finished right behind me and I immediately started whining. I was carrying on in the most miserable way. "Dad, I'm in so much pain. All I want to do is sit. I can't walk anymore."

As we walked to the family reunion area to meet Mom and Greg, I saw a chair sticking out the side of a massage tent and grabbed it. I couldn't help it. I needed to sit down. Dad kept telling me the best thing to do was to keep moving but I was being stubborn. "If you don't want to wait, that's fine, but I am sitting down," I told him. He patiently waited with me for a few minutes and I finally got up and we continued our walk to meet the family.

He didn't know what to do with me. I wouldn't stop whining and eventually he just tuned me out. We laugh about it now and it has become an ongoing joke in our family. He says he was amazed about how much I could whine over it all.

The next few days all I felt was the pain and *Thank goodness it is over.* But a smile came to my face when I thought about the marathon picture that was going to be on the wall. After all, that had been the goal all along.

In a while, I did start to feel better about what I did and was so proud of myself. And having everyone congratulating me made me further realize what a great accomplishment running a marathon was and that felt great. I was finally on the other side and could proudly say that I had successfully completed a marathon. The picture turned out fabulous. Even better, fun Jen was back!

The thought of doing another marathon was nonexistent at this point. I did my marathon, got the picture, and was happy that I had finished.

However, a few weeks later as I was looking at the Marathon Wall with my picture, I realized that the photographs from the New York City Marathon were actually better quality and bigger than the Chicago photos. That got my mind spinning and I realized that I had to have one of those as well. So here we go again. I had to run another marathon, specifically New York City, all for a better picture.

We decided to run New York City and my dad and I entered the lottery. The other factor in wanting to run New York City was that by now I had moved into the city and thought it would be cool to run my hometown marathon. But I didn't get in. My dad did, but he deferred his acceptance, hoping that the following year I'll get in and we can run it together.

In the meantime, Greg signed up to run Chicago. I still wasn't thinking of doing Chicago again. No way. I was through with Chicago. But then Dad decided to run with Greg and I didn't want to be left out, sitting on the sidelines cheering them on, so I decided to run it again.

My training schedule moved up a notch from beginner and I ran three 20-milers. At the start of my second marathon, I still felt nervous but confident. Right before the start, Dad and Greg went off to the bathroom one more time and I stayed behind. But somehow, they never came back. Dad disappeared, swallowed up by the crowd. I got so nervous I almost began to cry. The race started so I just stayed where we had all been standing, hoping he would appear, but there was no sign of him. I was freaking out, not knowing if I could run the whole thing alone. After all, the longest run I had done by myself was 12 miles. The guy next to me had a cell phone and I asked to borrow it so I could call my dad hoping to locate him. The man was kind enough to let me use it but I only got my dad's voice mail.

Finally Greg appeared but he didn't know where Dad was either. Greg offered to run with me, but I knew that would slow him down too much. I appreciated his offer but declined. I took a deep breath and said I'd go it alone.

At first I was scared, but after a while I realized I wasn't really alone. There were thousands of people around me all doing the same thing. If I needed to talk to someone, there were plenty of people right next to me. So I ran the race without my dad but it ended up just fine. I saw the race from a different perspective.

I finished in 4:11, almost 20 minutes faster than my first marathon. I guess that came from better training and being more focused. I don't think I am necessarily faster than my dad but I think I changed the pace more, according to the way I felt, knowing I didn't have another person at my side to follow. In the end, I proved to myself that I could run a marathon alone, if needed. This time, I took in the scenes and really appreciated the marathon in a different way. It also helped that I didn't hit the wall as badly, so crossing the finish line this time I did experience that euphoric feeling and rush of energy everyone speaks about.

My mom framed the picture from my first marathon to match my apartment in New York, but I insisted it stay home on the Marathon Wall so everyone can see it. After all, I couldn't be missing from the bunch when visitors came to view it. I don't know if I'll ever get a New York City Marathon photo, but these two are pretty special.

Will I run another? Who knows. I'll get back to you on that next year. I keep telling my friends to remind me what I felt like during the last few weeks of training. But you know what? When marathon registration comes around again, I'll focus on that feeling of crossing the finishing line, seeing the cheering crowds, and being in the best shape of my life. That's all it takes to forget the early morning long training runs and the weekend nights that I missed.

It would be extra special if my mom could run in a marathon with us. She has a bad knee so it is out of the question, but she is the greatest support crew any of us could have. She is the trouper who wheels around our suitcase of postmarathon clothes and food and is always at the finish line for us, taking the pictures, getting them framed and keeping our "Marathon Memorial Wall" picture perfect and up to date.

Even through all of this, I still don't think of myself as a runner. I just know this was an awesome time in my life where I achieved a goal and was able to do it in the company of Mom and Dad and Greg. Looking back as well as into the future, I realize that the months of training, the pain, and the whining are worth it and I encourage anyone who can run to try a marathon at some point in their lives. It is a feeling unlike any other. Who knows, maybe the "Running Lous" will make an appearance at the start of the next New York City Marathon.

# MARATHON GOAL: FINISH BEFORE THE TIME CLOCKS COME DOWN

**GARY MELLOR**

**D.O.B.: 10-29-53**
**RESIDENCE: WAYNE, NJ**
**OCCUPATION: OWNER, OMEGA**
   **ENVIRONMENTAL CONSULTING**
**FIRST MARATHON: 1999 NYC**
   **MARATHON**
**AGE AT FIRST MARATHON: 45**

*Gary is a self-described late-in-life athlete. A combination of high blood pressure, increasing weight gains and a hectic work schedule gave him the incentive to start running. For his 40th birthday, he joined the New York Road Runners and started a journey that changed his life. When he made the decision to run a marathon, he thought it was only a distance of 10 miles. He had a lot to learn in the next few months, starting with just how long a marathon really is.*

I don't fit the profile of a runner. No one would look at me and ever think I could run a marathon. And I'm not fast. On a great day I can pull out ten-minute miles. But none of that bothers me because I know I am a runner and that's all that matters.

Back in high school I was never an athlete; wasn't a jock, never got a letter in sports. I was the last one picked for intramural games. That feeling of being isolated from the popular athletic kids still haunts me. Playing on a team wasn't even an option for me as I had to work after school starting at age 15 to save for college. My parents didn't have the finances to pay for tuition. They did what they could but I still had to work. Sometimes I held down two jobs, one before and one after school. I don't regret that because it gave me a strong work ethic, which carried through to my adult life and helped me set up my business. However, I definitely missed out on a lot of high school social life.

I put myself through college and graduated in 1977 with a degree in environmental science and chemistry and then continued on to graduate school with a degree in environmental engineering. I got a desk job and my diet and health started to disintegrate. My weight ballooned from 156 to over 230 pounds. It bothered me, and I tried every diet out there to lose the pounds. The Atkins Diet, grapefruit diet, Weight Watchers, I did them all. The only thing I accomplished was a yo-yo cycle of losing and gaining, but I always gained a few more with every cycle.

I was also eating out about five nights a week while on the road with the job. I was in my mid-30s and not happy. Ironically, my job was going well but I was unsatisfied. Plus the commute was killing me. I was always on the road. The corporate life did not agree with me. I tend to be a real homebody, not a mover and a shaker. I was married with a daughter and never home with my family. Something had to give and I made the decision to quit my job and start my own company with two partners. One was a runner.

Opening my own business gave me the incentive to do other things in my life that I had put off for too long, such as losing weight and keeping it off. I also had high blood pressure and had become lethargic. What I didn't need was a new diet. What I did need was a new lifestyle, one that incorporated good nutrition and exercise.

I chose running because it wasn't dependent on time, equipment or location. I still remember my first run. It was a Saturday morning and I laced up my $10 sneakers, put on an old pair of shorts, and a paint-stained T-shirt, and ran out the door expecting to do at least 5 miles on an old country road in front of my house.

I ran as hard and as fast as I could and collapsed after a few blocks. Totally discouraged, I walked home. I had a strange sensation I was going to die because I couldn't breathe! I felt so alone and scared and thought no one would find me if I dropped dead from my first run. When I finally made it home I decided I would never do that again.

Two days later I tried it again but with a different approach. I did a walk-run for about a mile. I purposely did not go far because I wanted to make sure I could make it home in case I felt like I was going to die again. This paranoia stayed with me for quite a few years and affected my ability to run races or go out for longer longs. If I strayed too far from home, or started out too fast, panic set in and I worried that I would not be able to make it back.

It took me a year and a half before I felt comfortable with running. Being new to running, I kept getting injured. I actually thought it was supposed to hurt, that it was a sign of progress. Finally I got so frustrated I quit. Everything hurt and my blood pressure kept going up, not down. Why the heck was I running if I wasn't getting any of the benefits? Maybe I was just too old and too fat for this.

When I turned 40 I decided to try running again, but this time I decided to do it smart and joined New York Road Runners and signed up for running classes. At the first session, my group headed into Central Park and I froze. I had never been in Central Park before and my old paranoia and panic came back. *What if I get lost in the park? What if I get mugged?* All the old feelings of being picked last in gym class came flooding back and I almost quit and went home. But I didn't.

I needed to give this 100 percent before I quit again, and I was not ready to give up. After all, this was the first class. I stuck with it and found a great partner who was also a beginner, Jane Cates. Running with a partner made me feel safe. Jane and I connected and we helped each other learn about running.

After a month of classes, we decided to enter a 5K. It sounded like a good idea but the day of the race I was petrified. I didn't know anything about pacing, hydrating, pinning on a number, or wearing a chip. My palms were sweaty. The old feelings of panic and being abandoned or lost came back. What was I doing here?

Jane stayed with me the entire race. After 1 mile I started walking but she pulled me along and I started running again. After 2 miles I looked at her and asked if we were running a marathon instead of 3 miles. I couldn't believe I was running so far. I finished last, but it felt great. I didn't even mind being passed by the one-legged runner. For the first time in my life I felt like an athlete.

I was so impressed with myself, I suggested to Jane that we run a marathon. She asked if I knew how long a marathon was and I said, "Ten miles?"

After I found out just how long a marathon was, I still wanted to do it. I was so high from running my first race that nothing could stop me. The next week in running class I told the coach I wanted to run a marathon. This was February and the coach thought it was doable with eight months of training. When I saw the course map, I almost caved in. Ironically it wasn't the distance that scared me, but being in places that were strange to me. I had never been to Brooklyn or Queens or Staten Island. Again, my issues of loss and abandonment rushed in and almost made me give up. But I didn't.

Jane and I trained for our marathon all through the summer of 1999. The quality of our training wasn't that great, but we had fun. We ran from one water fountain to the next, took a walk break, then start running again. It took us close to three hours to run 10 miles and we thought we were flying!

Training for a marathon takes a lot of time, especially when you are slow. To ensure that I spent time with my daughter Kristy, I made her my coach. When I ran, she would ride her bike carrying my water and offering words of encouragement. She was great company and we discovered a new relationship together; she became my best friend. When I told my parents I was running a marathon my dad actually asked me if I had a chance of winning. He was more naive than I was about marathons.

I followed the running schedule obsessively. If it poured the day I was scheduled to do a long run, I ran in the rain. Never gave it a thought to postpone it even just one day. Training for the marathon became my religion. For one of our long runs, Jane and I entered a 15-mile race in Central Park. By the time we finished, the finish line had been dismantled. Our longest run was 18 miles—and it didn't go well. I couldn't believe how far it was. It took us over four hours in the pouring rain and for the first time we started to get doubts. By the next day, however, we were back to being psyched and blew off any lingering doubts.

With three weeks to go, we met in the park for our last 10-miler and suddenly decided to blow the whole thing off. We looked at each other and decided we didn't want to run the marathon. Jane was worried she wouldn't finish and I was worried I'd get lost. To alleviate our fears, we decided to drive the course. Halfway through, we looked at each other and said, 'Holy shit, this is far!'

To get through my fear of being lost, I bought a subway map and a token so I could get back in case I did get lost. I also brought money for a cab in case I couldn't find a subway. I had contingency plans up the wazoo for any emergency I could possibly think of.

The night before the marathon I couldn't sleep. At 4 A.M. I was up to catch the marathon bus into the city. It was cold, damp, and dark and I felt so unprepared. Fort Wadsworth was like one big party—a marathon Woodstock. I was among thousands of other runners but unlike me, they seemed to know what they were doing. Jane went off to go the bathroom and took forever to get back. I thought she was lost and I started to panic, thinking I would be alone. Finally she returned and told me if I had to go, I better go now because the lines at the Porta-Pottis were long.

We kept waiting for instructions about how to line up and start but couldn't hear a thing. We just kept going to the bathroom. Finally people started heading out, but we didn't know where to go. We tried to follow the crowd but got confused and lost and ended up dead last, the absolute two last people to cross the start line. It took us 16 minutes to cross the start and get on the bridge. Once on the bridge, we had to pick our way over all the debris of clothes and water bottles left from the thousands of runners ahead of us. Midway across the bridge we got excited and it finally hit us that we were running in a marathon.

The crowds were great and kept my mind off my fears and worries. Somewhere in Brooklyn I had to pee, but I was too bashful to pee in front of people so I held it. Jane kept saying, "What's the big deal?" but I couldn't do it. For 10 miles Jane and I argued about peeing in public. Finally I couldn't take it anymore and pulled over and just peed. I didn't realize we were smack in the middle of the Hasidic area of Brooklyn and when I finished my task, I noticed a young woman and her daughter staring at me. I was never so embarrassed in all my life.

At the halfway mark, coming across the 59th Street Bridge and rounding the corner onto First Avenue, Jane started to run out of gas. The thought of running alone petrified me so I kept encouraging her to run. Finally Jane stopped dead in the middle of First Avenue and gave up. What was I going to do? I was at a major crossroads. I wanted to finish but I needed her with me to accomplish that. I started screaming at her, "Goddamn it, run!" and I think I scared her into running again.

We started a walk-run routine heading into the Bronx for the next 5 miles. By now, it was getting dark. We had been out for over five and a half hours and the crowds were starting to thin. My legs felt like jelly and we were having a tough time even walking. Cold and tired, we had no energy left.

Somehow we managed to make it to mile 23 and entered Central Park. We had looked forward to this for the last 5 miles because this was where our friends had said they would meet us but somehow we missed them. Now we were really miserable. The only thing that kept us going was the knowledge that we only had 3 more miles to go.

When we finally saw the finish line, we decided to run. We didn't want to walk across the finish line of our first marathon. As the clock timed 5:58:00, we finished together and burst out crying. Crossing that finish line, I experienced a flood of emotion like I have never had in all my life. Our spouses were waiting for us and I sat down on the curb with my Mylar blanket wrapped around me, holding my medal like it was a lifeline rescuing me from the most horrific ordeal I had been through in my life.

I never made it to work the next day. In fact, I couldn't even get out of bed and had to force myself to move. I promised myself I would never run a marathon again.

The next few days, I went through a depression. I felt this huge letdown after such an incredible accomplishment. *Where do I go from here? Could I have run better?* Questions swirled through my brain. The only way to get out of my depression was to make the decision to run another marathon.

I trained better for my second marathon in three simple ways. First, I wasn't as obsessive about the scheduling. If it rained on the day of a long run, I postponed it. If I couldn't make a race, I didn't feel bad. Second, I upped my weekly miles from 35 to 43, and third, I ran a few 20-milers.

I chose a smaller venue for my second, the Hartford Marathon in Hartford, Connecticut. Instead of 30,000 runners like New York City, it gets around 3,000. Although I was still nervous at the start, I felt confident. This time, I felt I belonged there. It was also less stressful than running a big-time marathon. I felt relaxed instead of tangled up in wall-to-wall people.

I also set a goal this time, to break five hours. To help me attain my goal, my running buddies Maureen, Angela, Joan, and Jill decided to run the race with me. The course was flat and very scenic, but I missed the crowds. Instead of a city feeling, this one goes through farms and colorful fall foliage. Halfway through, I was on target to break five hours and felt great. I was running with a woman named Maureen whom I met at the start and we just fell in together with the same pace and goal so that was helpful.

At mile 20, I began to fade. Maureen fought with me to stay on target but I was dying. By mile 23 I was doing 16-minute miles and thought I would blow my goal and didn't even care. I threw up twice from drinking too much Gatorade. At mile 24, I didn't think I could go on. There was nothing left inside and I was so brain dead I couldn't even do the math to predict my finish time. I was mentally and physically exhausted.

The last mile of the Hartford course is downhill, which is the only thing that saved me. As I came down the hill I could see the finish and suddenly got a burst of speed and ran across the finish line. I remember thinking, *This is what it feels like to be a real runner*. I finished in 4:49, making my goal by ten minutes. I learned a very valuable lesson that day: The only reason I was able to make my goal is that I never gave up on myself.

Although my second marathon was very special, I will always remember my first one. Running a marathon took me to a place I never thought possible. It validated the fact that I was an athlete of the highest caliber. I finally got that high school letter in the form of a marathon finisher's medal.

I'll never be the slim, buff athlete breaking records or winning awards, but that's not important to me. I'm middle-aged and slow and all I want is for the finish-line clock to still be up when I finish my race.

Running is permanently integrated into my life. It's like a daily vitamin: I don't feel right without it.

# I DO IT MY WAY

GERALD OTTEN

D.O.B.: 9-15-54
RESIDENCE: HOBOKEN, NJ
OCCUPATION: DIRECTOR OF ENGINEERING,
   ELECTRONIC CONTROL SYSTEMS
FIRST MARATHON: 1978, RICHMOND
   VIRGINIA
AGE AT FIRST MARATHON: 24

*Gerry is one of the most unusual marathoners I have met. He loves to have fun, espe-cially eating and drinking decadently while running 26.2 miles. I would not advise doing as he does, but he seems to pull it off with flair and it does seem tempting. With his zest for life, Gerry will probably outrun and outlive all of us.*

I grew up on a street that was a four and a half-mile loop. My dad was a runner and encouraged me to come with him. He read the Jim Fixx book and was doing the 15-minute run exercise. When I was 12, I started doing the loop with him. I wasn't a jock at school so I was surprised that I enjoyed run-ning so much. Perhaps it was because I was with my dad, but it felt so natu-ral right from the start. We ran for pleasure and that has never changed for me. I would consider myself a consistent runner, not a serious runner. But more on that later.

I continued running with my dad and eventually we entered races togeth-er. What we enjoyed about racing was not so much the competition as the social aspects. I grew up in Colts Neck, New Jersey, but moved to Hoboken, New Jersey after college. In 1983 I decided to put together a race in Hoboken for people who liked to race and have a good time and that was the start of the Hoboken Classic, a 5-miler through downtown Hoboken. Since I was the race director, the race reflected my view on running—which was to have a good run followed by a great party. The race had everything: filtered water for the runners because I never liked the taste of tap water used in most races, quality chocolates at the finish, a Clydesdale division, and a super-Clydesdale division for the really big guys. This was special to me since I am a Clydesdale and wanted to acknowledge the struggles of a person with a bigger-than-average body. It's much harder running with that extra weight than it is for the normal waifs you usually see at the races.

We also had five-year age divisions, kiddie events, great bands along the route and at the postrace party, and each runner received a personal thank-you letter from me. We had 244 volunteers and an average of 1,000 participants. My partner catered to the fast elite crowd, whom I found to be a bunch of complainers. My personal favorites were the back-of-the-packers. If I overheard a runner complain about something I'd pull their number. I was doing this because I love running and socializing, not getting headaches. The grand prize was a lottery drawing for all participants for a trip to Europe so that slow runners had just as much of a chance to win the big prize as the fast ones. The best part of the race was that my dad ran it and that made me proud. The Hoboken Classic had a great run for 10 years but then it just got too big and out of hand and not fun for me so I quit.

Although that was the end of my race director years, I continued running. My younger brother talked me into doing a marathon, which neither of us really ever considered before or trained for but it seemed like a fun idea at the time. We were very inexperienced runners and I remember eating an entire submarine sandwich right before the race. It didn't seem to bother me and that sub sandwich, more than any other memory of that very nondescript first marathon, is what I remember. Somehow, food and marathons became intertwined in my psyche.

The marathon I do like to recall as one of my first memories of a really fun time is the 1994 Los Angeles Marathon that I ran with two friends from Hoboken. One is a chef, Chef Ed, who makes Hoboken Eddie Sauces, and my friend Briant who owns a construction company. Briant is my regular running partner and Chef Ed is my marathon partner. He only runs marathons and does it without any training. He just shows up at the start and runs with us. I initiated the idea to run the L.A. Marathon and the other two fell in line. Briant and I had trained for the marathon and we asked Chef Ed, who didn't train, to come along as the entertainment. As always, food was a big part of my marathon strategy and training.

I love preparing for the long runs, which I do with Briant and any friend that wants to come along. I do most of my long runs in New York City as Hoboken is 1 mile long. Running through all the different neighborhoods gives us an opportunity to really see New York up close and personal. There isn't anywhere I won't run. Whether it's taking a train out to Fire Island and running along the beaches, or going through some sketchy area where I've witnessed shoot-outs, it's always interesting and entertaining. I start by studying a map of the neighborhood where I plan to run so I know the streets where the restaurants and bars are located. Sometimes we'll go out and run the entire day and end up at Rose's Bar in City Island where I love the food, or Silvia's in Harlem, or Zorba's, a great Greek restaurant.

Getting back to my Los Angeles event, we planned to give ourselves two days in L.A. prior to the marathon to acclimate to the time change. On the morning of our flight Chef Ed, who is always late and never prepared, was surprisingly ready and on the curb waiting for us with bags of food. Seems he had been cooking turkey dinners all night to take to L.A. The steaming turkey dinners went through airport security and X-ray machines and onto the plane where the aroma is so good everyone keeps asking the stewardesses what the mouthwatering meal is. Chef Ed takes some turkey and gives it to the stewardesses and before we know it he is walking through the aisles giving away the turkey dinners and samples of his sauce. The stewardesses are so thrilled to have this entertainment they give out free drinks. Meanwhile, Briant and I are also working the passengers trying to find recommendations for the best restaurants in town.

We land in L.A. on a beautiful day in March and the first thing we do is head down to Malibu for Dungeness crabs. Then we head over to East L.A., and Chef Ed, who speaks Spanish, finds some great Mexican restaurants. After that we decide to go to Tijuana for some nightlife. It was supposed to be a one-night trip but we ran out of money so ended up sleeping in the car until the banks opened the next morning. On our way out we stopped for a quick drink that somehow lasted all night. Now it was the night before the marathon and we knew we had to get back to L.A., so about 4 in the morning I went for a cold swim in the ocean to keep me awake and we drove back to the hotel. Since we only managed four hours of sleep in two nights, we crashed for a few hours before the race, but when it was time to leave we couldn't get Chef Ed up. He waves for us to leave without him so we do. By the time we got to the start line it had already been dismantled. Eight miles down the road as we try to catch up to the back of the pack, we hear a loud "Tally-ho" from behind us and there's Chef Ed, bedecked in beads and a colorful tee shirt promoting his Hoboken Eddie Sauce line. We were all hung over but through years of training and very scientific studies I have found that a hangover usually goes away after the first 5 miles.

Ten miles into the course we pass a group of CHIPS, the California highway motorcycle police, and Chef Ed decides it would be a hoot to get a picture of a "fake arrest" so the cops consent to our request with the handcuffs and all so we goof around there for a while before heading on. Fifteen miles into the marathon we decide it's time for our first beer. Now, I have to tell you we have very strict rules for our bar stops. Rule number one is only fifteen minutes allowed per bar, and rule number two is we must stretch and eat something. It's really fun because we are treated like celebrities at the bars since we are paying customers, not just asking to use the bathroom. We started drinking Guinness but that took too long so we moved on to martinis.

There is also a scientific reason for stopping at bars: the sugar in the alcohol numbs the pain and makes us happier and revved up to go.

At the 22-mile marker we decided to look for the most decadent dive we could find and discovered a bar covered in plywood with no door and three guys in sombreros taking a siesta outside. Right away we knew that was the place. No one spoke English but it didn't matter. The spicy chips that we downed in handfuls were incredible and I had my first Corona stuffed with 12 limes. It was the best beer I had ever tasted and ever will taste. In fact it was so good I had three of them. We had such a great time with the locals that we violated the 15-minute rule. When we finally left, the bartender came out with a paper cup filled with another Corona. Four more miles to go and I tasted those spicy chips and beer in my mouth the whole way. Approaching the finish line we readied ourselves for what would become our traditional ending ritual, lighting a big fat stogie. At that moment, I am as happy as it gets.

I don't want you to think that I am a careless runner. On the contrary, I take my running very seriously; I just choose to have fun while running. My year-round training schedule consists of running two to three days a week with a long run on the weekends and a very long run every other weekend. For instance, I'll do two 5-milers then 11 on the weekend and the next week do a 5 and 6 miler and 24 on the weekend. It's a modified formula from Jeff Galloway's training book. I do get injured, but that's because I don't stretch. Yes, I should, but no, I don't. It's boring and torturous. I manage to fit in two marathons a year, although one year I did four back to back: Marine Corps, NYC, Philadelphia, and Berlin. That was a banner year. I also make sure to get in two, maybe four long runs of 24 miles before a marathon. Most runners hit the wall at 20 miles because that's as far as they trained. Yes, the crowds will carry you through the last 6 miles, but why not train a little harder and be better prepared?

I travel a lot for business so my life is constantly hectic and I don't ever know where I will be in a given month. But I always pack my running gear. My work takes me on ships so I do a lot of my running around the decks of tankers, which can average a half mile once around. One memorable run was on a tanker going down to Venezuela. We docked at a town on the outskirts of the Amazon jungle and at night I was sitting on the deck with the crew sharing a few beers and I got the urge to run. I had a tape recorder and I wanted to record the sounds of the jungle at night. My plan was to run 5 in and back for a nice 10-miler. I jokingly told the crew if I wasn't back by dawn to send out a search party. I was a little concerned about the panthers and snakes but I stayed on a trail. The run was amazing. Under a full moon at midnight, the jungle was eerily scary at the same time it was quietly beautiful. The sounds from the nocturnal animals were an orchestral cacophony. Just as I reached the turnaround point, the sight of three men standing in the middle of the path holding machetes startled me. The moonlight reflected off the sharp metal of their 2-foot-long blades. They just stood there staring at me. After a second glance, I remembered seeing them in the village the day before and had offered them my shirt. But meeting them here in the middle of the jungle was unsettling. They had menacing machetes and I had a tape recorder. Trying not to show fear, I nodded to them, passed them by, and was too scared to look back so I just kept running. I ran for another hour hoping they would be gone by the time I circled back to the boat. So my 10-mile run through the jungle turned into a 20-miler running for my life.

The 100th running of the Boston Marathon was another time Chef Ed, Briant, and I banded together to be a part of running history. We had never done Boston and figured if we ever were then this was the year to do it. Naturally, none of us had official numbers as we could never dream of qualifying, so we had to run as bandits. Usually I don't do that but I am a very respectful bandit. I don't drink the water on the course and don't try to go through the finishing chutes. With 38,000 runners, we knew the back of the pack would be crowded and that worked to our advantage. But first we had to break through the tight security so we studied maps of the area surrounding Hopkinton Square and found a railroad track that we could use as a place of entry. Chef Ed hitchhiked up to Boston. Don't ask me why a grown man with a successful business selling barbecue sauce to high-end retailers decided to hitchhike. That's just Ed. Briant and I flew in the morning of the race. A friend drove us to the designated meeting spot. For our race bibs, we used old race numbers and crayons. Chef Ed brought the food and we had a picnic at Hopkinton before the race started. Then we tried to start to mingle with the crowd but they are penned in with fences and security and we are outside the fences roaming like free-range chickens looking for a place to break through. The back-of-the-packers were in great moods and laughed at us with our Crayola numbers. Chef Ed started handing out samples of his sauces and we slowly managed to work our way up to the elite runners' area. Chef Ed was wearing tennis sneakers covered in sauce drippings, which is what probably blew our cover because this huge guard started stalking us and he locked on me like target practice. It became a game of cat and mouse but we finally lost him as we merged into the crowd and took off. It was a great run, well worth the insane tactics to get in but let me tell you something about Heartbreak Hill: It is very anticlimactic. Central Park has worse hills.

I don't believe in killing myself, I believe in having fun. In fact, I have a list of rules for marathons that I'll share. Number one is definitely to have a good time. Don't worry about the pace. Number two is the previously stated "15-minute" rule for bars. Number three, dress comfortably. No cotton touches this skin. Number four, don't take the race seriously. Talk to people. If you can't talk, you're running too hard, which breaks rule number one. Number five refers to running foreign marathons. Be careful of the food and water and avoid getting diarrhea. For instance, don't eat a bratwurst sandwich before running the Berlin Marathon. Number six, always carry money for food, beverage, and a cab if necessary. Number seven, carry a cell phone so you can call ahead to favorite bars and restaurants and order a meal so it's ready by the time you get there. This is a very good timesaving tool that can shave five minutes off your time. When I run the New York City Marathon I have my favorite bars programmed into my cell phone so I can call ahead to McRiely's Pub and order a bangers and egg sandwich with a martini to go, which I consume while crossing the Queensboro Bridge. Number eight: Get the longs in during training; that's the key to running a successful, happy marathon. My longest training run is 25 miles. That's an important part of my planning, as I want to be comfortable while I am running and not look like I'm dying or all beat up. Number nine: Make sure to rest and recover between races. The body needs to recover not only from the run but also from the food and alcohol. Number ten: If you're not feeling well, don't do it. There will always be another marathon to run. I truly believe more people would take up running if they followed my philosophy.

One of my biggest fears in life is that something will happen to me that will prevent me from running. Nothing will ever replace running in my life for me. Everything I do is scheduled around my runs. I choose vacations so I can run. Even my work affords me the opportunity to run. Being on board ships has brought me to so many exotic places to run, I feel extremely fortunate. I was on a tanker in the Arctic once and ran on the ice where I could see polar bears and seals and all sorts of wildlife I've never seen in their natural surroundings. The ice was so thick and it was so cold, I was jumping over frozen waves and icescapes. I have had unbelievable experiences through running. It is my therapy. Running should be fun and make you feel good. I can still remember that first run I took with my dad. It's an image I keep with me and that always makes me feel good.

# RUNNING FOR FRED'S TEAM

**CAROL PATTERSON**

**D.O.B.: 7-12-56**
**RESIDENCE: NEW LONDON, CT**
**OCCUPATION: DIABETES NURSE EDUCATOR,**
   **LAWRENCE AND MEMORIAL HOSPITAL**
**FIRST MARATHON: 2000 NYC MARATHON**
**AGE AT FIRST MARATHON: 44**

*When her mother-in-law was diagnosed with ovarian cancer and a good friend who had survived breast cancer ran a marathon, Carol decided it was her turn to run a marathon and along the way raise money for cancer research. If you were to ask Carol what was more difficult—raising the money, training for the marathon, or running the marathon—she would laugh and say just getting into the NYC Marathon was the hard part! Carol has a wonderful way of tackling life with a smile and a determination to always do her best whether she is running 26.2 miles, caring for her patients, or helping her children with their homework.*

I always enjoyed sports but was never what you would call an athlete. During high school I skied and played tennis but not at the varsity level. For me, sports were fun but not worth a big commitment. After college I moved to New York City and worked at Lenox Hill Hospital. I lived a great single life, had lots of friends and an active social life. This was my time to have a ball and sports took a sideline. After work I'd hang out with friends at neighborhood places, stay out late, and do what young single people do; party and have fun. No one was overly concerned with any form of disciplined exercise.

In 1977 a friend of mine knew someone who was running the New York City Marathon and we went to watch. Back then the running scene was still just a blip on the radar. Less than 5,000 runners entered the marathon that year and Bill Rodgers and Grete Waitz had yet to become household names. I remember standing on the corner of First Avenue and 76th Street watching the parade of people run by and was totally dumbfounded. To run 26.2 miles seemed amazing. I didn't know people could run like that. But it left an impression and I thought to myself that someday I'd like to do that.

Shortly after that I started running for social reasons. It was a great way to meet people. Everyone hung out at New York Road Runners on 89th Street or congregated at 90th and Fifth Avenue at the entrance to Central Park. I would run from my apartment to the park and do a loop around the reservoir. But I still didn't consider myself a real runner. In the spring of 1980 I entered the L'Eggs Mini-Marathon, a 10K in Central Park. It was a fun way to spend the day and that's all running was to me. If something else came up, I didn't sweat over not getting a run in that day. And if I had to make a choice between sleeping in on a Saturday morning or going for a run, most of the time I'd sleep in.

In 1983 I married and we moved to Connecticut where Bruce joined a dental practice. My husband wasn't a runner but he played golf and tennis. We both like to stay in shape. As soon as we got settled in New London, I became pregnant and eventually had three children all close in age. With three young kids there was no time to run, so I stopped running but stayed active with tennis and I was always pushing strollers and going for walks. Bruce had a family home on Martha's Vineyard where we spent part of the summer with his parents and we were always outdoors playing tennis and walking with the kids everywhere. Even though I wasn't running I managed to stay in shape.

From 1984 to 1995 I didn't run. During the summer of 1995 I started working out with a friend of mine, Ellen, a personal trainer and marathoner. She started our session with some warm-ups and then suggested we do a 1-mile run. After the mile, I had the endurance to keep going and we ended up running a few more miles. She was surprised that I could do that having not run for 11 years. After that we ran together, gradually getting up to 6 miles. At some point that summer I began to consider myself a real runner. The difference was in my mind-set. The new me got up in the morning, put on my shoes, and headed out for a run instead of the old me that would go for a run only if there was nothing better to do. The difference was I became committed to my morning runs and now they were a part of my routine. I was finally a runner.

I continued running with Ellen for the next four years, entered a few local races, and even did a half marathon. I also ran with other friends or alone when Ellen wasn't around. When Ellen talked about her marathons, the memory of watching the 1977 marathon came back to me and I casually mentioned that at some point in my life I would like to run a marathon. I was now in my 40s and thought maybe it was a good idea to start thinking more seriously about it but still wasn't ready to commit to the challenge just yet. Then a good friend of mine, Jill, a breast cancer survivor, ran the Rock 'n' Roll Marathon in San Diego. I thought it was remarkable that she not only recovered, but was healthier than ever before and ran a marathon. The following April of 2000 she ran the Boston Marathon. That's when I made the decision to run my own 26.2 miles and decided it would have to be New York for two reasons; One, having lived there, I thought it would be fun to go back and run it in New York City, and two, I wanted to run on Fred's Team and raise money for cancer research. Fred's Team is sponsored by Memorial Sloane Kettering Hospital and is dedicated to the memory of Fred Lebow, the founder of New York Road Runners and director of the marathon from its inception. Fred died of brain cancer in 1994. My decision to be part of Fred's Team stemmed from being inspired by Jill and my mother-in-law Janice Patterson's diagnosis of ovarian cancer. Running on Fred's Team just seemed like the perfect way to accomplish a personal goal, raise money for cancer research, and honor both my friend and Jan.

Joining Fred's Team does not guarantee entry to the marathon; I still had to enter the lottery. I'll never forget the day I scrolled down the website and saw the word ACCEPTED next to my name. It was very exciting. In the meantime, my neighbor Matt Greene also applied and got in. He wasn't a real dedicated runner and applied almost on a lark, hoping we would both get in so we could train and run it together. The big joke between us was that he never won anything in his life and now he wins a lottery to run 26.2 miles. After being accepted I then joined Fred's Team. They took care of hotel arrangements (the Plaza Hotel), meals, a private bus to the start, and VIP passes for family in a reserved tent right across from the finish line. All I had to do was train and raise $3,500.

Raising the money was the easy part. I dedicated my race to Jan and solicited some of my friends and my mother-in-law's longtime friends on Martha's Vineyard. They all responded most generously and I was able to raise $7,800. The best part of the fund-raising was Jan's reaction. She was overwhelmed with the generosity of her friends, exclaiming to me over and over again how she didn't realize so many people cared about her. It also gave her something to focus on besides her chemotherapy treatments. She asked about my training and how it was going. It became a special bond between us.

I followed Hal Higdon's book on marathons and religiously kept to his schedule. All I did that summer was run. My marathon goal was just to finish, so that eliminated any pressure to do speed work or anything less than long easy runs. It was easy to get the long runs in because the kids were older and I could leave them alone on weekend mornings if Bruce was busy. The skiing, tennis, and hiking always kept me in shape so my endurance was already at a fit level. I did some nice long runs on Martha's Vineyard with my friend LuLu. She never disappointed me and was always ready for our rendezvous to Ally's General Store, about a 12-mile point-to-point. Back in New London I would run with Matt. By the time training was over we had completed three 20-milers and two 18-milers. Higdon preaches that the key to running a marathon successfully is the long runs. We did two of the 20-milers by entering full marathons, running the course, and dropping out at 20 miles. It is a great way to practice running a real marathon and learning how to pace yourself among the different runners. And there's the added advantage of the water stops and bathrooms. We always paid our entry fee so it wasn't like we were bandits, using the course as our personal training ground.

Don't get me wrong about the difficulty of running a marathon; I'm not saying it was all fun and games. The training was sometimes difficult and it certainly put a dent in my social life. Friday nights were now off limits to any late-night socializing, as I had to be up early Saturday for my long runs. I also cut way back on tennis and golfing all summer and bike rides with my husband. I'd come home after a long run and Bruce would be waiting for me and say, "Come on, let's go for a bike ride," and I'd respond, "What are you crazy? I just ran 20 miles and I'm not going on a friggin' bike ride."

Having a running partner was a necessity for me. Matt and I were very compatible because we were so damn reliable. I would never stand him up— nor would he do that to me. Matt was as reliable as the sunrise. We took turns setting the course and putting out the water bottles ahead of time, and then picking them up afterward. The other reason I was so dedicated to my running is that my husband kept telling me that since I had already raised all the money, if I didn't run I'd have to return it!

The Friday before the marathon my family and I drove down to New York City. I wanted this to be a fun experience for everyone so we took in a play, had a nice dinner, and Saturday afternoon went to the marathon expo. That night we had a great Italian meal and I even had a glass of red wine. The book said not to do anything different than I normally would so what the heck, I decided to enjoy myself. Sunday morning we took the private Fred's Team bus to the start after eating an ample breakfast. Fred's Team volunteers handed out snack bags with protein bars and fruit and water. That certainly beats having to take the New York Road Runner buses to the start; they depart starting at 5:15 in the morning. Fred's Team is such a civilized way to run a marathon. Our families had reserved bleachers in front of Sloane Kettering Hospital on First Avenue to view the race and then they waited for us at the Fred's Team VIP tent at the finish. No walking miles through Sheep's Meadow in search of a familiar face in a sea of 20,000 people for Fred's Team participants. The best was, however, the gratification of knowing the money raised supported cancer research.

Matt and I wanted this adventure to be fun. We were both in agreement to enjoy it and stay together. Standing on the bridge at the start, it was a glorious day and as the gun went off we crossed the Verrazzano and were on our way. I loved running through all the neighborhoods. It is such a charge moving from borough to borough and through all the different ethnic sections. There is so much to look at that you forget about the miles.

Meanwhile, throughout the course Matt was peeing behind every tree and car he could find, but so far I was okay, didn't get the urge. We finally entered Manhattan and passed the Sloane Kettering bleachers and met with our families. That was a kick. We actually hung out and visited a bit. I even ate half a sandwich. It was fun. No worries about our time or anything; we were still having a ball. It was comforting.

At 18 miles we were still feeling great. We had made a prior agreement to split at that point if either one felt the urge to run faster. We were enjoying each other's company, talking up a storm and laughing the whole way. Matt was annoyed at me because my T-shirt had my name across the front and everyone cheered for me and no one called out for him. Matt carried food as well. He had lollipops and gum, goo, more food than we could ever need. I didn't know a Dum-Dum lollipop tasted so good.

Finally, at around 18 miles, the corner of 110th and First avenue, I suddenly had to go to the bathroom but there wasn't a Porta-Potti in sight. In fact, at this point in the course, there aren't a heck of a lot of spectators, period. Just lots of locked-up businesses. Matt advised me to hide between cars like he was doing but this was not just a pee. I knew this was going to be trouble. I ran over to a store and started pounding on the metal and the owner came over and said he was closed. I looked at him and said, "I have to poop." So he let me in and by now I was beginning to cramp I had to go so badly. He pointed to the back of the store and I was literally racing to the back with my shorts already down around my ankles when I ran right into a circle of men playing a card game. The bathroom was to their right, but it didn't have a door. I was so desperate I didn't even care and just sat down on the toilet and let it rip. I was only 10 feet away from them. To their credit, they turned their eyes to avoid looking at me and went on with their game.

I am sure they thought I was some crazed middle-aged woman and potentially more dangerous to them than the other way around. They were terrified of me and just didn't know what to do. I finished my business and as I got up and passed them on my way out, I gave them the $10 I was carrying with me for an emergency. If there was ever an emergency, this was it. I dropped the 10-spot into the middle of their game, thanked them, and ran out the door.

I couldn't stop laughing at my shamelessness. We now refer to the New York City Marathon as "The Big Crapple." The ironic part about this whole adventure is that just two blocks from where I stopped was the Adam Clayton Powell Recreation Center with big signs out front for bathrooms. Who knew!

Meanwhile Matt had kept going and I caught up with him on the Madison Avenue Bridge just past the Bronx and starting into Harlem. He was walking slowly and grimacing from a back spasm. We walked for a while. By now we were on Fifth Avenue with only 4 miles to go but he had no concept of our location. Having lived in New York, I explained to him the logistics of where we were and where we had to go and that we were almost at the finish so he felt somewhat better. We started running again very slowly. As he started to feel better, he picked up the pace. We were now in sight of the Plaza Hotel, with about a mile to go. But whereas he was feeling fine, I developed an intense pain in my left arm. It killed. I couldn't move it. Perhaps it could have been that we'd been running for over four hours and I was just tired. Fortunately, I knew where the finish line was and could almost taste it we were so close.

We crossed the finish line holding hands, glad to have the 26.2 miles behind us. Our time was 4:39, but I like to subtract my "rest stop" and make it 4:28. Our spouses were right there waiting for us at the Fred's Team tent and as we got caught up with the cheering, the congratulations, the hugs and tears, we drifted apart. I didn't see or talk to Matt again for a few days. When we finally spoke, we realized that we now share a life memory. It doesn't necessarily make us best friends but it bonds us in a way that is special and that I don't have with anyone else.

I felt fine the next day but didn't go back to work till Thursday. I took care of myself with mineral salt baths and lots of Advil. My mother-in-law sent me flowers with a nice congratulatory note and we talked on the phone about the race. Two weeks later we drove down to Pennsylvania to her winter residence to visit her in the hospital. I spoke with her a little bit and she asked if I'd brought my medal, which I had, but she was getting tired so we left. She died five minutes later. It was the night before Thanksgiving and I think she was just waiting to say good-bye to Bruce and her other children.

I discovered things about myself that I didn't know by running a marathon. I never really believed I'd ever run a marathon and when I made the commitment I realized I had the discipline to do it. I didn't quit. That impressed both my husband and me. I set out on a course, followed the book, and never diverted, never went off track. The marathon also gave me something to talk about with my mother-in-law when she was dying, and through the fund-raising she realized she had lots of friends who cared about her. That meant a lot to her.

The marathon was a thrill a mile. I wore a smile the entire way and laughed and joked with Matt for over four hours. There was no sense of disappointment if I didn't crack a time. I knew I would finish even if I had to walk it. We weren't under the burden of time. It was a just one of the nicest afternoons I've ever spent.

Mentally I often go back to the marathon when I am faced with something difficult. I'll say to myself, *Heck, I know hard. I ran a marathon. I can get through anything.* I also find that I can make time for things that otherwise I might put off. I found the time to train for a marathon so I should be able to find time for other things that I value just as much, such as volunteering at my

kids' school. I told myself at the start of the marathon that no matter how horrible it got I was going to finish: *After training for five months it will be over in
five hours and if you can't do something for five hours that's pretty pathetic.* In the
grand scheme of life, you can hang in there and make a difference. I use that
same metaphor with my kids when they rush through their homework. I tell
them one more hour is not going to make a difference in their night, but it
will make a difference in how well they do they their work and how much better they will be prepared for the next day.

I am absolutely going to run another marathon. It has to be a great place,
though. I need the excitement. New York was exciting because it's New York
and I used to live there. I will also definitely do it with Fred's Team. No question. It's the only way to go. Maybe Paris?

# MOM'S BIG MOMENT

**JENNIFER SAGE**

**D.O.B.: 2-1-66**
**RESIDENCE: EXTON, PA**
**OCCUPATION: MOM**
**FIRST MARATHON: 2000 SHAMROCK**
   **MARATHON, VIRGINIA BEACH, VA**
**AGE AT FIRST MARATHON: 35**

*Jen Sage is willing to share all the gruesome details of training for and running her first marathon, which she describes as a life-changing experience, all with contagious laughter. Putting on a few extra pounds after two children and needing some of her own breathing room, Jen decided to shake up her life and do something just for herself. The daunting challenge of a marathon was just what she was looking for, and she told anyone who would listen that she was going to run 26.2 miles. The training was more than she'd bargained for, but through a great support team that included friends from the Y, her husband and family, and the babies, she made her dream come true.*

I am still basking in the glory of my first marathon. Just the other day I told a group of friends that I ran my first marathon and they asked how long a run that was. Of course I couldn't wait to say it was 26.2 miles to see the look on their faces, which was priceless.

Words don't come easy when I try to describe one of the most incredible experiences in my life, especially when it truly was a life-changing event. People who know me find it hard to believe I can't find the right words as it is rare that I don't have something to say about everything. Let's just say it was almost as good as my wedding night.

To put things in perspective about my running career, I ran track and cross-country in high school and was better than average. I went to an all-girl school and the coaches were positive and motivational. But I never really applied myself. I had a natural talent but ignored it. Of course I am kicking myself now for not taking advantage of my talents and their training and wasting those youthful years and now wondering what kind of athlete I could have been if I applied myself. The other reason I liked to run is that in every other sport I was terribly uncoordinated. Couldn't handle a ball or a bat.

Couldn't even run the relay as I was always dropping the baton. That's why running appealed to me so much. It was just me and a pair of shoes. My parents weren't into sports and my sister was a good runner but not great. I was also an ugly duckling in high school, very unattractive and gawky. Just one of those kids who never come into themselves till later in life. Running was my outlet. I ran every race like it was the last one. Even in practice I never let up. It was my way of fitting in, of trying to be accepted.

After high school I put myself through college; lots of them. I transferred around quite a bit throughout Michigan, where I grew up. I'd go to a college for a couple of semesters, then have to work again for more tuition money then go back to school again. I stopped running because I was tired of the discipline and decided to major in drinking instead of running. And Michigan is not a good place for all-weather running. It gets really cold there. There were many mornings the locks on my car were frozen. Actually I couldn't wait to get out of that state where the natives give directions by showing the palm of their hand. I lived just above the second joint on the third finger.

It took me 4 years to get my associate's degree and eight more years to get my bachelor's but I wouldn't trade in those years for anything. I had a ball! In between school I worked at all types of jobs from manager of a country club to a hair salon. I totally believe in experiencing life before settling down.

Flash forward a few more years and I got married, moved to Pennsylvania, got my teaching degree, taught, and then had my first child. Then I had my second child. Prior to the children we were weekend warriors and we'd rock climb or bike or hike. I ran off and on, but without any real goal or motivation. Staying in shape wasn't a motivator, either, as I was always skinny. But after two children in a very short time I put on a lot of weight. Now I had a reason! I never recovered physically after my son was born. I remember nursing him when he was 10 months old and I was already pregnant with number two. Before discovering I was pregnant again, I flirted with the idea of running a marathon to get back in shape but that thought moved quickly to the back burner when I found out I was pregnant.

Thirty pounds heavier and two children later I felt like I was nothing but a fat mom and had lost my whole sense of self. Who was I other than a breeding milk machine? I used to be so much more than that and realized I needed something all my own. Everyone from the kids to my husband to the dog wanted a piece of me. I couldn't even read the paper anymore or go to the bathroom without someone looking for me. I felt I had lost a part of myself and needed to reconnect with the person I was before my life changed. Don't get me wrong, I love my life and chose this lifestyle, but along the way I think I left a part of me behind. And the weight gain bothered me. After having two kids too soon, my normal weight of 135 ballooned to 170. I remembered what it was like to be in shape and wanted to get back to that place. So I thought, *What the hell, I'll run a marathon.* I always admired marathoners and besides, I felt like I needed a really big challenge that would keep me motivated and get me out of the house. Also, the best part would be telling people I was training for a marathon just so I could see the astonished look on their faces!

I'm an all-or-nothing type of gal. When I make my mind up I don't start out small. It was a marathon or nothing at all. I actually thought of doing a triathlon but would have had to go straight to the Ironman so pushed that thought back for a while. A marathon was doable. When I was in high school I ran 10 miles and thought I was Grete Waitz. In fact I remember that Grete's bra strap always showed when she ran and on our high school team we would purposely show our straps to imitate Grete. But I never realized the training involved. Back in my heyday of track I thought I was invincible, could run forever, and now the reality of running 26.2 miles was becoming daunting. Although the training was harder than anticipated, it was also exhilarating. Each long run was like climbing a personal mountain and getting to dump all the crap of the week down the other side.

I followed a book, *The Non-runner's Guide to Running a Marathon,* which begins with zero training so that was right up my alley. I started with a walk-run sequence, 30 minutes, three times a week. My high school training kicked in and one of the rules I remembered was not going out too fast or too far in order to prevent injuries. The book also recommended picking the marathon date early on so that my training calendar would coincide with long runs and a nice tapering-off period at the end. Another recommendation from the book was signing up for the marathon early on and writing the entry fee check and then telling everyone about it. In other words, make it real. Make it a big event in your life. Well, I told everyone I knew about my marathon! When I was just in the walking stage, I'd tell anyone I passed, "Hey, I'm training for a marathon!" Even at the gym, with my shorts too tight and 35 pounds overweight, I'd tell people, "I'm training for a marathon." I'm sure they thought I was nuts and what they were really thinking was, *Sure you are. We know you. You're just a mother of two kids here at the local Y trying to lose weight. Don't try to fool us that you're training to run a marathon. Yeah, sure you are!* I certainly didn't look the marathon type but I was so into it.

Originally, my sister was also taken with the idea of running a marathon and said she would do it with me but as we got deeper into the training she had to back off, which was very disappointing to me. But I got great reinforcement from my parents, who were psyched for me. They babysat the kids for me when I went on my first 5-miler. I was gone over an hour and they were freaking out thinking something went wrong but it was just me being slow. They also booked flights to Virginia Beach to be with me for the marathon. But I know they were concerned that I was biting off more than I could chew because every once in a while they'd look at me and say, "How's it going? Are you all right? Are you sure you want to do this?" My husband was an incredible support as well. He always inquired how I was doing, how the training was going, always wanted to be there for me. He told all our friends and family I was running a marathon. Every time I felt tired or that my goal was impossible he would remind me how far I'd come and how hard I had worked to achieve that and it would make me work harder. He was proud that I had set this goal and was working so hard to make it happen.

Training for a marathon with two young kids was not easy and there certainly wasn't a chapter in the book dedicated to moms with kids. I was on a four-day running schedule. Three days of the week I ran on a treadmill at the Y, where I could leave the kids for two hours at the nursery. It was solid training but really boring and I could only manage 8 miles in that time limit. But I did meet a trainer at the Y who got interested in my marathon goal and told me I would also need upper-body strength. He showed me some exercises to strengthen my upper body and some core balancing exercises, and that made a huge difference in my running; I felt so much stronger.

After my three days on the treadmill, my husband watched the kids on Saturdays so I could do my long runs. It was so refreshing to be able to run outside and see things and smell things. I really appreciated being outside and I think that mentality also helped me get through the marathon. When I got tired during the marathon I thought to myself, *Well, at least you're not on that stupid treadmill at the Y!* My Saturday runs were usually done in cold weather and after my run I'd come home to a hot lunch prepared by my husband. I used to love to come home to a great-smelling kitchen, knowing he had prepared something that would really hit the spot, like a grilled cheese sandwich or soup. All I had to do was peel off my sweaty clothes, sit down, and eat to my heart's content.

I trained for six months, did three 16-milers and two 18-milers and was ready. I followed the schedule in the book to a T with a goal of just finishing. I didn't even think of a finishing time. The marathon was on a Saturday, so my husband and I piled the kids and all the gear into the car on Thursday night and drove down to Virginia Beach. Friday I did the expo and wanted to cry I was so excited and full of emotion. Picking up my race number was such a thrill after all the months of planning that I thought I would burst with bottled-up excitement. I hadn't felt that way since I attended the 1996 Olympics in Los Angeles. I went to see the track and field events and when I walked into the stadium and smelled the track I started to cry. That smell brought back my own track and field days and the memories came pouring out. I couldn't believe I was at the Olympics and here again I couldn't believe I was going to run a marathon. It was such a high. I'd never focused on this part of the event so it caught me off guard and I couldn't contain my feelings.

That night we did the premarathon spaghetti dinner and some runners from New York were drinking beer and I said, "What are you thinking? Don't you worry about puking it all up tomorrow?"

I went to bed at 10 P.M. and since I was still nursing my second child I had to wake extra early to nurse him before I left for the marathon. Then I took a shower because psychologically I wanted to be clean for the run! Ate a bagel but was too nervous to think about food. It was 42 degrees and overcast so I wore gloves and a jacket and shorts. When I headed over to the start to join the 2,000 other runners I couldn't find the start line. I felt nervous and apprehensive, as if at any minute the race officials would spot me and say, *Hey who is that 35-year old woman and what in the world is she doing in the middle of all these marathoners? Get her the hell off the course before she hurts herself!*

The adrenaline was racing through my veins as I started out. My goal was a pace of 11- to 12-minute miles. There were lots of first-timers at the start so I fell in with a nice group and we chatted and exchanged stories. I took it very slowly and stopped at every water station. At mile 8 I met an 80-year-old man who had just run a marathon three weeks earlier. Everyone was passing us until I was sure we were the last two on the course. I was having a great time and actually picked up the pace a bit and started running with another guy my age for the next 6 miles. By now the elite runners were passing us on their way back and we cheered for them. I was pleasantly surprised when some of them turned around and cheered for us. My new running buddy told me his wife was pregnant and that it was a girl but not to tell anyone. It's funny how you meet a total stranger and in a few short miles you know their life history and the sex of their unborn child.

My family was waiting for me at mile 14 and that was a real lift. Then I ran with a guy who was getting tired and complaining. We ran up an incline and when he referred to it as a hill I knew he was starting to hit the wall. I tried to help him through it but he was so full of negative energy I had to pull away before he brought me down. He wasn't drinking water and hadn't eaten anything that morning whereas I was drinking water at every stop and sucking down gel packs.

Then in the crowd of spectators I saw my two buddies from my YMCA who drove five hours from Pennsylvania to cheer me on. I hardly knew them but they used to talk to me while I was on that stupid treadmill and teased that they would show up for me—and there they were. I only knew them as Rufus and Jack, and Rufus was blind. They made me feel like a real celebrity.

At mile 20 I was still going strong and felt like I could have run an ultra; that 26.2 miles wouldn't be long enough. Even took a Dixie cup of warm beer from a spectator, which didn't taste so great but the crowds definitely made my spirits soar. Saw my family again at mile 21 and yelled that I would see them at the finish. Then at mile 22 the fatigue started to set in and those thoughts of doing an ultra disappeared. Just when I was beginning to whine to myself that I wanted it over and didn't think I would make it alive, a woman in the crowd shouted my number and said, "We are proud of you!" Just remembering that brings tears to my eyes now. It was just what I need-ed and I lifted my head and smiled and ran faster. She will never know that she made all the difference in the world to me at that low point in time.

With a half mile to go my legs felt wooden and I could barely lift them, but then I saw the finish line and couldn't believe it. I'd like to say that I sprinted across with an incredible pace but it was more like lumbering across. I remember running into the stadium and crossing the finish line and never wanting that feeling to go away. When they hung the medal around my neck I started to hyperventilate from emotion and couldn't stop crying. My face was blotchy from all the tears and one side was sunburned from the sun while the other side stayed pale. It wasn't a pretty sight but for me it was the best moment of my life, right up there with childbirth. After I went through the chute, I walked around in a daze looking for my family. When I found them the look on my husband's face was amazing; he was crying and kept saying how proud he was of me. My baby wanted to be picked up and my older one was parading around with his own tee shirt and medal from a children's race he ran that morning. It was quite an ending.

No words can describe what that marathon did for me. A sense of accom-plishment, completion, and relief all rolled into one. It was my moment of glory and I soaked it all up. This day belonged to me. Will I do it again? Definitely. Why? Because no one can run a marathon for me. If I don't put in the time, the training, the pain, and the effort, it doesn't get done. I own it. I guess in a way doing the laundry is the same thing—if I don't do it no one else will—but the level of satisfaction after completing a marathon is so much more greater than a pile of clean clothes.

Back home in Pennsylvania I got right back into the swing of the house-hold chores. No basking in the limelight for me at my house. But after all, if I can run a marathon, I can do anything—especially housework.

# I'M NOT JUST A JOGGER

**ROBERT SAWYER**

**D.O.B.: 5-22-49**
**RESIDENCE: SANTA PAULA, CA**
**OCCUPATION: REAL ESTATE**
    **ATTORNEY**
**FIRST MARATHON: 1999 LOS**
    **ANGELES MARATHON**
**AGE AT FIRST MARATHON: 49**

*Robert's story of how he came to run a marathon is very similar to men and women in their 40s who find themselves juggling family and careers. With limited time in the day to accomplish both, something has to give—and usually exercise takes a backseat. A runner and cyclist in his early stages of life, Robert got the incentive he needed to resurrect his running from his teenage daughter, who called him a jogger, not a runner.*

Before I ran my first marathon, I didn't understand why people ran marathons. Now that I've run two, I still don't.

I've been a runner off and on throughout my life. You might say I've had three running lives so far. My first started in high school. I was on the tennis team and ran cross-country for conditioning. I enjoyed the competition and surprisingly wasn't the slowest. I was never an outstanding athlete—no championships or awards—but I enjoyed it. During my first two years of college, athletics went by the wayside, which ended my first incarnation as a runner player.

In junior year in college I fell in with a group of cyclists and started some serious bicycling. Our campus had some supersteep hills and I picked up a reputation for being one of those weirdos who actually pedaled all the way to the top rather than getting off and walking.

After college I went to law school in Portland, Oregon, where I continued racing with an amateur bike racing team, but as the weather can get a bit wet there, I returned to running as a good way to stay in shape when rain or snow made the roads less than inviting.

Even after I graduated from law school and started my law practice in Southern California I stayed with the bike racing. But within a few years family and business obligations put an end to competitive cycling. I like to tell people that I left the sport after losing to the legendary Greg LeMond. It's a true story but not as exciting as it sounds. My last race was a road race in central California, where the 16-year-old LeMond had to get a special dispensation from the sanctioning body to enter the Category I and II race. At least he and I started at the same time but he finished, cleaned up, and accepted his winner's trophy while I was still struggling on the road with a pack of dropped, punctured, and fallen riders. He was on his way up in the sport while I was definitely on my way down.

That's when my second life as a runner began. I needed a sport where I could jump out of bed in the early morning, get a decent workout, and still make it to the office in time. Running fit the bill perfectly. In the process I got reacquainted with local running guru and childhood friend Chuck Smead, the legendary mountain runner who took the silver medal in the marathon at the 1975 Pan Am Games in Mexico City. Although his easy days were my hard days, and his hard days generally ended with his having to take a long double-back to find me, we had a great time working out together.

By my late 20s and early 30s I'd become a pretty solid runner, picking up an occasional age-group award at local 5- and 10K races. It was in the early 1980s and the running boom was in full explosion, led by Gary Tuttle, who'd returned to his hometown of Ventura after a successful collegiate and amateur career, and had opened up a running store, The Inside Track. He was a real mover and shaker, organizing local races and fun run, coaching, and generally promoting the sport.

But as my daughters came along and family and work took more time, my workouts got shorter and less frequent, and I got slower and slower. My racing narrowed down to the annual Law Day 5K, sponsored by the local bar association. Even though I wrote an optimistic goal of "run a marathon by age 40" in my planning diary, as I got closer and closer to that age I unconsciously morphed into a three-day-a-week jogger.

The turnaround, and the birth of my third running life, happened one day when my older daughter, by then 17 and running on her high school track team, was looking at my stash of ribbons and medals and said, "Gee dad, you should start running again." "But I do run," was my reply, to which she, with rapier-point accuracy, said, "No you don't. You jog once in a while but you don't run."

It was a rude awakening, but it made me realize how much I'd let my love of running stagnate. I went back to the sport with a ferocious appetite, going to Gary's coaching clinics, reading every running book I could get my hands on, keeping a detailed training diary, and actually training instead of just jogging around. A few months into this incarnation I happened to be watching the TV broadcast of the 1998 Los Angeles Marathon while stretching prior to a Sunday-morning workout, and, remembering my diary entry of more than a decade before, said to myself, *Hey, I could do that.*

With my decision made, I read everything I could about marathoning, both in books and on the Internet. I even found an old video at the local rental outlet, *The Marathon Challenge,* featuring British marathoner Ian Thompson preparing a group of eight first-time marathoners for the third annual Gloucester Marathon in 1984. I picked the brains of every marathoning friend and teammate I knew. I also signed up for one-on-one coaching from Gary Tuttle.

Why the marathon at 49? Because it's such a symbolic event. You've got all the trimmings of myth and legend, starting with that heroic Greek messenger Phidippides dropping dead after running from the Plains of Marathon to Athens. You've got more than a century of American history at the Boston. You've got unforgettable mental images of Ethiopia's Abebe Bikila winning the 1960 Rome Olympic marathon barefoot, as torches lit the path along the Appian Way. Then there's Frank Shorter's stunning marathon victory at Munich in 1972, and even Oprah Winfrey running the Marine Corps Marathon in 1994.

But with all this glamour and fame, I also realized that the average person running a marathon was no different than me. When I watched the Los Angeles Marathon I saw people who looked to be in worse shape than me, still having the time of their lives. I knew I could do it.

I started extending my distance in the summer of 1998, a slow build to long distance. Gary Tuttle's training program was simple. Eighteen to twenty weeks to train, a combination of increasing basic speed with increasing distance, gradually building up to weekly long runs of 20 miles or more. There's no magic to it. In fact, what I learned over time is that the training becomes more mental than physical. I'd be out for an hour and cover 6 miles and wonder to myself if I had the mental stamina to stay out 3 or possibly 4 more miles.

I've always been an early-morning runner, fitting it in before work or before the heat of the day. But I particularly remember one long run I took at night. I had another commitment in the morning, but my training schedule said it was the day to do an 18-miler, so I ran it after work. I started after the winter sun went down and ran on the frontage road along the beach so I could use the car headlights to see where I was going. It turned out to be one of my better runs, and I figured if I had the commitment to run then, I could run anytime.

My family was supportive during my training and occasionally my daughters would accompany me for 3 miles or so on my long runs or run a 5K race with me. My wife was also supportive and a great coach. She would read subtle changes in my moods or my sleeping patterns, for example, and suggest I take a day off. However, the training does eat into family time and that wasn't always met with a favorable response. It wasn't so much the time I was out running as much as the extra "nonrunning" time that gets eaten up by marathon training. Like on Friday or Saturday nights when I'd go to bed early so I could prepare for a long run, and forgo a party or a dinner out at a restaurant or whatever the social calendar called for. And the night after a long run was also cut short, as I was too tired for much of anything. Twenty weeks of training was a big chunk of time out of our lives, so I made a promise that marathoning wouldn't turn into a regular thing.

I chose Los Angeles because it was close by, and because it was big. I wanted the benefit of lots of people. To sustain my focus when I race, I tend to play head games with the pack. I'll look for people I can pass, and I knew I would have lots of material in a mega-marathon like L.A.

As the day came closer, I felt confident. I had monitored my training well and Coach Gary was pleased with my efforts. As part of his final coaching strategy, though, two weeks before the marathon he had me race a 10K as fast as I could go. His rationale was that anything could happen in the marathon, and if I had a dismal day, or dropped out, at least I could look back and say I had one of the best 10Ks of my career. Sort of a consolation prize. I was prepared not only physically, but mentally as well. I was excited and felt that no matter what happened, even if I was picked up by the sag wagon, I was going to experience the thrill of a lifetime.

Prior to running the marathon I entertained the idea of doing it as a fundraiser, but didn't want to raise the pressure level that high. Instead, I decided to run wearing a cap with the Rotary Club emblem on it, and figured I'd use that as a way of soliciting some charity funds from my fellow members of the Santa Paula Rotary Club, after I'd actually done it. It turned out to be the perfect way to go. Not only was I surprised how much attention my cap drew during the race from other Rotarians in the pack, but when I passed my still-sweaty hat around at my regular club meeting the day after L.A. I was able to raise nearly $400 for the world health efforts of the Rotary International Foundation.

The day before the marathon my wife and I checked into the Biltmore Hotel in downtown Los Angeles, which was offering a special rate to marathon entrants. The special turned out to be a tiny room looking out into an airshaft, but still, it's a grand hotel, and we didn't mind. We got all dressed up and had a fancy dinner to celebrate my next day's event. In the morning, we walked to the start together and I kissed my wife good-bye through the security fence. It was as if she'd seen me off to the train station as I started my morning commute.

I was on the start line a half hour before the gun, lining up behind at least 10,000 folks who'd decided they wanted to get a faster start. Listening to

Randy Newman singing "I Love L.A." at 4 trillion watts on the sound system really got me pumped up. Once the gun went off it was a long shuffle before the crowd started to thin out and I could pick up my pace. A few miles later I caught up with those mythological marathon heroes, the Marathon Elvises. At around 15 miles I shook hands with the famous L.A. coach Pat Connolly as he stood in the middle of the street encouraging everyone. The fanfare was spectacular but the experience was harder than I expected. I tried not to go out too fast too soon, but I kept fooling around with my pace, attempting to speed up while I was still feeling strong. Somewhere after the halfway point, however, my brain started yelling at me, saying, *Hey fella, you're lucky we're not slowing down. Stay with the pace I give you or we'll stop altogether.* I never really hit the wall, but around the 20-mile mark my back started hurting and I had difficulty keeping an efficient stride. At the beginning I actually considered running negative splits and thought I could finish under four hours, but even before my back started acting up I knew it wasn't going to be possible.

Thankfully, the crowds were just as amazing as I had hoped, and helped to pull me through. Spectators two and three deep, church congregations singing and clapping, bands playing lively tunes, even the other runners made the event like one big rolling party.

Near the finish the race crossed a freeway overpass where the lack of a sidewalk discourages spectators, but as you come off it you hit downtown and take a sharp left turn to the finish. I'd figured that by the time I finished the winners would have accepted their medals (and new Hondas) and the crowd would have drifted away, but I was shocked as I hit that final turn to find an incredible crowd, 10 deep, making an incredible roar up the canyon of buildings leading to the finish line. I couldn't believe that these thousands of people had stuck around for over four hours just to cheer for me. I crossed the finish line in 4:23 and thought to myself, *Dang, I just ran a marathon.*

While I was crossing the finish line, my wife was back in our marathon special-rate room, trying to watch it all on the TV. Her focus was interrupted when a leaking pipe in the floor above us caused the ceiling in our bathroom to collapse in a rush of water and plaster—an ending that was even more spectacular than mine!

Even though my legs were dead, I walked the few miles back to the hotel. I didn't think that was possible but there I was, walking in downtown Los Angeles with my Mylar silver cape and my marathon medal proudly draped around my neck.

As I reflected on my accomplishment, my first thought, besides trying to ignore my sore, aching body, was to run another. Why? First, I simply love to run. I enjoyed the whole experience, and found it exciting, interesting, and just plain fun. Second, I wished that I had trained more effectively and had made my goal of four hours. I felt it was doable.

Before I started tackling my second marathon, I needed some distance. As I mentioned, the training takes too much away from the family social life, and I owed them a break. I also wanted my body to heal, and finally I wanted to find better ways to train and prepare for my second one.

Two years later I was ready and decided to do something different. I have friends who run L.A. every year, but I wanted to mix it up. I had done "big," and now I wanted something more intimate. I chose the Sutter Home Napa Valley Marathon because of its beautiful scenery and the fact that it is billed as low-key and rural. I was also inspired by the late legendary Northern California running figure Walt Stack, who had run it every year in his 70s and 80s.

With a goal to break four hours, I did longer long runs and upped my top weekly mileage from 45 to 60. I also added stretches to my workouts, both before and after. There were other and more subtle changes, but I think the higher mileage made the difference. I felt better prepared mentally and physically and my confidence level was much higher. I also went back through my running diary to make sure I was ahead of my L.A. schedule. My last long run was 25 miles.

Although Napa was supposed to be beautiful, at 3:00 A.M. marathon morning I woke up to a howling storm. The race starts at 7:00 A.M., so we were loaded onto school buses at 4:30 to get to the start. In the dark on the buses, driving through a pounding rain, we felt a bit like soldiers going off to battle, unsure just how we'd make it back. When we got to the start it was still dark and wet, and no one wanted to be the first to get off and start warming up in the deluge.

I didn't really mind the rain, and I figured it'd have to let up eventually. Instead, it just got worse. And it got chilly. But I was doing well and hit the halfway mark in 1:57. I was pleased to be on track for my 4:00, but soon after wicked headwinds kicked up, and within a few miles I knew I'd never make my goal. I finished in 4:19, a time that really pleased me, given the conditions.

Crossing the finish line of my second marathon still gave me that incredible rush. The main difference was the weather. Whereas L.A. was perfect, I was cold and wet and for the last 10 miles kept wondering if that darn finish line would ever appear. I also missed the crowd support. Because of the narrow course, spectators are only allowed at crossroads, and while those that braved the rain cheered mightily, supporters were few and far between. There were maybe 30 people at the finish line, but on the plus side the small field gave the race director the chance to check incoming numbers and announce each finisher's name, age, and hometown as he or she crossed the line. It was really something to slog out of the drizzle and into the finishing chute at Napa's Vintage High while hearing a voice over the P.A. announce, "And now finishing, from Santa Paula . . ." (Another reason I got a great lift from finishing Napa was that this time I'd prepublicized my marathon among a bunch of local Rotary Clubs, and had raised nearly $1,400 in pledges for the Rotary International Foundation. All I had to do was put on that same hat and run another 26.2 miles.)

So why am I planning to run a third marathon? If you enjoy running, it is a natural event to do, part of the smorgasbord of what the sport offers. Honestly, mentally I find racing an all-out mile tougher than running a marathon. It amuses me when fellow running club members who haven't run a marathon, but who I know, if they ever entered one, would finish in an hour or more less time than me, make a big deal about it. It's also a great sense of accomplishment in general. *Marathon* has become a descriptive word in our society for the highest level of achievement. It doesn't make me a better person, but it makes me feel a little better about myself. And it's fun when people whom I know have worked harder than I have, have faced tougher times, and accomplished a lot more in their lives, look at me and say, "You ran a marathon? Wow!"

# SO LONG, CHEESE STEAKS AND BEER

**TIM SHIELDS**

**D.O.B.:** 12-20-71
**RESIDENCE:** STATEN ISLAND, NY
**OCCUPATION:** MANAGEMENT
   CONSULTING
**FIRST MARATHON:** 2001 GRANDMA'S
   MARATHON, DULUTH, MI
**AGE AT FIRST MARATHON:** 29

*When Tim crossed the finish line of his first marathon, it was the thrill of his lifetime. You would have thought they were handing him the Nobel Prize or an Olympic gold medal. Tim worked very hard to get that finisher's medal so his unchecked emotions are understandable. After an unspectacular high school running career, he drifted away from running—in fact, from all exercise—and put on the pounds. To put it bluntly, he got fat. Wanting to get back to his former self, he knew it would take a miracle—or a marathon—to do it. It wasn't easy and he almost gave up a few times but through perseverance, more than a few aching muscles, intense shin splints, and encouragement from his family who were waiting for him at the finish, he accomplished his goal. Now a self-described "runner for life," Tim's new goal is to qualify for Boston when he gets better and stronger at his new sport. He likes his new outlook on life— and his new body isn't bad either.*

I grew up on Staten Island in the shadow of the Verrazzano Narrows Bridge. The family house was less than one-quarter mile from the start of the New York City Marathon. Our sleepy block was transformed for one Sunday each November as hordes of skinny people in skimpy outfits competed for the few prized parking spaces that would allow them to avoid the organized chaos of the bus trips from Manhattan.

Marathon Sunday was my favorite day on the calendar. I loved the energy and the nervous anticipation. I loved seeing Mayor Ed Koch and nationally prominent sportscasters. And I could never get over the wonder that a number of internationally renowned athletes should travel from all corners of the world to come right here, to my own neighborhood. That amazes me to this day.

Security is much different now, but from the late '70s through the mid-'80s, spectators could intermingle freely with the runners at the start. I was sufficiently mischievous and ignorant to occasionally join the runners for 100 yards or so after the cannon went off, and after separating myself from the real runners, I'd work with the volunteers to collect the left-behind warm-up suits and caps. Then I would run home and watch the TV coverage.

If the New York City Marathon sowed the seeds for my interest in running, it was my dad who actually got me to find out what running was all about. He had begun jogging at the local college track when I was 10, and I usually tagged along. He would do 1 or 2 miles, and I did my best to struggle through a half mile.

Two things happened as a result of these jogs with Dad. First, my dad and I became much closer. The daily jog was a great way for him to unwind. He led a stressful career as a homicide detective within the NYPD, and I think he partly got through his days of dealing with the most troubling elements of society by thinking about the time he and I would spend circling the track that evening at the College of Staten Island. After our jogs we would walk a bit to cool down, and he would feed me the answers to all the world's problems. I would fill him in on the exciting developments in the sixth grade, such as how many games our school basketball team needed to win so that we could move up to next-to-last place.

The second development was that I started to become competitive about my running. Over my junior high years, my goals evolved from running as far as my dad did to running as fast (I will never forget the thrill the first time I beat him over a mile). Finally my goal was to lap him as many times as possible.

No surprise that high school meant track. My very first organized race was run along the renowned cross-country trails at Van Cortland Park in the Bronx. On that morning my dad and I had gotten caught in traffic and we also had some trouble with the directions once we got to the park. I remember saying "Dad, I think that's my race" as we drove past a line of 50 or 60 boys standing in a single horizontal row, all at the ready. I jumped out of the car and began screaming "Hold the race! Hold the race!" as I sprinted in full panic toward the start. The starter held the race.

The sound of the gun terrified me, but off I went into the Bronx woods, not at all sure how I was supposed to do this. It was certainly different from jogging with Dad. It all seemed so serious, and I was having trouble staying in front. When I encountered the very first hill of my running career, I lost five places.

Eventually, the course brought us out of the woods and onto an enormous open field. I had no idea how far I had gone or where the finish line lay. And the race boiled down to myself and one other runner. I looked down the seemingly endless path before me when I noticed a hysterical, screaming figure off in the distance. Dad? It sure was, and as I got closer I could hear him cheering me on: "You got 'em! Don't give up! You can win this!" I decided to engage him in this conversation. With whatever breath I could muster I asked "Dad, where's the finish?" He yelled, "It's just right there! Those two poles!" I was confused. The only two poles I could see were far, far off in the distance. Those were the poles. Summoning my waning reserves, I mounted a final kick and won the race by half a step. I promptly collapsed, having won the 1.5-mile race in 9 minutes and 42 seconds. My coach was excited and congratulated me, but added that I might have had less difficulty if I would have worn running sneakers. Sneakers specifically for running? Neither my dad nor I had ever heard of such a thing.

I went on to a satisfying, albeit unspectacular, high school running career. I was a reliable runner on a good team, but I was not a superstar. I enjoyed the camaraderie and the opportunity for travel that track offered. My personal highlight was competing in the Milrose Games at Madison Square Garden, where my relay team brought home a silver medal. More exciting than this, I was able to meet the heroes of the day—Eamonn Coghlan, Johnnie Gray, Mary Decker—in a forum where for at least that evening I could consider them colleagues.

When I went on to the University of Pennsylvania, I thought about continuing competitive running, but I decided against it, concerned that the time it demanded would detract from both my studies and social opportunities. I also did not want to face the reality that I would clearly be in the back of the pack, and the medals and glory I had piled up in high school would be in short supply in NCAA Division I athletics.

My intention was to keep up the running on my own, but that did not happen. I worked in the student dining hall and had a tough academic workload, so I always had a convenient excuse for not exercising. I also discovered cheese steaks and beer during this time. The pounds piled on, but I shrugged it off, telling myself that that was why retailers made larger clothes. Leaving college and entering the workforce, I no longer even bothered with excuses. Health and fitness fell entirely off the radar.

This lasted for years. By 1999 I was no longer simply an ex-runner; I was fat. In November of that year, now living in Manhattan, I found myself walking along Central Park West when the balloons and the closed-off streets alerted me to the fact that it was Marathon Sunday. It had been years since I had bothered to notice or care.

I wandered into the park toward the finish-line area and took my place among the hundreds of thousands of spectators waiting to cheer on the elite athletes and the masses who followed them. It all came back to me: the beauty and the freedom of running, the excitement of competition, and the memories of my childhood at the other end of this race. As thousands of exhaust-ed but obviously elated runners passed in front of me, there was no doubt but that my own joy at watching this was intermixed with considerable envy and sadness, as I felt unworthy to be in the presence of dedicated runners. At that moment I made up mind: I would run a marathon.

My training began that very evening. I went back to Central Park and decided to start off by running two laps around the reservoir, a flat, easy, 1.6 mile path. Less than halfway around my first lap, I stopped. My muscles were aching and I had no breath. I walked back to my apartment, shocked and ashamed that I could not even complete a simple jog. When I got home, I realized I had been crying.

I didn't give up, but it wasn't easy. I fell into a pattern where I would have one good run, develop intense shin splints, try to run through the injury, and become incapacitated for three weeks. Then I would have one good run, develop intense shin splints, try to run through the injury . . . I became very frustrated. I don't know this for sure, but I think the problem was that I was trying to run at a much faster pace than my body could handle. I was fat and out of shape, but the only pace my body "remembered" was from the time when my goal was a sub-two-minute half mile.

I refocused my efforts on losing weight through other means, and spent endless hours on StairMasters and stationary bicycles. Months later, having shed some pounds and feeling more fit, I tried running again, and this time I managed to have the patience to start off running appropriate distances at appropriate speeds. Things started to click, and soon enough I began to feel like a real runner again, and started to think not just about running a marathon, but also which specific marathon I would run.

A coworker of mine, Thorn, from my company's Minneapolis office, told me about Grandma's Marathon in Duluth, Minnesota, and that he was plan-ning on running it. He suggested I join him. I agreed. On some level I have to admit I felt like a bit of a traitor for not choosing the New York City Marathon for my first race, but I was anxious to get started with serious marathon training, and Grandma's takes place in June, a full five months before New York.

Training was definitely challenging. My work schedule typically included late evenings and weekends, so I often found myself on treadmills past mid-night, or in Central Park in a freezing rain at 4 A.M. Also, I had never run far-ther than 8 miles in my life, and even that was more than a decade earlier. But the difficulties were matched by the rewards. Every other Sunday I ran farther than I ever had in my life, and each time I was amazed at what I had just accomplished.

Around the time I began my 18-week training schedule I stumbled upon *First Marathons* in a bookstore. I bought it and immediately became engrossed in the stories. I even had to force myself to slow down the pace of my reading because I did not want to finish the book too quickly. I enjoyed the stories of the elite athletes, but drew little inspiration from them: Their goals and their talents seemed superhuman, and I couldn't relate. But the stories of the everyday folk were tremendously helpful to me. Many of the runners had overcome both running and life difficulties far in excess of anything I'd ever had to face. Whenever my legs screamed for mercy, or whenever I woke up and stared at my sneakers for 15 minutes before deciding that indeed I would go running that day, I thought of the struggles and triumphs of Dick Traum, Lauren Fessenden, and Ileta Coley. But mostly I thought of Tom King, who had been beaten down in life repeatedly as an obese child and somewhat irresponsible adult. What I saw in his story was not only an incredible triumph over difficult circumstances, but an appreciation of running as a gift and a joy. He became my unwitting training partner, encouraging me through the toughest miles of my long runs.

Also encouraging was knowing that my dad and the rest of my family would be there with me. No one from my family had ever been to the Midwest, and they seemed genuinely excited about the trip to Minnesota. More touching was that three of my sisters, none of whom had ever participated in a race of any kind, all entered a 5K, which was scheduled for the night before the marathon.

As race day approached, I was starting to feel good about my training. I had been able to maintain the schedule without injury and was confident I could finish. I even began to wonder about my time. With effectively no benchmark, I had no idea how long it would take. Although I knew I should concentrate on simply finishing, I silently wondered if I could actually run fast enough to qualify for the Boston Marathon. But with less than two weeks to the race, I woke up one morning and could not get out of bed. My back was completely out. I saw three different doctors, all of whom told me there was no way I would be able to run this race. The intense pain grew worse over the next few days, and I was forced to use a cane to walk. Coworkers laughed as I insisted that I would run the race, even though it was now taking me 10 minutes to hobble down the hall. I put on the best front I could, but inside I was completely heartbroken.

The constant pain did begin to subside over the following few days, but even light jogging induced sharp pain after only a few steps, and I would have to stop immediately. And then all of a sudden it was time to go to Minnesota. So I went.

Upon arrival in Duluth it was clear that the city was prepared for a big event. The whole town—from the airline workers, to the hotel staff, to the shopkeepers—welcomed the thousands of runners in town for the weekend. My family had no idea what to expect, and the enthusiasm of the city gave them a sense of how much this meant to the city's residents and the runners. The running expo, with great speeches given by legends Hal Higdon, Kathrine Switzer, and Billy Mills, gave them an introduction to the strange world of long-distance running. I was excited and proud to give them a glimpse into this world—my world.

My mom even went a made a friend on her own. She described meeting a delightful older woman in the hotel. My mother was impressed that a woman several years older than herself should dare enter as daunting an event as a marathon. My mom asked the woman what brought her to Duluth. The woman responded "I was invited," to which my mom answered "Me too! My son invited me here." I was with my mother when she met the woman again. I instantly recognized her from *First Marathons:* it was elite runner Toshi D'Elia, who unlike my mom had been invited by the race directors.

Toshi was wonderful, congratulating me on getting set for my own first marathon. She signed my copy of the book, and told me to relax and enjoy myself. She even gave me her favorite energy gel to carry with me. Meeting Toshi reminded me of how I'd felt many years earlier when I found myself warming up with the superstars in the lower level of Madison Square Garden. That someone like Toshi d'Elia would welcome me as a colleague and fellow runner was a tremendous honor.

The morning of the race itself I was remarkably calm. I was very concerned about my back and whether I would be able to start, let alone finish, but I wasn't overcome with the intense anxiety that used to grip me before my high school races. My lack of nervousness made me nervous.

As Thorn and I rode on the bus that would bring us to the starting point in the town of Two Harbors, we simply could not believe how long the bus ride was taking. I think this was the first time I had any notion of how far 26.2 miles actually was. Gosh, it's far.

The race started and I cautiously took my first few steps. No pain. I breathed an enormous sigh of relief. My back felt fine, and I relaxed tremendously. Over the course of the first mile I slowly built up to a comfortable pace. I was surprised at how it went in the early miles. Swept up by the energy of the other runners, the support of the crowd, and the beauty of the course along Lake Superior, the mile markers seemed to come very rapidly. This was going remarkably well.

I reached the midpoint in 1:35, and realized that if I ran the second half just a few seconds faster, I would qualify for Boston. But perhaps I overreached. At mile 16 I was able to spot the large Aerial Lift Bridge at the finish area. It looked dishearteningly small. I was immediately deflated, and stopped to take my first walk. I had hit the wall with 10 miles to go.

Knowing that Boston was now out of reach, I determined to sensibly pace myself to get to the finish line. I began a pattern of running a mile, walking

100 yards, and then running again. It wasn't exactly how I had hoped to run, but on the other hand, things did not become appreciably worse as the miles went on. I reached mile 25 in 3:20, and realized that if I could maintain an eight-minute-mile pace for the remainder I could break three and a half hours. It took everything out of me, but spotting my family with three-quarters of a mile to go—including my dad screaming just the way he did so many years ago in the Bronx—gave me the energy I needed to cross the line in 3:28. What a wonderful feeling to finish, giving me a sense of accomplishment on a scale I had never felt before. Judging from my reaction, you might have thought the finisher's medal I was handed was an Olympic gold medal.

Now that it's over, I would like to get better. One side benefit of having lost over a decade is that I can expect considerable improvement over the next several years. I want to be stronger and faster. I want to qualify for Boston. I want to jog from the family house on Staten Island to the start of the New York City Marathon.

I'm proud I've become a runner again. I think I appreciate the sport more now than I did as a teenager. I know what I lost, and I won't let that happen again. I intend to be a runner for the rest of my life.

# SWIM, BIKE, RUN INSTEAD OF RUN, RUN, RUN

**LISA SWAIN**

**D.O.B.: 4-16-58**
**RESIDENCE: FAIR LAWN, NJ**
**OCCUPATION: EVENT COORDINATOR,**
    **FUND RAISER, SWIM COACH**
**FIRST MARATHON: 1981 NYC**
    **MARATHON**
**AGE AT FIRST MARATHON: 23**

*Lisa loved the marathon but found it too hard on her body and decided to give it up. Looking for a replacement, she learned about triathlons and got hooked. She finds them easier to train for and just as rewarding. However, 18 years after her last marathon, she still gets the bug to do another. I wouldn't bet against Lisa's chances of filling that void.*

I was the original tomboy. Growing up, I couldn't find other girls to play with because I wanted to hit tennis balls against the wall, roll down hills in Central Park, and ride my bike as fast as I could and they didn't. Why should I sit by and watch the boys have all the fun? I didn't consider myself a jock or an athlete; I just did what was fun for me, and keeping up with the guys came naturally.

In high school my number one sport was tennis. I started playing in college at the University of Rochester, but tennis was mostly indoors since the outdoor season is so short, and I didn't like that. I preferred to be doing something outside.

I met a guy who was a runner and he tricked me into my first run ever. He told me 1 mile was 8 times around the track when in fact it was a distance of 2 miles. After 4 laps I thought I'd die and had to stop. When he told me I had already run 1 mile, I was shocked, and thrilled. From that moment on, I wanted to be a runner.

There was one slight problem with my plan to become a runner: My college didn't have a women's track team. So I decided to start one with a friend who was a runner in high school. We grabbed any woman who seemed remotely interested and recruited them. For three years we maintained a club status, and by the time I graduated in 1980 it was a sanctioned team.

I never considered a marathon when I was in college. My longest-distance run was 7 miles, and I thought I could do more if challenged to do so.

After college, I moved back to New York City. That October I stood on First Avenue and watched the New York City Marathon go by. Everyone was having so much fun and I wanted to be a part of it. And as a runner, the marathon is the ultimate challenge so I had to do it.

I was already a member of a running club so I hooked up with members who had run marathons and trained with them. I gave myself six months to get ready for my first marathon. We took long runs of 18-20 miles on the weekends, and during the week I did speed workouts. Our long runs started across from Tavern on the Green in Central Park and then we headed out across the George Washington Bridge or through the boroughs, close to the actual marathon course.

I can't say the training was easy, but I enjoyed it. I was very excited to be running my first marathon and was definitely ready and geared up to go by marathon morning. I started out with some guys from my club who were experienced marathoners. They kept warning me not to go out too fast and actually had to hold me back at the start because I just felt like flying across the Verrazzano Narrows Bridge.

I stayed with them for the first 14 miles but I felt as if I could go faster. Since it was my first time I kept listening to their advice but after I crossed the 59th Street Bridge and headed into Manhattan, I picked up the pace and left them.

I finished my first marathon in 3:54 and although I was physically and mentally exhausted, I was thrilled and danced all night at the postrace party. However, the next day I couldn't walk down a flight of stairs.

It was a significant accomplishment, the hardest thing I had ever done. I felt as if I could conquer the world! It was such a major milestone in my life that a few years later I used my marathon experience as my essay for graduate school.

Within days, I knew I would run another. My first one was for the experience—testing the waters, so to speak. The next one would be for speed. I needed to test myself and see how well I could do, especially after I had held back due to the advice of my friends.

All through the next year, I trained harder, added more speed work under my belt, and did more races. A year later I ran my second New York City Marathon and still had that same, *Wow, I'm here!* feeling as I did when I stood at the start of my first marathon.

I finished my second marathon in 3:25 and came to the conclusion that this would be a part of my life; that I would run a marathon every year. In fact, it only took another six months before I did my third. I ran the London Marathon in the spring of 1982 and did 3:24. This was only the second running of the London Marathon and there were only 200 women in the field. The cheering for us was amazing. It was awesome.

In 1983 I entered the New York City Marathon again and unfortunately it turned out to be my last marathon. Instead of fulfilling my dream of running a lifetime of marathons, I only got to number four.

That year was my best running year on record. I was setting PRs (personal records) at every race I entered, running hard, and training well. I was at my peak and couldn't wait for the marathon.

The 1983 New York City Marathon was cold and rainy. I went out fast but didn't hydrate enough and hit the wall at mile 23. I bonked. The last 3 miles were torture. I don't know how I finished, as I was blacking out and having out-of-body experiences. Despite my mental and physical breakdown, I finished in 3:16, but felt no euphoria. I was too drained.

I was 25 years old and quit the marathon for good. It was too tough on my body. I kept getting injured all that year and had chronic tendinitis and plantar fasiciitis. I had to drop my weekly mileage from 60 to 40. It was time for something else.

That something else turned out to be triathlons. This was new to me and sounded interesting. I had read about Mark Allen and Scott Tinley in my running magazines but had never even given triathlons a thought. But this was just what I was looking for—something to replace the marathon.

I was already swimming once a week but had never done it competitively, so I signed up for a triathlon swimming course with Doug Stern, the guru of deep-water running and tri-swim classes. He put me through workouts that left me drained and tired: right-arm laps, left-arm laps, swimming with one arm, all different training techniques for competitive swimming.

Then I started cycling around the Central Park loop, putting in 18 to 24 miles at a clip. I was always a recreational cyclist, but now I needed to beef up on my speed and race techniques, as competitive cycling is more about gears and technique than just speed.

During the summer on early morning weekdays a group of us would ride 10 miles to a pool, do some laps, and ride back. On weekends I would ride and then I would quickly change my shoes and go for a run. It was great training.

Although I felt prepared for my first triathlon, I still felt a bit weak with the swimming portion. But I've come to learn that most triathletes have one weak segment and for me it was the swim.

What really got me nervous was the new concept of the transition area. Runners don't have separate staging areas. There's the start and the finish. Period. In triathlons, each event (the swim, bike, and run) has a staging area, or transition area, to prepare for the next event. I started reading up in triathlon magazines on how to get through the transition areas as I kept hearing from seasoned triathletes that the race takes place in the transition area.

Kind of like the marathon mantra that the marathon starts at mile 20.

I liked the training for a triathlon so much more than a marathon because I was always doing something different. During my marathon training I was constantly worried about injuries or running too much, too long, too fast. With triathlons, there's none of that. You swim some, bike some, and run some. You don't do any one sport for a long duration. Plus, the training took a shorter amount of time. I trained for less than two months for my first triathlon whereas for my marathons I put in four to six months of training.

I should mention that I was training for the sprint-distance triathlon, usually a half-mile swim, 14-mile bike ride, and 5-mile run. The next triathlon level is the Olympic distance, a 1-mile swim, 25-mile bike, and a 6.2-mile run. Then there is the Half Ironman (sometimes called the Tin Man), a 1.2-mile swim, 56-mile bike, and a half marathon (13.2 miles). And the grand-daddy of them all, the Ironman, is a 2.4-mile ocean swim, 112-mile bike, and a full marathon (26.2-mile) run.

In 1985 I did my first triathlon, the Greenwood Lake Sprint Triathlon in Greenwood Lake, New York. Back then not many people were doing triathlons, so the field was only about 300, with very few women. No one wore wet suits and clipless pedals hadn't made the scene yet so it was sort of an old-fashioned triathlon compared to what I see today at events. In 1987 I started doing the Wyckoff Sprint Triathlon in Franklin Lakes, New Jersey. I've done this same triathlon almost every year since. In 2002 the field has swelled to 1,000 and everyone wears wet suits and has high-end performance bikes. Triathlons have definitely moved up to center stage in the sports arena.

I had so much fun start to finish. There was a craziness to the swimming, seeing all the heads bopping in the water and then running out of the water into the transition area and getting ready to jump on the bike. It was totally wacky and I liked that. And then changing from the bike to the run was just so comfortable for me I breezed to the finish. And afterward I wasn't burned out or in pain or suffering the next day. I was hooked; I had found my replacement for the marathon.

The following year I volunteered at the New York City Marathon, and that was a real test to see if I could be enticed back to the marathon. It was very hard to ignore the pull to do another one but in the end I didn't. I volunteered a few more years but it was a strange and lonely feeling to be helping out instead of running so I stopped volunteering at the marathon, although I continued to volunteer at shorter distance races. It was just too painful to watch the marathon and not partake.

I began to take my triathlons more seriously and moved up from doing them for fun to seriously competing. I invested in a better bike, trained harder, and entered more triathlon events. Then I met my husband-to-be, who was a runner, and he got intrigued to do triathlons with me so he got hooked as well. We did our rides and runs together.

Since my first triathlon in 1985 I've done over twenty, two or three a year. I stick with the sprint distance since I now have two children, and that adds more time constraints to my training schedule. I have competed in the Olympic distance a few times and my husband and I used to think about doing the Ironman distance but that doesn't look like a possibility at this stage in our lives. Many triathlons offer a relay team option which is great if you are unable to train for all the events.

Why did I switch? The marathon was just too tough on my body. When I train for a triathlon, I'm constantly using different muscle groups so I don't get injured. The recovery is much easier as well. I also get to meet a different group of people, not just runners. I meet swimmers and cyclists and runners. The marathon has one focus—running. I like breaking up the routine with swimming and biking so I never get bored.

I still think of myself as a runner first. The ironic thing is that most triathletes are burned out or injured runners like myself. First they pick up swimming and before you know it all they have to do is add the biking and they become triathletes.

I must add that running is still the easier sport to adopt; no equipment except a pair of shoes, and you can run just about anywhere. For triathlon equipment I not only need a pair of running shoes, I need a bike—a good bike—and swim gear. The equipment can get costly, with the helmet alone averaging $160 for one that will save your head in a fall. The cost of a bike, depending on style and performance criteria, can soar into the thousands.

The training schedule can also be more difficult than marathon training. It's not just run, run, run. I swim twice a week in the morning, bike twice a week, and run every other day. And that has to fit in with the other scheduling in my life juggling two daughters, a husband who works late hours, and my freelance work as an event planner.

I couldn't do it without the support of my husband, who is also committed to triathlons. Usually, when I return home from my bike ride, he starts his.

Sports are a lifetime pursuit for us and we are introducing them to our kids. They are already good swimmers but I don't push it. At their ages they should be experimenting with all sports and enjoying them for fun, not competition.

They entered their first bike race this summer, a 100-yard dash, at a family fun-day event that my husband and I also entered, at a longer distance. They wore their helmets and matching racing outfits and had a ball, the way it should be. It was an accomplishment tailored to their level of fitness. We all went home with the satisfied feeling that comes from knowing we pushed ourselves just a little bit harder that day and reaped the physical and mental rewards.

The triathlon is now an Olympic event. Maybe that will give it the exposure it needs to get more people into the sport earlier in life. In Florida and other states down south the triathlon event seems to get more exposure than in the Northeast.

I have to be honest and say that I still miss the marathon. It's like a dormant virus inside me that is waiting to erupt. I always think to myself, *Maybe I'll do one next year.*

# PERSONAL GOAL: A WORLD WITHOUT CANCER

**CATHARINE TROISI**

**D.O.B.: 3-31-46**
**RESIDENCE: SENECA FALLS, NY**
**OCCUPATION: OWNER AND DIRECTOR,**
**    THE PRE-SCHOOL COMMUNITY**
**FIRST MARATHON: 1992 BOSTON**
**    MARATHON JIMMY FUND WALK**
**AGE AT FIRST MARATHON: 46**

*Cathy's marathon accomplishments are impressive: 104 marathons in eight years. But more than that, she is driven by a personal goal to help erase cancer from our world. Through her charity fund-raising marathons, she imagines a world without cancer and believes in the effort toward making that goal a reality. Soft-spoken and unassuming, Cathy deflects any praise heaped upon her as she insists she is just one person who has found an avenue toward the elimination of cancer as a life-threatening disease.*

I have to start by saying one of the best things you can do for your life in general and particularly your running life is attend Jeff Galloway's running camp. He single-handedly changed my life.

When I first attended Jeff Galloway's running camp in 1994, I had never run a step. I had already walked five marathons but had never done any running. I was never athletic. In fact, one of my friends said the term *couch potato* was coined just for me. In high school and college, my athleticism was confined to the physical education requirements necessary for graduation.

In 1991, when I was 45, I started walking with my daughter who had just graduated from college. We walked daily for two weeks until she went off to a job in Albany. Although I missed her companionship, I continued to walk every day, and that New Year's Eve I made a resolution to walk at least 1 mile every day. I found a friend to walk with me and soon we were up to 5 miles a day, which seemed like a big deal. Eventually my friend's early morning family responsibilities kept her from our daily predawn walks but I continued on. For the next three years I logged 2,200 miles a year.

In 1992 there was an advertisement in *Walking Magazine* about walking the Boston Marathon. I showed it to a friend who agreed it would be fun to do. When she asked how far is a marathon, I said, "I don't know but I think it's far—about 10 miles."

When I called the Boston Athletic Association, I asked about walking the marathon and the woman gently laughed and said, "Oh honey, no one walks the Boston Marathon!" When I mentioned the advertisement, she told me it probably referred to the Boston Marathon Jimmy Fund Walk, a fund-raising marathon for Boston's Dana-Farber Cancer Institute, and the only group sanctioned to officially use the Boston Marathon course.

That appealed to me, especially since my best friend from college had died from melanoma cancer. So I walked my first marathon and to this day I still participate in the Jimmy Fund every year. To prepare for my first Jimmy Fund walk, I mapped a 5.5-mile loop around my neighborhood and completed it five times to make sure I could physically go the distance. My neighbors questioned my sanity as they witnessed me walking in circles for hours. I finished my first Jimmy Fund walk in 6:35:34.

Some people don't consider the Jimmy Fund an official marathon. I count it! An application, registration fee, T-shirt, pasta dinner, certified course, finisher's medal, and finisher's photograph make it as official as any other marathon. However, my first "official" marathon was the Los Angeles Marathon in 1994. I walked it; that's all I knew how to do. I wasn't yet a runner. During that marathon I saw a volunteer being a guide for a blind runner through the Achilles Program and thought I'd like to do that. But first, I would have to become a runner.

Even though I was a walker, I subscribed to *Runner's World* and saw an article on running camps and decided that was the best way I could learn about running. The nearest camp to me was in Boston with Jeff Galloway. I didn't know who Galloway was or what a running camp would be like. I just hoped this would help me reach my goal of guiding a blind person through a marathon. Little did I know how this camp would change my life forever.

When I arrived at camp I was concerned that I would be the oldest and the slowest. I was 48 years old. Turns out I wasn't the oldest or slowest, although close on both counts. My goal was to learn about running long distances. I learned I don't have speed but I have endurance.

The basic philosophy of Jeff's run-walk marathon program is that the marathon is basically an endurance event and anyone can complete it injury-free by using walk breaks. Walk breaks allow your running muscles to recover before they are fatigued or injured and also help to conserve energy, which builds the endurance needed to finish. This was the breakthrough formula I needed to become a runner and not become injured or burn out.

Running camp was in August. Eight weeks later I entered my third Boston Marathon Jimmy Fund, did the run-walk program, and finished in 4:48:46. Ecstatic with my sub-five-hour finish, I started to focus on the possibility of running the Boston Marathon as a charity runner for the Dana-Farber Cancer Institute the following April. I was also excited to have completed two marathons in six months and taking more than an hour and a half off my Los Angeles Marathon back in March, which I walked in 6:23:26.

I felt invigorated and energized and decided to run the New York City Marathon in November, making that my third marathon for 1994. I wanted to have a sense of the course on my own before I volunteered to run it with a blind person.

I made significant progress in one year, going from a recreational walker to entering a walking marathon, and continuing on to run-walk two more marathons. To me this success served as stepping-stones to achieving my goal to be an Achilles volunteer in 1995. And I could never have achieved these goals without the knowledge, experience, and guidance gained at Jeff's camp.

1995 turned out to be another banner year for me. In April I ran my first Boston Marathon, which I did as a charity runner, again for the Dana-Farber Cancer Institute. In September I did my annual Jimmy Fund marathon followed by the Wineglass Marathon in upstate New York in October, the Marine Corps Marathon later that same month, and finally reached my goal as an Achilles volunteer at the New York City Marathon in November. Since then, I have been an Achilles marathon companion to a blind runner, wheelchair athletes, cancer patients, and cancer survivors.

Despite five marathons in one year (three in one month), I felt fine. No injuries, no problems. Thank you, Jeff Galloway.

Since speed was not my forte, my goal for each marathon was to finish within the official time before the finish line was dismantled, usually five hours. That time has since been moved up to six hours and more at many marathons but not when I was starting out. In 1996 I did seven marathons, in 1997 I did nine and my first 50-miler. That's when things became interesting as I decided to add ultramarathons to the scene.

I'll say it again and again: I owe all my accomplishments to Jeff Galloway's program. If you look at my tally, I have 85 marathons and 19 ultras in a span of eight years, and I have never been injured. Not once. My best clock time was the 1998 Boston Marathon, when as a Dana-Farber charity runner I ran four minutes/walked one minute and finished in 4:00:42, a qualifying time for the next year's Boston Marathon. In 2001 I completed 16 marathons, a 50K, a 50-miler, a 100K, and the 72-mile race around Lake Tahoe. I consider myself proof that Jeff's run-walk program works. Jeff is very dedicated to his people. He cares about everyone in his program and they become like family. Although there are many lessons, one of the most valuable for me, and one I use often during marathons and ultras, is to do a mental form check while running. If you can maintain your form, you don't expend unnecessary energy and it is easier on your body. Also, Jeff makes you believe in yourself. He has a charisma and he can make you believe that a marathon is within the realm of possibility. And with his program, it certainly is.

My biggest problem is fitting in all the marathons I want to do. So many marathons, so few weekends. Thankfully, I am very organized and have a great staff at work. Otherwise I don't know how I would have the time to do as many marathons as I do. I also have a supportive family. The nice part is, running so many marathons I am generally always race-ready.

The other part of this scenario is that I believe in fund-raising for cancer research through running. Losing family and friends to cancer has made this a personal mission. The Jimmy Fund each fall and the Marathon Challenge in April, both fund-raisers for the Dana-Farber Cancer Institute, are marked in ink on my calendar every year. When my friend died of melanoma, it took me nine years to put closure on the sense of loss I felt. Another friend just had a double mastectomy. My dad had colon cancer, and other family members have had cancer scares. We can't do enough to fight this disease. I need to be actively involved and I do it through running marathons. My ultimate goal though all this is not to lose another friend or loved one to cancer.

I've raised over $40,000 for cancer research. Some years I just put aside $25 a week toward the goal and don't bother to fundraise. One year I decided to forgo the fund-raising because it is time consuming and difficult but when a three-year old showed up in my classroom bald from chemo treatments, I decided to go all out in fund-raising. With several factors contributing to a feeling of total meltdown, I didn't think I would finish the Boston Marathon that year. But during the race I kept thinking that almost nothing could be as bad as going through chemotherapy and radiation treatments. I kept thinking of the little three-year-old in my classroom and all the other people I knew who were dealing with cancer or who had died from cancer and somehow I kept running and set my marathon PR. I also set my fund-raising PR.

Even after running consecutive weekend marathons, I am rarely a victim of DOMS, delayed onset muscle soreness. My legs and muscles are fine. The day after a marathon is spent traveling back home. I have no problems walking and don't have to walk backward down stairs.

I'm setting new goals for the future and plan to do other 100Ks, continue the Jimmy Fund and Marathon Challenge for Dana-Farber and finish my 50 states plus D.C. goal. I have 19 states to go. And I keep telling Jeff I am going to start a new age division, the 100-plus division, and keep on going.

When I was turning 50 in 1996, I wanted to do something different so I decided to run the JFK 50-miler. Fifty miles, fifty years. Sounded good. When I am out there running for so long I think about people I know who are dealing with cancer and what they endure daily. I think about Jeff's camp and everything I learned from him and try to put it into practice during the run.

I think about future marathons and ultras.

I was once pegged as a onetime marathoner, and now running and marathons are an important part of my life. The marathon is 100 percent discipline, desire, dedication and determination. I'm also stubborn and tenacious, which helps for the long run. I don't think I do anything unusual or grand. It's just my thing. Besides giving me a healthier lifestyle, it has also given me a different perspective on life. My association with cancer patients helps me put my own ups and downs in perspective and realize that everything is relative.

Right before my friend died of melanoma cancer, I called and asked if he would like to go to lunch; he said sure, whenever I was in the area. I hung up the phone and hopped a plane from New York to Texas and took him to lunch. He was in shock when I showed up at his doorstep. We had a great time together sharing lunch, memories, and hours together. He died soon after and I will be forever grateful that we had that time together.

My best friend's dad always said, "Never forget who you are or where you came from." Although he was referencing one's personal life, that also applies to my running life. I remember my less-than-auspicious unathletic lifestyle. I remember my years walking mega-miles annually. I remember my 1994 Galloway camp experience and subsequent marathons and ultras. And underlying all of it, I remember my hope and dream of a cancer-free world that will make a difference in a life for a lifetime.

# DOING IT FOR RUTHIE

**ABRAHAM WEINTRAUB**

**D.O.B.: 2-3-10**
**RESIDENCE: BROOKLYN, NY**
**OCCUPATION: RETIRED JACK-OF-ALL-**
**TRADES**
**FIRST MARATHON: 1990 NYC**
**MARATHON**
**AGE AT FIRST MARATHON: 80**

*Photo courtesy New York Road Runners*

*Abe Weintraub is an unlikely headline grabber. He is shy, quiet, and reserved. Yet headlines such as* 90-YEAR-OLD SETS RECORD AT NYC MARATHON *follow him wherever he goes. He didn't plan on running his first marathon at 80; he did it for his wife, Ruthie. When asked how he does it, he just shrugs and says all he does is put one foot in front of the other and just keep running. That's all. No big deal. A son of Russian immigrants, Abe grew up during hard times. Bullied and picked on in school, he learned early that life was going to be a tough act. And then later on when married with children, he faced even harder times during the depression. However, he credits his background with his ability to run marathons in his 90s. After all those hard years, Abe has finally aged to perfection.*

It took me four years to learn to run so that I could participate in the New York City Marathon and then I ended up walking it in eight hours. I never reported my finish time because I didn't run it. I didn't think walking counted so I had to go back the next year and run it again. Everyone makes a fuss over me, saying things like how amazing I am to be running marathons in my 90s, but I don't think I am amazing. I just know how to fight. I am a survivor and that's what it takes to run marathons.

My parents came over from Russia and settled in Brooklyn. I was one of six kids. I probably had some kind of learning disability because I never did well in school but my mother was so busy raising six kids she never took notice. In school I was picked on and bullied and beaten, even by the teachers. It was a very hard life and as a little kid I learned that you have to fight to the finish, no matter what, in order to survive. I wasn't smart enough so I became tough enough.

I was a pretty good basketball player in high school but never ran. And then after I got married there wasn't any time for things like sports or recreation of any kind for that matter. It was tough times during the depression.

The other lesson I learned in life is not to trust anyone unless you've known them for 23 years. That rule comes from being deceived by my best friend of 20 years. We were buddies from the neighborhood and all through school. We even double-dated when I had my first sweetheart. Turns out, he was also dating my girlfriend on the side. I couldn't believe that after 20 years of friendship he would risk it all on a girl. Never spoke to him again. Then I met Ruthie. She had the most beautiful smile and was the love of my life for 58 years. We married during hard times but I did whatever it took to keep food on the table for her and our four kids.

It wasn't easy getting jobs during the depression. I'd have a job for a week and then get laid off. I was a toy manufacturer, worked in a dairy, lumber yard, textiles, and a shipyard, among other things. During the war I worked on the battleship *Missouri* as a riveter.

I also trained the women who came into the factories to help out in the war effort while their husbands were overseas. Most of them ended up as welders because the riveting gun was so powerful it was hard to handle. I always had an issue with those "Rosie the Riveter" posters because the majority of women were welders. But I guess nothing rhymes with *welder* so they made them riveters.

After the war Ruth and I settled down in Brooklyn and raised the three kids. We would go for walks along the river and watch the Verrazzano Narrows Bridge being built. Over the years, my beautiful wife developed Alzheimer's and I would push her in a wheelchair on our walks. I thought it would be fun to give her a different view of the bridge, one from the top, and decided to enter the New York City Marathon so I could push her wheelchair across the top span. I called the New York Road Runners but my request was denied; they thought it would be too dangerous. Determined to give Ruthie her view, I decided to enter the marathon on my own. Maybe if I ran while pushing her wheelchair they would allow it.

During the next four years I learned how to run with the help of New York Road Runners running classes. I do have good joints and bones, and longevity runs in my family. My parents lived till 80 and I have two older siblings, a sister who is 96, a brother who is 94, and the baby is 71. I've always maintained a good diet, even during the depression. When I was working at the shipyard, one of the loading docks handled food from all over the world. I became a gourmet eater. I know good food when I see it and eat it. When I go for my long walks I look for all the best specialty food shops. I buy my pastries at Balthazar's but not the bread. I know a better place. And I've always held the belief that a great lamb chop is better than a porterhouse steak. It's all in the cut.

I never really train for my marathons, but I'll go out and walk for eight hours, covering 14 miles on a good day. When I race I never really break into a run; I keep to a simple jog or walk. I don't stretch or have a consistent running routine. I probably do everything wrong but it works for me. Finally, in 1990 I got to keep my promise to Ruth, but she had passed away. Determined to still keep my promise I ran the marathon in her honor. I kept to myself and thought about her all through the race. I didn't need to talk to anyone; I just focused on my pace and on Ruthie. I knew she was by my side. Twelve years and 15 marathons later she is still my inspiration.

After my first marathon I got the running bug and continued to enter races. My son was living in London at the time so I decided to run the London Marathon and have been doing that ever since. I'm the oldest runner at the marathon and the British Broadcasting makes a big deal of it, putting me on television. A Jewish newspaper also picked up my story, which was seen by a charitable organization called Age-Concern, which is like the Salvation Army. Now I run on the Age-Concern team but I still don't get any money. Like I said before, no one wants to give money to the old-timers. London is a nice flat course that winds through towns. Some it is on cobblestone, which is tough on the feet but it's not so bad. You get used to it. I've also ended up in the London hospital two times. Even though I am in good health you never know what will happen to the body during a marathon.

I also try to participate in the weekend NYRR races in Central Park. I get in 40 or so races a year, including the marathons. My favorites are New York City and London. My son now lives on Martha's Vineyard so I race there in the summer, competing in the Vineyard Scoops 5K and Marianne's Run the Chop 5-miler. My one gripe about the running community is that they only like to sponsor the young runners. I'd like to be sponsored and have someone pick up my flights to London but no one seems interested.

I love to run; I love to talk about running. I feel better at 92 than I did at 80. For my second marathon, I decided to train harder and took almost one hour off my time. Then in 1994, at 84 years old, I set a personal record with a finish time of 6:32. And I'm setting world records. I didn't start out to set any records; I just keep a steady pace until it's over. When I was 90, I set the world record for my age group in the 2000 New York City Marathon with a time of 7:25:12. Like I said, I just kept a steady pace and that does the trick. I never know if I am going to finish or not when I start a marathon. No one can ever be sure, not even the elites. I don't care who you are, a marathon is too unpredictable to call.

I'm not the only senior running out there, either. I belong to a running group called the Ash Can Runners. Our members include Charles Feldman (85), Willie Rios (84), Vince Carnevale (84), Frank Brownstein (83) and Ted

Corbitt (82). We tease Ted about being the kid in the group. We formed the group about 20 years ago when seniors were coming on strong in running. Most of the guys were serious competitors at one time and now we're all over the hill but that doesn't stop us. We're still pretty competitive among us and needle each other. Anything to get under one another's skin, but in a fun way. We love to egg each other on and tell lies about our racing times and what we used to do. I'm the oldest member of the group. We love to get together and talk about running or World War II stories, as they are all vets. I think the older women runners are jealous of us so they are thinking of starting their own team as well. It's always great to see different generations of people being active.

Recently I wasn't feeling well and my daughter took me to the hospital. Turns out it was an ulcer. When you're 92 years old and have to go the doctor, an ulcer is good news compared with other stuff he could have told me. The doctor doesn't want me to run for a while, but the London Marathon is coming up and I need to train. I got up at 5:30 the next morning to get my prescription filled and had to walk until 6 A.M. before I found a place open. That's one way to get my walking in for the day.

People have it too easy in today's world. They don't know what it's like to work really hard and make sacrifices. That's why everyone thinks I am so amazing to be running at my age. Heck, anyone can do it if they want it bad enough. I was never given anything in this world. I've had to fight for everything I ever had, including the marathon. It all boils down to hard work and a little bit of luck. That's what makes the difference. I plan to keep running marathons until I can't walk. When I finish a race I am the happiest man in the world.

# THE ACCIDENTAL MARATHONER

**ED WHITLOCK**

**D.O.B.: 3-6-31**
**RESIDENCE: MILTON, ONTARIO**
**OCCUPATION: RETIRED MINING**
   **ENGINEER**
**FIRST MARATHON: 1976**
   **MONTREAL MARATHON**
**AGE AT FIRST MARATHON: 45**

*Soft-spoken, lean, and handsome in a silver screen leading-actor kind of way, Ed Whitlock is very humble about his very impressive running career. With a degree in mining engineering, he left his native England for Canada to mine metal. He had run track and cross-country in school but no one ran in the cold of northern Ontario. Twenty years later he picked up running again with his two sons, but not of his own doing. When his 15-year-old son announced he wanted to run a marathon, Ed reluctantly ran as well to be with him. That was the beginning of Ed's new career as a marathoner. Today, at 71, Ed considers himself fortunate to be running at all and takes it one day at a time. That said,* Runner's World *magazine dubbed him the Age Group Ace for being the oldest person, at 69, to break three hours for the marathon.*

I am really not a marathoner, just an old miler. However, circumstances throughout my life kept pointing me toward the marathon so that's where I just happened to end up.

I grew up in England in the suburbs of London. During high school I ran track and cross-country. I was good at it, but what I liked even more than being good was being part of a team. My best time was a 4:31 mile at age 17 and at London University, where I majored in mining engineering, I was the 3-mile champion with a time of 14:54. I knew I was an above-average runner but upon graduation I quit running altogether. Graduating from the college I attended was like taking out immigration papers to leave England. The only mining left in England was coal and I didn't care for that so I packed up and went to Canada to mine metal, primarily gold. Canada at that time was the world's number two producer of gold. Northern Ontario had a big gold mining center so after mining nickel in Sudbury for a while I ended up in Timmins.

One of the reasons I quit running was the cold. Nobody ran in northern Ontario. This was in 1952, prior to the running boom, and I just wasn't ambitious enough to keep it up on my own. I wasn't one of those running pioneers, just a 21-year-old kid right out of the university looking for a job.

Twenty years later, living in Montreal, married with two young boys, I got back into the sport but not by my own endeavor. As most things in life, it came down to chance. That, and my wife and my elder son. It was sports day at his school and my wife showed up to help. They were short a running coach for the kids so my wife volunteered my services. However, when I got there they didn't need me after all. But once there I thought, *What the heck, I'll run around the track a bit.* I surprised myself; I wasn't in such bad shape after all those years. I did some refereeing of my boys' soccer games and gardened a bit and did a fair amount of walking. I played some soccer in junior school and rugby at the high school. In England they say that soccer is a game for gentlemen played by hooligans and rugby is a game for hooligans played by gentlemen. Anyway, by my early 40s I was in decent shape from all these activities. Oh, I forgot to mention shoveling lots of snow.

Gradually I did a bit more running every time I went to the track, running with the teenagers. The final thing that brought me back to competitive running was a relay competition. Again, it wasn't my doing that got me back into the sport. The teenagers needed another body on their relay team and asked if I would step in so I entered my first race after 20 years' retirement. I ran 1,500 meters and we did quite well. This was before the masters movement so it was the only outlet for me to race. Slowly I was starting to get the bug to run full time and make it more than a casual comeback.

By now, 1972, the masters movement was beginning to pick up. Frank Shorter had just won the Olympic gold medal for the marathon, and the running/jogging boom was starting. But in Canada running was still unusual for older people. I was looked upon as a weirdo as I ran through the streets. Running and biking were still for kids, not grown-ups and not as sports.

In 1971 a fellow by the name of David Payne in San Diego got a group of older runners together to compete in England. As word of this spread, it began to attract the Canadians, then the Aussies, and finally it evolved into the World Amateur Veterans Association (WAVA). Roger Bannister was at the first meeting. It was a huge success and I joined the following year. There was always a bit of confusion with that name in the United States, as it has nothing to do with war veterans. In England, the word *veteran* does not connote military experience; it just refers to older people. In 1975, the first world championships were held in Toronto and I attended. Following that, championships have been held every two years. In 2001 the name was changed to the World Masters Association (WMA). Somehow or other I got involved with the Canadian executive management of the organization. I keep the road records.

So now I was running most of the time either with WAVA or still with the kids. Along the way I had converted from a cross-country runner to an 800 and 1500-meter runner. Getting back into running felt natural, as if I'd never quit. In fact, I ran faster times as a master than I ever did as a kid. Of course, better equipment helped; no long spikes and broken-up cinder tracks!

My entry into the marathon was, once again, not by my own choice. This time it was the fault of my younger son Clive, then 15 years old. He ran cross-country in high school and got the notion in his head to run a marathon. I said I would go around with him to train, so I ended up running my first marathon just to accompany my 15-year-old son. He did most of his training by himself, getting help and support from our running club. I have no idea why he wanted to run one but I was somewhat concerned, which is why I decided to run it with him.

I didn't seriously train for this. I knew that 800-meter runners were largely not suited for the marathon and I had a healthy respect for it. My normal mileage was 40 to 50 miles a week, with a long run of 15 miles on most Sundays in the winter as I put in background mileage as a base for the summer track season. So I did have some base for running the marathon even if not optimal. I really had no business running a marathon other than wanting to accompany my son.

The marathon was in March, in Montreal, and it was cold and windy. This was in 1976 and there were 400 participants, small by today's standards. My son didn't seem nervous, but I was somewhat worried for him. There were no water stops. It would have frozen anyway if there had been water to drink. I don't recall us drinking at all. He was beat and hit the wall at 22 miles. It was a bit of a struggle for him but he kept going. I would have quit and dropped out but he wanted to finish. We crossed the finish line in 3:09. He was 15 and I was 45. I thought it was pretty amazing for him. I didn't think much about my time because I didn't approach the marathon for myself. I had no personal ambitions except to be with him. I certainly didn't have the desire to convert to a serious marathoner.

We ran another one three months later. Things had warmed up a bit by then and he was determined to break three hours. We finished that one in 2:58 and he was happy to meet his goal. The following year, 1977, we won the father-son team competition at the Ottawa Marathon and finished in 2:52. Then he quit. He was all of 17 years old.

The following year, 1978, elder son Neil, who also ran cross-country at school and was 18 at the time, decided he wanted to try a marathon as well. I won't go as far to say this turned into a competition between the two boys but they did have a healthy sibling rivalry. Over the years Neil has been a more serious runner than Clive and still runs competitively. We ran the Ottawa Marathon and finished in 2:48.

Never having intended to run a marathon, within the course of two years I ran four. Finally in 1979 I decided to run a marathon on my own. I had luke-warm ambitions that maybe I could make something of this. Distance running was now getting popular and more people were doing it. My club had more or less converted from a track club to a road runners' club and all the teenagers that I used to train with had either grown up or moved on. A friend from the running club wanted to run a marathon so I said I would train with him.

During that winter I decided to train properly for a marathon. I wanted to see what I could do and started putting in 100-mile weeks. I finished the March Montreal Marathon in 2:33, coming in second in the race. I was 48. It wasn't a big marathon but then again, no matter what the number of participants it's always the same distance, 26.2 miles. Two months later in Ottawa I did 2:31, my personal best. Even after this, I still considered myself a track runner and felt that the distance training would be good for the track. That same year I won the world championships for WAVA in the 1500 meters so my theory held true. I received a gold medal but speaking professionally as a mining engineer, I don't think there is much gold in the medal. It wouldn't pass the bite test.

During these years I was working full time, training, and raising a family. I used to go out at 10 P.M. at night in the dark and cold to get my runs in. There was no money in it for me so I guess I truly enjoyed it. I was very organized then, which certainly helped to get everything done. It is interesting to note that I was more organized when I had less time. Now that I am retired and have the time, I am less organized.

When I retired at 58, I entered my self-described third career as a runner. My first career was marked in my school years. My second wave came in my 40s when I ran with the club and did my marathons with my sons. I scaled back a bit in my 50s but after retirement came back full time to running. At 69 years old, I competed in the Columbus Marathon and became the oldest person to break three hours for the marathon. People have started to acknowledge me nowadays and even Bill Rodgers paid me a compliment. The records people have indicated that on age-graded tables I am running the equivalent times of a 25-year-old man. My goal is to be the first person 70 or older to break the three-hour marathon but I am injured at the moment so I don't know whether that goal is still within reach—but I'll give it my best. I gave it a shot last spring but missed the goal by 24 seconds.

As for running, I don't think I fit into the typical runner's mold. I am not a compulsive runner; I do it because I am good at it. It does not give me the solace it seems to bring to others and I have never experienced the so-called runner's high. Competition for me is mainly personal, against myself rather than against others. I wouldn't like to compete in tennis singles where it is one against one. I don't log my miles; I track my time. My usual course is one-third-mile loops around a cemetery. I just put in the time and do virtually no speedwork. Whenever I start to do speedwork, my Achilles tendon starts to complain but it never says a word on my distance runs. I don't race much in the winter. Come spring, I am a bit sluggish, but after a few races the speed comes back. I don't cross-train either. Can't swim a stroke. Growing up in England the water was always too cold and there weren't any indoor pools. One of the best-kept secrets is that no English sailor can swim.

I don't dislike training but I don't look forward to it or really enjoy it, either. I get nervous and feel awful before an important race. I feel euphoric when it is over, especially when I have done well. I don't like to disgrace myself. In my experience, long-distance runners are universally good people with great spirits and very supportive. I enjoy being around other runners. Basically, I take it as it may come. As I said, I am an accidental marathoner.

# PART TWO

## THE ELITES

The elites are different but in some ways the same. They learned to run by putting one foot in front of the other, just like everyone else. They put in the months of training, just like everyone else. They suffer through the distance and feel the pain after mile 20, just like everyone else. And sometimes they drop out of a marathon, just like everyone else.

What makes them different is their intense, no-distraction dedication to their training, their weekly mileage (up to 200 miles a week) their pace (averaging five-minute miles), their mental state (obsessive about winning, not just finishing), and maybe some god-given talent or good genes (although we haven't seen any Rodgers or Shorter offspring yet at the start of a marathon).

Most of them started their running career in high school or college, not as a midlife crisis. Most don't eat any differently and are as prone to eating junk food as the average runner. It all boils down to extreme training, which most average runners are not willing to do or cannot fit it into a life already full with job commitments and perhaps a family.

Legendary marathoner Bill Rodgers doesn't like the word *elite*. He prefers to be called a professional, and is always impressed by folks who run this crazy race no matter what their pace or how long it takes to finish. He swears he couldn't stay out on the course much longer than his usual marathon finishing time of 2:10. "I am always amazed and in awe of the people who have the stamina and dedication to stay out for four or five hours, or longer. I couldn't do that."

Rodgers also acknowledges that faster runners are born with the ability to utilize oxygen more efficiently, which allows them to run faster than someone who doesn't. This ability, usually referred to as $VO_2$ max, can be measured in a state-of-the-art laboratory. When he was 16, legendary Tour de France winner and cancer survivor Lance Armstrong had his $VO_2$ max tested at the Cooper Clinic in Dallas, Texas, the research lab and birthplace of aerobic exercise testing. His numbers are still the highest ever recorded. He also produces less lactic acid than most people, which enables him to endure more physical stress. Rodgers, Armstrong, and others like them do have a physical edge over others whose tests results aren't as high.

Then there's the muscle fiber twitch effect. Elite marathoners have a greater percentage of slow-twitch fiber, which enables them to run long distances at a fast pace. Sprinters have slow-twitch fibers, allowing them to run at high speed for short distances. The twitch test requires needles poking into muscle fibers, so not many runners do it.

So, yes, the elites are different. I can run my heart out, do hill work, speed-work, intervals, and repeats up the wazoo, increase my weekly miles to 60, even 80 a week and still not get my times down to equal an elite in my age group because my $VO_2$ max is most likely not as high.

Regardless of whether you are in the elite category or not, what we all share is a common passion and love for the marathon. When we lose that, when we don't have the spirit or the will or the desire, it doesn't matter what our $VO_2$ max is.

Running a marathon is serious business. But it is also a gift, regardless of fast you run. Even though the elites are physically and mentally at a higher level than most runners, we are all joined together on the same course because of the challenge ahead and the rewards that await us at the finish line.

# NEW YORK CITY OR BUST

**GORDON BAKOULIS**

**D.O.B.: 2-14-61**
**RESIDENCE: NEW YORK CITY**
**OCCUPATION: EDITOR, WRITER,**
**RUNNING COACH**
**FIRST MARATHON: 1984 NYC**
**MARATHON**
**AGE AT FIRST MARATHON: 23**

Photo courtesy New York Road Runners

*Gordon Bakoulis is a perfect example of a woman who has combined her love for running with her career as editor and author without losing sight of her first priority, her two sons and husband. A force to be reckoned with on the racing circuit, Gordon placed first in her age group at the 2001 NYC Marathon with a time of 2:41:43, which also was 17th overall female. Not bad for a new masters runner. Her other running highlights include qualifying for the U.S. Olympic trials marathon five times and being a finalist in the 1992 U.S. Olympic 10,000-meter trials. The former editor-in chief of* Running Times *magazine, Gordon is also the author of three books on running. A true professional in every sense of the world, Gordon is gracious and unpretentious and always willing to give back to the sport that has given her so much.*

Running was not my first sport. I loved lacrosse and played that as well as field hockey at Princeton High School. What I loved about lacrosse was the lack of any boundary line. You could step outside the lines and still be legal. That appealed to me. Running as a sport didn't. The only time I ran was for conditioning. I guess the first time I actually ran with any type of a routine was in the fall of 1978 when I started running with a girlfriend in the mornings. And even with that, the whole idea was to get into shape for the spring sports season.

Running wasn't something I identified with till later in life. In high school, it was always a means to an end. My family is pretty athletic although I wouldn't describe us as jocks. We kept busy with chores like raking leaves or cleaning the house and we would take family walks. Exercise was centered more around being naturally active, such as riding my bike to school, than structured sports.

The best description of me in high school is a skinny geek; definitely not

one of the jocks. I was also totally uncoordinated. Even though I loved playing lacrosse, I was really bad at it. I had no eye-hand coordination. So in my
senior year I switched from lacrosse to track and finally felt like I was good at
something. Our team was terrible but I won all my races. I went to the states
that year and met Carl Lewis. We were both 18 and he was the first runner I
ever met who had star quality. You could tell he was going far in the sport.

After high school I attended the University of Virginia. I wasn't recruited
for the track team but thought I'd look into it and spoke with the coach. He
quickly made me realize college track was a whole other level of running than
what I was used to. In high school I had fun and this was not going to be fun.
It would have meant lots of hard work and commitment to keep up with the
team, and I wanted to drink beer, eat pizza, and stay out all night. Basically
I wanted to experience the whole college life, and if I ran on the team that
would have to come first. So instead of running, I chose to have a blast and
enjoy my four years.

Even though I wasn't associated with a team, I continued to run on my
own and did intramural sports like field hockey, racquetball and squash. I also
got very involved with the school newspaper. I had a very well-rounded college life. I did do a race my freshman year, the Charlottesville 10-miler, and
won. It was a hard race so winning was a great feeling. I didn't train or anything, I just showed up and ran. I was beginning to realize I had a natural talent for running but still didn't do anything structured. My senior year at
school I ran a half marathon in Richmond with my cousin. Again, I didn't
train for it, just went out and ran. My time was 1:34, which is close to a seven-
minute pace. It was also the hardest thing I'd ever done. A full marathon was
also scheduled for that day and it was the first time I ever saw a live marathon.
I knew how hard it was for me to finish the half and this looked much harder. But it didn't intrigue me, I didn't even consider running one. It was off my
radar screen for the time being.

The only other racing I did through college was a mini-marathon in
Central Park, New York. My dad was a member of New York Road Runners,
and he would occasionally get me out to run with him. There were very few
running clubs in New Jersey back then so he joined the New York club and
would drive in from Princeton for the races. He's 69 now and still makes the
effort to get out and run, and my mom walks every day. He was probably my
first running role model. He and I volunteered at the 1983 New York City
Marathon. He had run it three times and wanted to give back so we both
helped out. Our job was to scan the runners' bar codes at the start of the race,
which isn't done any longer. It was the equivalent of the chip used today. After
we scanned in all the runners it was only 9 A.M. so we drove back to watch
the finish. It was a very exciting finish that year with Rod Dixon and Geoff
Smith dueling for the lead the last 3 miles. It was quite an experience for me

as I watched the parade of humanity pass by. I thought to myself, *If these peo-ple can do this, I can, too.*

After graduation in 1983 I moved to New York City and got a job with *Ms.* magazine. During college I concentrated in journalism and always want-ed to be a writer from when I was young. After *Ms.*, I worked at *Glamour* magazine as a health and fitness writer. I lived near Central Park, so that became my running turf. That year my dad gave me a New York Road Runners membership for my birthday so I decided to run the marathon the following year. I guess the inspiration to run came from watching my dad run it and also convincing myself I could do it.

I knew that once I decided to run a marathon, it would have to be New York City. I knew the crowds would be great and that it would be a very excit-ing event. And the idea of running through the five boroughs intrigued me. I wasn't familiar with any of the boroughs outside of Manhattan and thought this would be a great way to see them. I was on pins and needles as I waited to hear if I made the lottery drawing. When I got in, it was very exciting for me and I started training in July.

When I look back at how I trained for my first marathon, I have to laugh. I didn't know anything about the sport. I never kept track of my mileage and didn't do any speed work. I had moved out of the city to Weehawken, New Jersey, and ran along the Jersey waterfront for my long runs. I'd be out run-ning by 6 A.M., then back home, wash up and take the bus to the city. I start-ed running with a guy named Paul I met and soon realized he had other inten-tions beyond running. After we talked it over we were able to remain friends and running partners. He was more knowledgeable about training so he taught me quite a bit. Soon I was keeping a running log, learning to take flu-ids during long runs, and just being smarter about my running. Some run-ning techniques came easy to me, like the concept of hard-easy. I knew if I did a long run or speed work one day, then I had to take it easy the next so my body could recuperate. I've always been a believer in listening to my body. Paul also knew a lot of history about the sport and would talk about some of the great runners. I only knew about Joan Benoit Samuelson and Grete Waitz who had just won her umpteenth New York City Marathon so it was fun and interesting to learn more.

After a few months of training I could tell I was getting stronger as I could go farther on my long runs. I never did worry about speed. As the date got closer I got more excited and told everyone that I was running a marathon. Back in those days it was a real status symbol to run a marathon, especially for a woman. However, I still didn't see myself as a runner, didn't take it on as my identity. It hadn't become part of my essence as it is now.

Paul told me to set a finishing goal but I resisted. I just wanted to finish without the added pressure of worrying about a time. It became an obstacle to our training as he kept insisting this was important and I just wanted to finish and have fun. I felt he was putting undue pressure on me and I had to tell him to back off. Having seen a marathon, I had a healthy respect for the distance and knew it would be hard. And I had recently done a half marathon race and totally bombed. I ended up walking the last few miles and finished with a time of 2:08. I think that's another reason I didn't want to set a time. It was the one area where I was really being smart and believing that I knew what was best for me. In the end, being patient turned out to be the best thing I ever did as the heat factor we faced during the marathon made all the runners throw their expected times out the window.

By the end of my training I had done two 18-milers and one 21-miler and they were tough. We ran along the New Jersey side of the Hudson, carrying our water bottles. I also did some short-distance racing just to get used to the pace and the crowds.

Marathon morning I took the bus from the New York Public Library to the start. I wasn't nervous but I was very excited. I knew this would be different from anything I had ever done before. My parents came in to watch and my dad was especially psyched—and proud. It was a particularly hot October day, 79 degrees, high humidity, and full sunshine. Everyone was obsessing over the weather and how the heat would affect their times and health. We were constantly warned to drink lots of water and wear sunscreen. Since I was a sports and health writer, I knew the conditions could be potentially dangerous and took the necessary precautions and ran slower than normal. I also had it in my mind that if I had to walk it would be all right. I wasn't obsessed with running the entire distance and again, I think that mentality also helped me on such a hot day.

I stood at the start with my friend Amy. I had stayed at her New York City apartment the night before and we were both psyched. There was a lot of downtime waiting for the marathon to start so we just milled around going to the bathroom a zillion times. Finally we started and it took us about three minutes to cross the start. After 10 miles I picked up the pace and left Amy.

The whole marathon experience was just so great. It was hard but I never felt like I wasn't going to finish. In fact, during the second half I must have passed hundreds of people. It wasn't that I was so fast; I wasn't. But I was running smart. Always took water, paced myself evenly, and was consistent with my energy output. And most importantly, I enjoyed myself. I didn't talk much, just tried to focus on the run. Consistency was the key. I enjoyed running through the boroughs and seeing how they connected. Not being a native New Yorker, I was always somewhat mystified by the five boroughs and finally it all made sense to me! I remember thinking as I ran the route, *So, this is Brooklyn. And next comes Queens, which is linked to Manhattan by this bridge and then another bridge linking Manhattan to the Bronx and then back to*

*Manhattan*. The puzzle was finally solved. I felt like a tourist. I was never bored and didn't talk much to the other runners. I was too busy looking around.

Once I got to Central Park South I knew I had only 1 mile left and even though I was really tired I knew I could do it. The crowds were awesome, loud and very supportive. I was thinking that the elites had been done for an hour by now but that didn't matter to me, I was going to enjoy every minute of this. I was also psyched to talk about the race with my dad afterward and share the experience with him. I felt great at the finish and definitely knew I would do another one. My time was a respectable 3:40:03. Meanwhile, my friend Amy finished about 15 minutes behind me and threw up at the finish, declaring it was the hardest thing she'd ever done and she hated the whole experience!

I didn't run for three months after the marathon. The big event was over and since I didn't think of myself as a runner yet, I didn't feel the need to keep it up. It wasn't until two years later that I ran my next marathon, and I was decidedly a different runner by then. During those two years I had been recruited to run for a team. I took to training right away and loved it. I tried to run the 1986 NYC Marathon but had to drop out at 8 miles with plantar fasciitis. I never should have started because I knew I was injured and just made it worse. Finally in 1987 I ran Grandma's Marathon in Minnesota with a finishing time of 2:46, carving almost an hour off my first one. My whole focus had shifted since my first marathon and I was now a competitive runner. All that training and my natural abilities came together and I finally saw myself as a runner.

I enjoyed my fast marathon as much as my "fun" marathon, but in a totally different way. I was now serious about it, no longer the tourist. And because I came into the sport as a recreational runner first, I'll be able to retire someday and not worry about staying competitive; I had my one fun marathon and can go back to that. Some elite runners have trouble continuing to run once they stop winning and setting records because they never had a "fun" marathon; they don't know what it's like to just enjoy running. It can get scary when you start setting up performance goals and tie your entire identity in with your running goals. Luckily, I have been able to manage my identity as an elite runner along with my roles as a mother, wife, and career woman.

I went on to compete in the Olympic marathon trials in 1988, '92, '96, and 2000 and have already qualified for the 2004 trials. I've run 22 marathons with a personal best of 2:33:01 set at the 1989 New York City Marathon. My next biggest event was becoming a masters runner last year. That was a big step but I love it. It's a wonderful time to be running. In my first NYC Marathon as a masters division runner, in 2001, I placed first female masters with a time of 2:41:43. It doesn't get better than this!

I am often asked for advice by people running their first marathon. My main piece of advice is to enjoy the process. As important as it is to set goals in running (and life), I really believe it's more important to embrace each individual moment and experience it to its fullest. Training for a marathon, and completing the race itself, is hard work, no matter what your level of fitness. It takes tremendous time and energy, and if you resent the drain on your physical and emotional resources, you will not enjoy the training or the race itself. Before you commit to a marathon, accept that it will be hard, at times tedious, and require plenty of sacrifices.

As for the race itself, it may be the hardest physical thing you have ever done—so hard that you cry, curse, and wonder what in the world possessed you to start. Only you can decide whether it's worth it. The feelings of satisfaction that result from crossing the finish line are, for most people, an incredible conformation that, yes, it was worth every sweaty, struggling moment. That's certainly true for me—but I've met more than a few runners who have finished a marathon and said "Never again!"—and meant it. And that is fine.

I also tell people that it's impossible to fake your way through a marathon. If you haven't put in the training for *this* race, you will not perform to your potential, no matter your gifts or your past accomplishments. The body is not designed to run 26.2 miles without stopping, so it's essential to prepare to overcome the many, many physical messages to quit that you will receive along the way. Do the long runs, the tune-up races, the speed workouts, and get the proper rest and nutrition/hydration preparation in the weeks before the race. You'll still hurt, but you will survive—and go on to complete many other marathons.

I believe it can be healthy and life-affirming for many people to continue to run marathons well into old age. It may not suit every person's temperament, and some of us may develop infirmities that make marathon running a poor choice for health enhancement. But for the majority of healthy, fit people, a marathon is doable, and enjoyable. On top of being a wonderful process in and of itself, it can be a wonderful symbol of so many things in life that are worth striving for.

# SHORTER, RODGERS, AND WHO?

## DON KARDONG

D.O.B.: 12-22-48
RESIDENCE: SPOKANE, WA
OCCUPATION: SENIOR WRITER,
   *RUNNER'S WORLD*; COACH;
   SPEAKER
FIRST MARATHON: 1972, THE WEST
   VALLEY MARATHON,
   BURLINGAME, CA
AGE AT FIRST MARATHON: 23

*A self-described wayward runner, Don had an illustrious collegiate career as a track and cross-country runner, and then moved up to the marathon, eventually becoming the third member of the 1976 Olympic marathon team in Montreal. A Stanford University graduate, he ran in the glory days against legends such as Prefontaine, Shorter, and Rodgers. After the 1976 Olympics, he helped establish the Lilac Bloomsday Run, one of the more famous and loved events on the circuit, in his adopted hometown of Spokane. A past president of the Road Runners Club of America, Don is also a humorous writer of running books and has an additional career as an online coach. Likable, engaging, and always ready to lend a helping hand, Don is the consummate ambassador to the running community.*

I grew up in the Seattle area before there were many runners. In those days, the majority of us were the competitive type, either running for school teams or clubs. Green Lake was the favored place to run, and if you saw other runners there, you knew they were from a rival high school team or the University of Washington. Almost no one ran for fitness or fun in those days. This was before the running boom of the late '70s and early '80s. In fact, I never heard the term *running boom* until 1977. The first person I ever heard of who ran just for the fun of it, or perhaps for fitness, was a roommate of mine back in 1972. He ran the Bay to Breakers Race in San Francisco. I was surprised that someone would do that, run a race just for the fun of it, with no real competitive aspirations.

After high school I attended Stanford University and ran on the track team. I was mostly a 5000-meter guy, and I dabbled with the 10,000 too.

Back then the marathon was a huge unknown for me. I was vaguely aware of the Boston Marathon because it was famous. Other than that, there weren't too many marathons around. There were a couple in California, but marathons were few and far between, and the ones that did exist had very small fields, no more than a few hundred participants. I did know of gold medalist Abebe Bikila's famous barefoot run in the 1960 Rome Olympics. That story captured every runner's imagination, and I certainly admired him. I had a measure of awe and respect for the marathon distance, and somewhere in the back of my mind I thought it might be an event I could do well at, but mostly I kept training to race shorter distances.

I stayed in the Stanford area after graduating, because the 1972 Olympics were coming up and I thought I had a shot at making the U.S. team. I worked a few odd jobs, but basically all I did was eat, run, sleep, and read books. It was a great lifestyle.

There were runners in the club I had joined—the West Valley Track Club—who had done marathons, like Bill Scobey, whom we called "Mad Dog." The president of our club was Jack Leydig, who had a good job in the high-tech industry, but who spent most of his time organizing club races and activities without pay. One of those events was the West Valley Marathon, and Jack suggested I run it. That's about all the prodding I needed. I was training really hard that year, putting in up to 140 miles a week. It wasn't unusual for me to run two 10-milers a day. My longest run was 15 miles, and since I was mostly racing 5000 meters or less, I didn't think I needed to do more than that. The marathon was scheduled for the morning after an indoor meet I was planning to run in Oakland, but that didn't really matter to me. I ran the 2-mile indoors in the evening and set a personal best of about 8:34. That was the important race of the weekend.

The marathon the next morning was a lark, a glorified training run, and I didn't take it very seriously. Mostly I ran it because Jack had asked me to. Maybe 100 runners showed up. Back then, the streets were never closed off for a marathon. No one in their right mind would ask the police to close down streets for a running event. The course was five 5-mile loops through the city of Burlingame, plus a little extra at the end to make it the full marathon distance. It wasn't very scenic, either; in fact, you could see the Bayshore Freeway from several points on the course. Having zero experience with running a marathon, I basically did whatever I saw the experienced marathoners doing, or whatever they told me I should do. They were very helpful, and mentioned a few mistakes I was making, like running on the slope of the street instead of the flat part. I don't remember drinking any fluids, though, as I had never done that in a race before. The first four laps felt really easy, but by the time I started the fifth lap I was running out of steam. Then, with only a mile to go, I really, really felt awful. I was slowly breaking down, and it was sheer torture to keep going. Early on the 5:10 pace I was running seemed easy, since I usually raced shorter distances at 4:25 pace. Even as late as 25 miles the pace felt okay. But I hadn't eaten anything or taken in any fluids along the way, and the steady draining of glycogen reserves finally left me totally depleted. After 25 miles I thought to myself, *How can I possibly make it the rest of the way?* Somehow I did, of course, and when I heard I had run 2:18:06 I was stunned. I knew that was a very good marathon time.

That time qualified me to run the Olympic marathon trials later in the year. I had already qualified for the 10,000 meters, but now I also had an entrée to the marathon trials. Back then, the U.S. Olympic trials were scheduled a bit different than they are now. They staged them just like the Olympics, with the track and field events first and the marathon at the end of the week. Nowadays they hold the marathon months before the track and field trials. Anyway, with the schedule they had then, I was able to run the 10,000 early in the week and the marathon at the end.

Unfortunately, in about April of that year, 1972, I came down with mononucleosis. The trials were in July, which didn't give me much time to recover and train hard again, and the Munich Olympics were scheduled two months after that. So I really didn't have enough time to recover and train for either. I ran the marathon anyway, though, and placed sixth, not nearly good enough to make the Olympic team. Of course Frank Shorter went on to win the gold medal in the marathon at Munich that year, and the U.S. running scene was never the same again.

Even though I didn't place at those Olympic trials, I knew I had potential as a marathoner. My trials time was about 2:24, and that was coming off an illness. The possibility of making the Olympic team in the marathon was simmering in the back of my mind. After the 1972 trials I attended the University of Washington for two years, and earned a degree in English and a teaching certificate. During that time I would sometimes spend all morning running with my training partner, a steeplechase runner named Jim Johnson. We'd run 15 miles or more in a workout, combining distance, long intervals, and track work. It was awesome training, and I ran some of my best races in that time period. After I graduated I moved to Spokane, where I had landed a job teaching sixth grade.

I kept training for the 5000 and 10,000, which, as I learned, is also the best way to train for a marathon. Train as you would for a fast 10K, but add a few long runs in the 20-mile range. If you do that, marathon pace should feel relatively easy. My training plan was to keep running high mileage but also to stay fast by doing high-quality speedwork. I ran one more marathon, in Eugene, Oregon, before the 1976 Olympic Trials, which were also in Eugene. When I got to the Eugene airport a few days before the trials, I ran into a 5000-meter runner named Paul Geis, who was heading out of town for a race.

He told me I was nuts to be running a marathon only a month before the track and field trials. He thought I should have stayed focused on the 5000. I just really believed, though, that I had a shot at the marathon. Like most people, Paul saw me as a track runner who was fooling around with the marathon, but I thought the marathon might be a better event for me, and more suited to my character. I knew I could handle the distance, and I thought I could manage the concentration a marathon requires. In any case, I was up for the challenge. You have to dig deep for the marathon, more than in any other race. It doesn't come easy, but it definitely appealed to me.

And, of course, it worked out. I qualified in Eugene as the third man on the U.S. team, which also included Frank Shorter and Bill Rodgers. Those two were clearly top marathoners, and everyone looked at my qualifying as a fluke. I remember people talking about Frank's gold medal and how he was likely to win another one. And they'd talk about Bill Rodgers, the up-and-coming marathoner who had just won at Boston. And then there was me, a 5000-meter runner with no real marathon credentials. People would pause, then say, "Don, you'll love Montreal. Pretty city, nice restaurants. You'll have a good time." It seemed like there were only two people, my mom and I, who thought I had a chance to get a medal.

But I definitely believed I had a shot. My plan was to run an easy pace for the first 10 miles, and then go all out and catch runners who had fallen off the lead pack. Most marathoners in big races go out fast and try to hang on to the lead pack, and most of them can't sustain the pace. So my plan was to hold back for about 10 miles, then start moving up and eventually move into the top three. I didn't want to blow my Olympic opportunity by going out as hard as possible, because I thought that would backfire. So I was determined to relax for the first 10 miles, run on autopilot, and keep my mind off the competitive part of the race. To relax, I developed a plan to keep myself amused. At each aid station, after I finished with my water bottle, I would throw it into the crowd, yelling "Olympic souvenir!" I looked for kids to throw it to because I knew they would get a kick out it. I was thinking about my sixth-grade students, who had been really excited to send me off to the Olympics. Just before I left school, they had held a pep rally for me and presented me with an athletic sock filled with coins. It was supposed to help pay my way to Montreal. Of course the Olympic committee was paying my expenses, so I didn't need a sock filled with coins, but one of the teachers convinced me to keep it and let the kids feel they were part of my Olympic adventure.

Anyway, I kept this up for the first two aid stations, throwing my bottle into the crowd. Around 9 miles, the crowd had thinned a bit as the course went through a residential area. There weren't any kids to throw to, but I saw three guys sitting on the front porch of their house, so I decided to throw my bottle to them. I gave it a good toss, and I watched as the bottle made a big arc toward the porch. Then all of a sudden I realized it was on target to hit a big picture window the guys were sitting in front of. I couldn't believe it! Here I was in the middle of the Olympic marathon, the most important race of my career, and I was about to break someone's window. The three guys were curled up with their hands covering their heads in anticipation of the impact. Fortunately, the bottle just barely caught the eave of the roof, then rolled along the roof and bounced harmlessly to the grass. After that, I decided to focus on the race.

My energy level was high at that point and I started passing people. Of course, it got progressively harder as I starting catching faster and faster runners. At some point I passed Bill Rodgers, who was having a very bad day. He had been hobbled by a foot trouble for some time and his training was off, and he ended up finishing somewhere around 40th place. At about mile 19, someone shouted, "You're 30 seconds out of a bronze medal." I knew I was closing in on the leaders, but that was the first time I realized I had gotten that close. I could see three runners up ahead, and I figured those were the three I had to pass to move into third place, but it took me another 3 miles to finally catch them. At 22 miles, they all moved to the side of the road for water, but I had decided to skip the rest of the aid stations, so I kept running and passed them all. I was in third place!

Unfortunately, I wasn't at the finish line yet. And just at the point when I needed it most, my body started to seize up and cramp. Even so, I was convinced that if I could just relax and keep moving I would get a medal. Then, at 25 miles, I heard footsteps. I looked back and saw a runner catching me. It was Karel Lismont, one of the three runners I had passed a few miles earlier. He caught up to me, and for the next mile we ran side by side, each of us looking for a way to get ahead. Finally, as we headed around a cloverleaf and downhill toward the stadium, he surged. I simply couldn't keep up with him without my legs cramping up. Lismont surged onto the track, and I did manage to close a little bit on him during the lap and a half before the finish, but in the end I lost by 3 seconds. Ironically, my time of 2:11:16 was faster than the marathon had been run in any previous Olympics.

One of the first people I saw after I finished was Kenny Moore, who had placed fourth in the 1972 Olympics. Obviously, he knew how I felt. He tried to console me by saying, "I'll bet if you knew ahead of time how fast you were going to run today, you would have thought you'd won the gold medal." Other people have said that if I had actually broken that window at 9 miles and those guys had come after me, I would have run at least three seconds faster than I did.

I've looked back on the race many times, wondering how I could have run any better, and in all honesty I don't see it. I ran as well as I possibly could on that day. When Lismont caught me, I remember saying to myself, *I'm going to beat this guy or die trying.* But when he surged on that downhill, my legs simply would not allow me to stay with him. So I really don't think I could have run that race any faster, and that's comforting. I ran the fastest marathon of my life, set a personal best by two minutes, and I'm proud of that.

Of course years later we learned that the East German who won that race was part of a systematic drug doping program East Germany had at the time. After the evidence became public, there was some momentum to disqualify him, which would have given the gold to Shorter and the bronze to me. But so far it hasn't happened. The interesting thing about the '76 Olympic marathon was that U.S. runners were at the top of the world at the time. We expected to be in the medal hunt in any marathon. Shorter had won the gold in Munich, Rodgers was an up-and-comer, Kenny Moore had taken fourth in '72, and there were dozens of guys who were capable of running great times. We were a strong presence not only on American soil but internationally as well. There was never the feeling when toeing the line that we couldn't win.

Those were fabulous times to be a distance runner. I ran with—and against—the best runners of that era: Prefontaine, Shorter, Rodgers, Galloway, Bacheler, Moore, and many others. Prefontaine was brash and outspoken, but he always backed his words up on the track. He did not have the typical introverted personality of a distance runner. Today it's a much harder international arena for American runners. However, the beauty of the marathon is that it's unpredictable—that's its main attraction. Weather, pacing, a bad stomach, or almost anything can upset the favorite and give a dark horse the opportunity to win.

After the Olympics I returned to Spokane to teach for another year, and then I opened a running store. By then the running boom had begun in earnest, and I felt I could earn a modest living through the store while continuing to run competitively. That's about as much as I wanted at the time. It would have been nice to be a full-time runner, but there's something to be said about a runner having a real job, like Rod DeHaven and Christine Clark do. It's not easy to train and hold down a job, but at least fully employed runners don't have to rely on prize winnings for their sole support. As a result, they can be more focused on running well, and not worried about taking a chance and losing a paycheck in the process.

I guess I wasn't content to just run, either, as I got involved with the local running scene and helped launch the Lilac Bloomsday Run. What started out as a local run has turned into an annual event with 50,000 entrants. Spokane is flooded with people from all over the region and all around the world, and it's a great celebration. I also went on to be president of the Road Runners Club of America (RRCA), a group with a shared passion and commitment to running. During my tenure as president I brought with me a belief that you get more done if you're having fun. The most fun thing we did was kick off

National Run to Work Day. Clearly, it only appeals to a few people, but it has been a great success. It's like a runner's holiday. If you think about it, running is what people do in their free time, so it ought to be fun.

It's amazing to me how much the sport has changed in the years since I ran in the Olympics. Running as an activity is clearly more popular now than it ever has been in the history of the world. The biggest change I've seen is that when I started running the organizations and clubs were basically competitive in focus. Now they are much more social organizations. The typical club member is much more interested in running for fun and fitness than for competition. That's a huge shift in attitude.

I think it's likely there'll be another "golden era" for American distance runners, I'm just not sure when. Initiatives like the RRCA's Roads Scholar program, which provides grants to developing American runners, certainly help. An increase in support from the athletic shoe companies would also help. I think they should be more involved in supporting up-and-coming runners, putting more money into helping develop postcollegiate runners.

Today running is still my livelihood. I log about 40 miles a week, but I earn my income from speaking at race banquets and club functions, doing some online coaching, and writing for *Runner's World* magazine. This past fall, for example, I ran—and covered—the Marine Corps and New York City Marathons, which were a week apart. I've run about 44 marathons and try to keep myself in good enough shape that, at the drop of a hat, I can take on whatever running assignment my editors think up, and live through it. I don't run fast, which keeps me from getting injured. And I've found there is always something to write about, whether it's running a marathon in an unusual place, like Vietnam, or running under unusual circumstances, like covering the Boston Marathon while talking to people around the country on a cell phone. The running life has been wonderful. I wouldn't have done anything differently—except maybe run a few seconds faster in Montreal.

# DNF TO THIRD

**ANNE MARIE LAUCK**

**D.O.B.: 3-7-69**
**RESIDENCE: HAMPTON, NJ**
**OCCUPATION: PROFESSIONAL**
    **RUNNER**
**FIRST MARATHON: 1993 NYC**
    **MARATHON**
**AGE AT FIRST MARATHON: 24**

Photo courtesy New York Road Runners

*Anne Marie (Letko) Lauck is a racing phenomenon with a USA Track & Field biography that covers two decades of achievements and a career highlight of being a two-time Olympian ('96 and '00). Raised in New Jersey, where she currently resides with her husband, Anne Marie took up track in high school because they didn't offer base-ball, her first love, to females. Always finding support and encouragement from family and friends, as well as a competitive streak from her brothers, 12-year old Anne Marie fantasized about running a marathon after watching Joan Benoit Samuelson and Grete Waitz. Later on, her dreams also included making the Olympic team. She credits her success with always being encouraged to work hard and finding ways to improve and having the fortitude to turn her dreams into reality.*

I know I sound old fashioned when I say this but when I was young, kids seemed to be more active than they are now. I was always running around with my three brothers, riding our bikes, playing ball, walking where we needed to go. Our activities did not revolve around organized sports; it was more like tag and kick the can. And with brothers, I learned early to be competitive if I wanted to play with them. I was definitely a tomboy.

My parents were also very encouraging of our love for sports and the outdoors. If we showed an interest, they supported it. When I wanted to learn to surf I practiced first on a Styrofoam board and when they saw I was serious about it, they bought me a surfboard. My dad was the one who actually got me started with running. In 1983, when I was 14, he started jogging around the block and I tagged along to keep him company. I had never run before but he made it fun. Soon I was running on my own.

One summer afternoon while out on a run I met an older woman who was impressed that I was running and invited me to a race later that month that she and her husband were putting on, the Hampton Classic 7-miler. Honored that she noticed me and intrigued by the idea of a race, I entered my first competition. I successfully completed the hot and hilly race and even won my age division. I was hooked! A lady by the name of Lynne Lauck won the overall female division in that race. Little did I know that 12 years later she would become my mother-in-law.

In high school, I would have preferred to play baseball, as I grew up playing hardball in the Hampton community league, but females were resigned to softball only, which held no interest for me. My older brother encouraged me to try out for the cross-country team the fall of my freshman year. Little did I know that my school, North Hunterdon, was the premier running school in the state. I showed up clueless with no real running experience under my belt and struggled to make the varsity team. Some of the other freshman girls were members of the Hunterdon Harriers, a big running club in the area, and came with impressive credentials. In contrast to them, I was horrible as I had poor form and little speed. What I did have going for me was a competitive nature and the desire to improve.

I truly believe that those early years of having to struggle and work hard are what laid the foundation for my future success. In order to develop, I had to work and push myself beyond anything I had ever done before. I wanted to become the best and I was voracious in my desire to achieve my goal. After a race I analyzed my run to see how I could improve. I still do that today. I try to analyze everything because there is always something that can be done better. You just have to take the time to find out.

As I continued to improve and became more experienced in running, my family got caught up as well. I remember sitting with my entire family when I was 15 years old watching the New York City Marathon on television. Grete Waitz was my hero. I also subscribed to *Runner's World* magazine and tore through every issue. Like a baseball junkie, I learned all the stats of the elite runners. Joan Benoit Samuelson had just won the first women's Olympic marathon in 1984 and that became my fantasy.

By the end of my sophomore year in high school I had broken 11 minutes in the 3200 meters (a distance just short of 2 miles). That summer I decided to gradually increase my mileage by adding 5 miles per week until I got up to 90 miles a week. I then lowered it to average 70 miles a week for the fall cross-country season. It was amazing to see how much stronger and better I became from all those miles. I also attended a running camp organized by Pete Squires and Bill Dellinger, the legendary coach of Steve Prefontaine and Alberto Salazar, among others. There I met a woman who had a dramatic effect on me. Doris Brown-Heritage was in her 40s at the time I met her and was already a running legend, kind of like the grandmother of running. She looked like superwoman to me with her lean athletic body and charismatic attitude on fitness. I watched her jump up and grab a tree branch and knock off a bunch of chin-ups like it was no big deal. She gave a motivational talk to the camp participants and I was so awestruck and inspired by her that I asked to speak with her one-on-one in our dorm room. We spoke all about running and I revealed to her my dream to one day run in the Olympics. She told me to follow my dream and never stop believing that I could achieve this dream. After this encounter I went back home and worked even harder, both mentally and physically. I credit Doris with getting those sparks flying.

Back at school, in my junior year I went from 20th place in the state for cross- country to a solid number two. I was developing into a great runner but was haunted by always being number two. It just so happened that the number one runner in New Jersey was also my teammate. It was tough to face her every day at practice, in every race, no matter how big or small, and try to beat her. The competition between us became too intense and our initial friendship suffered in the end. This scenario kept me trying harder, though, and I was ranked All-American my last two years in high school.

I was offered close to 100 scholarships to colleges around the country for my running accomplishments and settled on Wake Forest in North Carolina. Unfortunately, that was not a happy time in my life. Plagued by injuries and a contentious relationship with the coaches, I left after two and a half years. To give you an idea of how bad it was with my coaches, when my mom was diagnosed with breast cancer they told me to shake it off, that she wasn't really sick. My mother passed away in 1995 from that horrible disease. Reflecting on that time, I think I just wasn't cut out for collegiate running. Some say I am too strong-willed and obstinate, but I believe in a mutual give-and-take relationship with a coach. I needed someone who treated me like an individual with specific needs and long-term development. Don't tell me what to do and then expect me just follow it without my input. The irony of my time at Wake Forest was that when I went home over the summers I would get healthy and strong doing my own training and would even set PRs (personal records) at local competitions. But once I arrived back at Wake Forest my performance and fitness suffered. The summer before my junior year I hooked up with a local Nike running club that was directed by Tom Fleming, a former elite runner who had won the New York City Marathon in 1973 and '75. Under his guidance I made some impressive breakthroughs with my running and racing. He was very supportive and that summer I even placed fifth in the women's national 10K road championships and ran under 34:00.

When I returned to Wake Forest again that fall the downward spiral continued as I got injured again and had to hear the same negative talk from my coaches. I decided to leave the end of that fall of my junior year, and it was a bitter split. Not only would my coaches not release me to compete for the entire next year in collegiate competitions, they continually bad-mouthed me for the longest time.

After leaving Wake Forest at the end of 1989, I transferred to Rutgers and lived at home. I continued training with Fleming and my career in running began to really flourish. I began to place high in some bigger competitions where prize money was offered. I initially gave back the money that I earned to keep my collegiate eligibility, but soon I realized that I did not want any part of collegiate running anymore. The remaining two years of college I was able to support myself running professionally. I felt proud being able to pay my tuition and make a nice living from my race earnings. The 1990s were a great time for my running. The goals I dreamed about as a 12-year old were finally coming true. I was sponsored by Nike and ran with a club instead of a college.

On weekends I flew all over the country and the world to compete and during the week I went to school to study and learn. After school I drove to workouts with my coach every day. It was not easy to follow this untraditional approach but it was definitely worth it. While in school my running career took off; I won the World University Games in the 10,000 meters, made the world championship track and field team in the same event, and was ranked second in the country at that distance. I received my BA in English from Rutgers in 1992, but my career was running.

The one piece missing from my career was running a marathon. In 1993 I told Tom I was ready and wanted to run the New York City Marathon. I had just placed eighth in the world for the 10,000 meters at the worlds in Stuttgart, Germany. Tom tried to talk me out of it, as he didn't think it was the right moment for me to move up. He also didn't think my first one should be New York City. The course is difficult and any marathon is tough on the body, so why choose one that just makes it harder? He also felt it was too high profile for elite first-timers and he worried about the press and the media having a field day with me. But I was ready and in my mind it had to be New York City.

That year the female elite lineup included Uta Pippig, Olga Appell, and Kim Jones, but that did not intimidate me. I had actually finished ahead of Pippig in the 10K at Stuttgart. The media predicted that the final miles would come down to Pippig, Jones, and myself. Confident I would win, I felt no pressure. I was excited and in top shape. I soaked it all up—the press conferences, the questions, everything.

Race day dawned warm and muggy, unusual for November in New York City. But not even that bothered me as I had done some summer training in Atlanta and at times New Jersey can be like a tropical rain forest in the summer. I stood on the start line with the other women and felt like nothing could stop me. When the gun went off, it was just awesome. Crossing the Verrazzano Bridge I wanted to run even faster but knew I had to hold back and reserve my energy for the long haul. At 5 miles my time split was 27:30 and my 10K mentality was telling me to run faster, this was too easy!

Uta took the lead and held it most of the race. Since she was an experienced marathoner I felt she knew what she was doing and that I was on track with my pace by keying off her. Everything was working for me except for one lapse—hydrating. I wasn't drinking enough fluids for such a warm and humid day. It was 71 degrees with 61 percent humidity and that eventually took its toll on the runners, including me.

Up until mile 19 I felt great. Then it hit me. A little fuzzy feeling at first, not like totally hitting the wall, but something was off and I knew it. By mile 20 my pace went from 5:30s per mile to 7 minutes. Still, I was in second place but then watched as Olga Appell literally flew by me and there was nothing I could do about it. It felt as if I was in slow motion. My legs were too cramped to work any harder. I began to panic as other runners started passing me. I made it into Harlem but was so out of it I took shelter on the steps of a church, sitting slouched over wondering what to do next. Although I was sitting on church steps, I felt like I was in hell.

I knew the course well enough to know there was only 4 miles to the finish, and I thought I could at least shuffle my way down Fifth Avenue and into Central Park. I pulled myself off the steps and did a very pathetic imitation of a run. As I entered Central Park, which is right at the 23-mile marker, my fiancé, Jim, was waiting for me with a horrified look on his face. The last time he'd seen me I was in second place, so he knew something was wrong when I didn't enter the park with the other elite women. He tried to talk to me but I was so out of I kept trying to push myself past him, convinced I could finish. I was out of my mind and shivering. We actually scuffled as I fought to keep running. As a runner himself, Jim knew I was in serious trouble so he finally dragged me off the course and got me to a hospital. I have little memory of any of this taking place. It was a horrifying end to a fantastic beginning.

It took me a long time to shrug off the wounds of my first marathon. It was humbling and embarrassing. My self-esteem took a dive as well as my confidence level. After taking a break, I went back to road racing and went on to have the best year of my career. I used my previous failure to my advantage and became a stronger person because of my will to overcome struggle. I won many very prestigious road races and these wins boosted my confidence. And against everyone's advice and warnings, I went back to the New York City Marathon the fall of 1994, and came in third. Talk about pressure! The press grilled me with questions about my '93 DNF disaster and how I expected to do better.

I did better by learning from my prior mistakes and lack of experience. I trained better, and more specifically for the marathon, and implemented some half marathons into my racing schedule. And I practiced drinking more fluids on my runs. When I finished the 1994 New York City Marathon I was so well hydrated that the first thing I needed to do was find a toilet.

I am the last American woman to finish as high as third in the NYC Marathon. Though a lot of time has passed, I have only run a limited number of marathons since 1994. In 1996 I qualified for the Olympics in Atlanta by placing third in the Olympic trials marathon and placed 10th in the Olympic marathon. Four years later I finished third again in the Olympic trials but due to some bad politics only the first-place finisher, Christine Clark, went to Sydney for the Olympic marathon. However, I placed fourth in the 10,000 and fifth in the 5000 at the track and field Olympic trials, and because two Olympic qualifiers eventually withdrew from the 5000, I was able to compete after all so my Olympic dream came true a second time around in Sydney.

I feel very blessed for what running has given me. Professionally it has afforded me with a great career that has financially supported me very well. There are many opportunities available and that makes me strive even harder to succeed. And I love what I do. Running is my passion and on a more emotional level it is a way of experiencing and understanding life. There have been countless runs where I sort out problems or dilemmas; running can be a refuge during times of personal strife. When I separate the competitive aspect of running, I appreciate running for its pure and simple art. Running is taking in life. It's an experience that is hard to put into words, but I'll try: When I am out on a run I feel as if I become one with my surroundings, with nature. Time and thought disappear and the sense of euphoria abounds. To me, an experience like this is what life is all about.

# ALL THE SATISFACTION
# WITH NONE OF THE PAIN

**JEFF GALLOWAY**

**D.O.B.: 7-46**
**RESIDENCE: ATLANTA, GA**
**OCCUPATION: COACH, WRITER,**
   **RUNNER**
**FIRST MARATHON: 1963 ATLANTA**
   **MARATHON**
**AGE AT FIRST MARATHON: 18**

*Jeff Galloway's first job after graduate school was a fourth-grade teacher in Raleigh, North Carolina. But he missed the excitement of traveling and racing so he combined his love of running with teaching and opened a running store, withdrawing his life savings to fulfill his dream. Twenty-six years later Galloway owns a worldwide company, and his books and running programs have taught tens of thousands of people to run— and enjoy—a marathon. A 1972 U.S. Olympian, Galloway has dedicated his life to his passion and dream to make the marathon accessible to people of all athletic abilities. He organized the first Avon Marathon for women, which contributed greatly to the inclusion of women in the Olympic marathon distance in 1984. He personally answers an average of 50 e-mails a day posted on his personal website, RunInjuryFree.com, from fans who follow his every word to the finish line.*

I can identify with the struggles of sedentary, overweight adults and kids, because I was one. When I was in eighth grade, my school required sports participation every quarter. Not being athletic and never having run, I enrolled in a track conditioning program. With my first run at 13, I was immediately intoxicated with a beginner's enthusiasm, the feeling that my body had vast capabilities. Of course, I tried to maximize every thrill on that first run and then had to hobble around for the rest of the week, almost too sore to move. But once the soreness diminished, I was back out there running again. I was hooked.

I was also a very average runner. It wasn't until my senior year in high school, after four years of running, that I qualified for the state high school championships in Georgia. After high school, I attended a small private liberal arts college in New England, Wesleyan University, and by coincidence my college roommate was another young runner, Amby Burfoot (Boston Marathon winner and editor of *Runner's World* magazine). Another college buddy was Bill Rodgers. I have to laugh when I look back on the Wesleyan yearbook picture of our track team. It was an auspicious beginning. I kept up my running, training harder and learning through my mistakes.

My first marathon was a fluke. I was a freshman in college and home for the year-end holiday break. I had heard that some local race directors had organized an Atlanta Marathon so I went down to check it out. A huge trophy was being awarded to the winner of the marathon, and I had never won a trophy before so I decided to enter. I really wanted that trophy. My longest run up to that time was 15 miles.

I knew that my only competitor would be an older man who was well known in the Atlanta area for being a strong, solid runner—and rumor had it that he had also run a few marathons. He was 30 to my 18 so I considered him an old-timer. I told myself that if he showed up to run this marathon I would drop out because there was no second-place trophy and that was the only reason I was willing to run the marathon in the first place.

On race day, I went to the park and didn't see him so I filled in the race entry, paid my fee and was ready. There were only 10 of us and I knew I would win so I was getting really psyched about owning that trophy. Then at the last minute a car came screaming around the corner and out popped Ken, my nemesis. Well at that point I was all ready to go so I thought I'd run up to 15 miles and then drop out. No sense running a full marathon when I wasn't going to win.

The course went through a city park, ten and a half times around. There were no water stations or aid stations back then but we did pass a water fountain and a golf shack if anyone did want a drink but that meant stopping so I don't remember seeing anyone take water. Part of the course cut through woods with no path at all. It was like running cross-country, jumping over streambeds and stone walls.

By mile 15 I was tired and as planned was ready to drop out. I passed the race director and told him I was finished but he surprised me by saying I was in first place! I was shocked. What about Ken? Isn't he in front of me? No, Ken dropped out two laps ago. With that news I kept running because I knew I would get the trophy. But I was tired and feeling pretty beat up by now. I ran another lap and when I saw the race director again I asked if he was sure Ken dropped out because I didn't want to run the entire 26.2 miles for nothing. Yes, he was sure Ken dropped out and I was in first place. The trophy was waiting for me.

By mile 20 I couldn't continue running so I took walk breaks. But I took them the wrong way! I waited too long to start walking and then had trouble picking up the pace again. It was a miserable experience. But I did finish and went home with the trophy.

I felt terrible afterward for days. It was just a horrible experience and I did everything so wrong. I didn't prepare well, didn't train properly. I hit the wall. I couldn't imagine ever running another one. But I'll tell you what—that marathon propelled me to rethink how to run distance. I decided to learn how to do it right so I could spare other people the miserable experience I had. To this day, whenever I run a marathon or hold a clinic, I think back to that run and all I did wrong and use it as an example of how not to run a marathon.

That first Atlanta Marathon continues on to this day and is held on Thanksgiving. I go back every ten years to run it and so far have never dropped below my initial time of 2:56:35, although it gets harder to do that with each new decade. I've run about a total of 119 marathons to date, three or four a year. And the last few years I have enjoyed running them more than ever because I follow my own walk-run program. Believe me, it is much more fun and rewarding to run a marathon and get all the personal rewards and satisfaction, and none of the pain!

It took me two years to get the courage up to run another marathon. I took a break from school in the '60s and took an all-expense paid trip courtesy of the U.S. Navy, where I learned how addicted I was to running. After two or three weeks pent up on a ship, all I could dream about was my first run when we entered port.

After my tour with the navy, I returned to Georgia and worked for my dad at his school, The Galloway School, as the PE coach. In the afternoons I coached distance runners at Georgia Tech and that summer won the first annual Peachtree Road Race. Years later I got involved with the organization of the race, which draws thousands of runners a year to Atlanta.

In the fall of 1970, I enrolled in graduate school at Florida State University with two missions: get a master's degree and qualify for the 1972 Olympic Trials. I teamed up with running buddies Frank Shorter and Jack Bacheler and we trained together. We spent two months prior to the trials in Frank's home state of Colorado for high altitude training at Vail. Our hard work paid off and I qualified for the 1972 Olympics in the 10,000 meters. I also ran in the marathon trial with Frank and Jack. Frank came in first. Since I already had a spot on the 10,000-meter team, I paced Bacheler through the marathon trial and then dropped back at the finish so he could take the remaining spot on the marathon team along with Kenny Moore. I became the marathon alternate. That 1972 Olympic Marathon opened the floodgates for Americans, both runners and nonrunners, when Shorter took the gold medal.

I returned to Atlanta and opened a running store called Phidippides, named after the Greek messenger-runner in 500 B.C. who was sent by the Athenian generals to deliver a message from Marathon to Athens, a distance of 25 miles, to announce they had won the battle against the Persians.

Phidippides sped the 25-mile distance and, in a now famous story, collapsed and died as he uttered, "Rejoice, we conquer."

As I look back on my career of over 121 marathons, I spent the first 20 years trying to run as many miles as I could as fast as I could. Then I spent the next 20 years trying to figure out how to run the least amount of miles needed to finish a marathon. I've come to the conclusion the second way is much more enjoyable and less prone to injury. And for the record, I have run a slow marathon and it was my most treasured. I ran with my 75-year-old father in the 1996 Boston Marathon in 5:59:48. He likes to tell folks that if I hadn't been there to slow him down, he'd have run much faster.

Progress is a matter of learning, maturing, and knowing yourself; one stage leads logically to the next. Not everyone has the same aspirations; all runners are not seeking a gold medal or a record-breaker run. Most marathon runners simply want that thrill of achievement of having conquered a seemingly insurmountable goal. The overwhelming number of first-time marathoners that swell the start line of marathons around the world do so because of the unequaled positive boost in attitude, significant stress release, and overall increase in vitality, focus, and creativity.

The key to a successful, injury-free marathon is my secret weapon: the walk break. Short walks interspersed with timed running will prevent you from pushing yourself to exhaustion and injury. And don't let veteran marathoners pooh-pooh the idea of partially walking through a marathon. Just tell them that four-time Boston Marathon winner Bill Rodgers has publicly acknowledged that he walked through his water stops at all of his Boston wins. Walk breaks allow your running muscles to recover before they get injured and also help to keep your endurance levels for those last 6 miles.

If you don't want to take my word for the success of the walk-run program, ask the thousands of people who have completed a marathon using walk breaks; some of them probably beat your best time! You'll see them out there on the course timing their walks and runs. They are usually the ones with big smiles on their faces because they are having so much fun.

Through my walk-run approach to the marathon, it is my mission to help others avoid the aches and pains, while experiencing all of the accomplishment and attitude enhancement, which running bestows better than anything in life.

# LIFE IS FOR PARTICIPATING

**KATHRINE SWITZER**

**D.O.B.: 1-5-47**
**RESIDENCE: NEW YORK AND**
**NEW ZEALAND**
**OCCUPATION: PROGRAM DIRECTOR,**
**AVON RUNNING, GLOBAL WOMEN'S**
**CIRCUIT; DIRECTOR, WOMEN'S**
**HEALTH AND FITNESS, RYKA**
**FIRST MARATHON: 1967 BOSTON**
**MARATHON**
**AGE AT FIRST MARATHON: 20**

*Every time a female runner enters a marathon, a small offering should be made to Kathrine Switzer. Through her tenacity, stubbornness, and belief that women can too run 26.2, she challenged the male bastion of the Boston Marathon that barred women from its race and helped to open its doors to women, which it officially did in 1972. Switzer then put her degree in journalism and her love for running to good use and furthered the cause for women in sports through her work at Avon and RYKA shoes. When not traveling the globe promoting women's walking and running, Kathrine can be found taking her daily run through Central Park. Among her many citations and awards for her work to advance women's sports is the Runner of the Decade commendation from* Runner's World *magazine. She was also honored as a member of the inaugural class of the National Distance Running Hall of Fame.*

When I was 12 years old I wanted to be a cheerleader. Like many pre-pubescent girls I thought if I were a cheerleader I would be popular and boys would ask me out and I would end up dating the captain of the football team. When I told my dad of my aspiration he looked at me and said, "You don't want to be a cheerleader. That's silly. Life is for participating, not spectating. The cheerleaders lead cheers. You should play sports and have people cheer for you. You like to run and be active. Why don't you go out for field hockey?" I wasn't a tomboy, but I always thought a girl could do anything a boy could so I took his advice to heart. My mother was a great role model in that sense as she did everything. She worked a professional job, cooked the meals, tended a garden, and raised us to believe there were no limitations on what we could do. My dad supported that and encouraged us to think beyond traditional roles.

With my dad's encouragement, I started to get in shape for field hockey by running a mile. No one ran on the streets back in 1959. The only runners I knew were the track and cross-country runners at school. But when I realized that running did in fact build my endurance, it became my secret weapon. I knew it would make me better at other sports. I didn't know anything about training or conditioning, but I knew that running was the key. By high school, I was up to 3 miles and felt like the cock of the walk. No girl I knew anywhere could run 3 miles a day.

I continued playing field hockey at Lynchburg College in Virginia but was somewhat disappointed in the skills and commitment of the other women. Most of them were not very dedicated to the sport and didn't care whether we won or lost. I cared deeply and played hard, taking practice and the games very seriously. After practice I would run a mile. When the coach found out she got very angry, accusing me of not working hard enough at practice if I still had the energy to run a mile afterward. What she didn't understand was that mile was my alone time, my solace. One day while I was finishing up my mile, the men's track coach approached me and asked if I would run a mile on the men's team. There was a big meet coming up and he needed another member on the team to qualify and I looked like I could do it. I had no problem with that and agreed. Well, all hell broke out when word got out that a woman was going to run on the men's team. Lynchburg was a small religious-affiliated school and I was doing something almost sacrilegious. On the day of the meet, the campus and field was swarming with local and national media to capture me, this woman who dared run with men.

The media hype made me nervous and I knew I had to do well to uphold my athletic honor. I finished the mile in 5:58 and was pleased. But I wasn't thrilled with some of the hate mail I received over the incident, telling me God will strike me dead for running with men. I learned a valuable lesson that day. I was being judged not on my athletic ability but on being a woman. It dawned on me for the first time that there would be no sports programs for me after college. Either it just wasn't done or it wasn't available. Billie Jean King had just come out as a professional woman's tennis player and there were some female golf pros, but those sports didn't interest me. Since I loved sports but didn't feel I could participate on a professional level I decided to become a sports journalist and transferred to Syracuse University in 1966.

I was still serious about my running and wanted to continue it at Syracuse. Along the way, running had evolved from being my secret weapon to my first love. It was something I could do by myself, didn't cost anything, didn't need a lot of equipment—and I loved being outdoors. I was also good at it. I knew that running was going to be a lifetime sport for me. I've often felt that if field hockey were an Olympic sport I would have stayed with it because I did love it and never would have become a runner. But those avenues were not available to women back in the early 1960s. Women today have so many choices, from soccer to basketball to snowboarding—almost anything they desire. For me, it was running.

At Syracuse I went to see the men's cross country coach and asked if I could run on the team since there wasn't a women's team. He looked at me a bit startled and said, "I've been coaching for thirty years and have never had a woman ask to be on the team. I can't let you run officially because it is against the NCAA rules but you are welcome to come and work out with us." With that, I started running with the team but was miles behind them. That's when I met Arnie Briggs, who was the postman for the university. He finished his job at 3 in the afternoon and then worked out with the team. He did this for years until finally he became the unofficial manager of the team. He was also a marathon runner and had run the Boston Marathon 15 times. When I met him he was 50 to my 19. He had a bad knee and all sorts of injuries but could still run slowly, which was faster than what my pace was. And of course, he still had the endurance for long runs. He was excited that a girl was with the team and sort of adopted me. Actually I think he felt sorry for me because as soon as the team headed out for their runs, I would lose sight of them and wouldn't know where to go. He took me under his wing and taught me about running.

In the winter when the team went indoors for training, Arnie and I stayed outside and ran in the cold and the snow. We were running 6 to 10 miles a night and Arnie would keep me entertained with stories of the Boston Marathon. He'd tell me tales of Clarence DeMar, John Kelley the Elder, John Kelley the Younger, Tarzan Brown, all the legends. I was entranced and fascinated. Finally one snowy night I said, "Let's stop talking about Boston and just go and run the damn thing." He turned to me and said, "Women can't run the Boston Marathon. Women aren't capable of running 26.2 miles. It's the law of diminishing returns." I told him he was crazy; that if I could run 10 miles, why couldn't I run 26? He *had* to believe a woman could do it, because I had read in *Sports Illustrated* that Bobbi (Roberta) Gibb had run the Boston Marathon in 1966. She hid in the bushes until half the runners had passed and then slipped into the pack. She finished but her time was not recorded as she didn't wear a race number and was not officially entered in the race. When I told this to Arnie, he was enraged and didn't believe it. I was deeply upset at his reaction. I felt our friendship was at a crossroad if he truly didn't believe a woman could run a marathon after all the training and the long runs we had enjoyed together. He thought it over for a while and said that if any woman could run the distance, he believed it was me, and if I could prove to him that I could indeed run 26.2 miles, he would personally take me to Boston.

Now I had a coach and a goal and it was all business from them on. I trained consistently and bumped up the long runs from 15 miles to 17 to 18 miles and so on. It wasn't always easy. At my first attempt at 18 miles I hit the wall. But I kept going and finally we set the day to run 26.2 miles. I was hot to trot, so excited. It was an early-April day with snow still on the ground. We mapped out about four 10K loops and as we were finishing up the last loop, Arnie turned and said, "I can't believe you are going to make it. You are really going to complete a marathon." It was such a big deal for me. All of a sudden I put on the brakes and said, "What if we mismeasured the course and we're short of 26.2 miles?" I wanted to be absolutely sure of the distance and began to doubt we had measured accurately. Just to be totally sure, I wanted to add another 5 miles. Arnie was astonished, but said if I could do it, he could do it. During the last 5 miles of this now 31-mile run, Arnie began weaving back and forth, his legs like jelly. I put my arm through his and steadied him for the last mile. Back at the car, our finish line, I threw my arms around him and slapped him on the back screaming that we were on our way to Boston, and he passed out.

The next day he came over to my dorm with the race entry form. I knew that Bobbi Gibb didn't wear a number, so I somehow thought I'd just show up and run. "Oh no," said Arnie, "Boston is a serious race, you are a serious runner, you are a member of the Amateur Athletic Union [AAU], and you don't mess with Boston. You have to do it right and officially register." I wondered if it might be against some rule, remembering that I was allowed to run in the conference at Lynchburg College but not with the NCAA at Syracuse University. Arnie had anticipated the question and had the current *AAU Rulebook* with him. The book listed "Men's Track and Field Events," "Women's Track and Field Events," and then a third category, "The Marathon," which listed nothing about gender. We laughed that nobody would think about a woman running a marathon since only crazy men ran it anyway!

The application also called for a medical certificate. In lieu of that I could have opted to have an on-site physical exam at Boston, but Arnie didn't think I'd want to stand in a hallway with a bunch of naked men getting a physical. So I went to the Syracuse Infirmary for my physical and got the medical certificate signed. Anyway, I filled out the entry, plunked down my $3 entry fee, and signed my name, K. V. Switzer.

Now, the reason I signed K. V. Switzer instead of Kathrine is that I always signed my name that way. Ever since I was a little girl I wanted to be a writer and K.V. was going to be my signature name. It seemed to my young mind then that all the good writers used their initials—like J. D. Salinger, e. e. cummings, T. S. Elliot, W. B. Yeats—so ever since I was 12 I signed all my papers K. V. Switzer, thinking I was totally cool. It was my signature.

Arnie sent my application in with the rest of the track guys from Syracuse who were also planning on running the marathon. Actually, I was the only one who had really trained. That night I went out with my boyfriend Tom Miller, who was a graduate student and a hammer thrower. He was very amused with all this and would ask me how my "jogging" was going. When I told him I was running the Boston Marathon, he fell down laughing. He said if I could run a marathon he could, too, and decided to sign up. He weighed 235 pounds but that didn't discourage him. He just felt if I could do it he could. To prove his point he went out and ran 9 miles and declared he was ready. So we all went to Boston.

The day of the race was horrible. Sleeting, snowing, windy, and cold. All the runners had on big baggy sweats with windbreakers and hoods. I wore my worst stuff because Arnie said when we got warmed up we'd throw away our old sweats and just leave them behind. As I pinned on my number, the other runners around me noticed I was a woman and got very excited and supportive. They thought it was great that a woman was going to run Boston. We all lined up to go through the starting pen and as I went through the pen, I had to lift my sweatshirt to show my number. Will Cloney himself, the co-race director, pushed me through the starting gate. More people were noticing I was female and congratulated me, all very supportive and excited for me. Arnie, my boyfriend Tom, John Leonard from our cross-country team, and I were in a little group. Our plan was to stay together for a while but if anyone wanted to split off we would meet at the finish. The race started and off we went.

Four miles into the race, the media flatbed truck loaded with photographers came through and we all had to get out of the way to let it pass. A bus followed the truck with the journalists and on that bus were co-race directors Will Cloney and Jock Semple. The photographers saw me first and started shouting, "There's a girl in the race," and then slowed up in front of us and started taking pictures. By now, I'd thrown away my top sweatshirt and my hair was flying. I didn't try to disguise my gender at all. Heck, I was so proud of myself I was wearing lipstick! When the journalists saw me, they started teasing Jock that a girl had infiltrated his race. They looked up my number and saw K. Switzer and started heckling Jock some more. "She doesn't look like a Karl," they'd say. Their bus was still behind us. I was unaware what was going on behind me as we were waving at the photographers in front of us.

Jock was well known for his violent temper. He seethed for a while, and then he erupted. He jumped off the bus and went after me. I saw him just before he pounced, and let me tell you, I was scared to death. He was out of control. I jumped away from him as he grabbed for me, but he caught me by the shoulder and spun me around, and screamed, "Get the hell out of my race and give me that race number." I tried to get away from him but he had me by the shirt. It was like being in a bad dream. Arnie tried to wrestle Jock away from me but was having a hard time himself and then Tom, my 235-pound boyfriend, came to the rescue and smacked Jock with a cross-body block and

Jock went flying through the air. At first, I thought we had killed him. I was stunned and didn't know what to do, but then Arnie just looked at me and said, "Run like hell," and I did as the photographers snapped away and the scribes recorded the event for posterity.

The rest is history. My infamous run at the 1967 Boston Marathon is recorded as unofficial and does not post a time, although it was around 4:20:00. Despite that the Boston Athletic Association wanted nothing to do with me, the fact that I ran with a number made headlines around the world. *The New York Times* reported the story but inadvertently said I didn't finish. I was furious and personally called the reporter to correct his mistake, saying, "Just because you filed your story while I was still out running didn't mean I didn't finish!" It was this incident as much as any other that made me determined to become a better runner, to prove I could also be a real athlete, as I certainly never was a quitter and even with all the dreadful stuff at Boston I would have finished that race on my hands and knees to prove that a woman could do it.

Afterward, I decided to use this experience to ensure that other women who wanted to run would not be subjected to the same treatment. I became an organizer and an outspoken proponent for women's physical capability. The first thing I did when Arnie and I got back to Syracuse was form the Syracuse Track Club and encourage women to join. We staged regular meets with full opportunities for women. I felt the most important thing I could do for women was to create the forum for their acceptance in sports.

Back in Boston, Bobbi Gibb continued to run without a number, as did the other women who were coming on the scene as well. In 1969 three women, including Nina Kuscsik, ran unofficially. I stayed away from Boston until 1970. That year, four other women also ran. This time they recorded my time, 3:34. By 1971 myself, Nina Kuscsik, and Sara Mae Berman ran Boston and afterward we united our efforts to try and force the arm of the BAA to officially allow women to run. We wanted to lift the ban in Boston as well as the exclusion of women running long distance in the Olympics, including the women's marathon.

Finally, in 1972, for the first time ever women were officially welcome to run the Boston Marathon. It was a big breakthrough—at last we could be *athletes*. After this momentous decision, I continued fighting for women's rights in sports, but for a while I moved my concentration on being an athlete to my first priority. I was 25 years old and knew I had a window of opportunity left and trained my brains out. I didn't want to get to be 40 and not have tried to go all out. I'd do a 20- or 27-miler every Sunday just to be ready for anything. Some years I did seven or eight marathons a year. Probably too much, but guess what? I got good! I went back to Boston eight times, and ran a personal best of 2:51:37 in 1975. I also won the New York City

Marathon in 1974. When I ran my 2:51 I was thrilled. I thought of the time I could only run a mile, then 3 miles, then ran my first marathon at 4:20 only five years ago and here I broke the three-hour mark. I am constantly amazed at what the human body can do. Really, I felt if I could do it on my limited talent, I thought thousands of women could do it, and they really deserved the chance to try.

And after running the 2:51, I really wanted to concentrate on making that happen. I was hoping it could become my career, too, somehow. I parlayed my journalism and writing skills with running and set out on a career in public relations and sports marketing promoting races, doing sportswriting, which evolved into doing TV commentary of running events. I also created the Avon Running Global Women's Circuit, a series of running events for women in many countries. I am most proud of this program because it led in great part to the inclusion of a women's marathon in the 1984 Olympics Games. At the same time, the Avon program and the work I do with RYKA women's sports shoes has allowed me to introduce running to women in 30 countries around the world, giving them the tools, the motivation, and the courage to run or walk a race. I've seen 400-pound women show up at a clinic with sullen faces of disbelief, wearing flip-flops, and 11 weeks later they are sporting smiles and a medal around their necks from their first race.

As an aside, Jock Semple and I became great friends. Five years after the 1967 event he had to welcome me, as well as all the women, as official competitors in the 1972 race and he was very impressed with our performances. We grew from there. For example, in the late 1970s I was invited to Boston for a book signing on a book about his life, called *Just Call Me Jock*. The promoters of the event thought it would be funny to surprise Jock during his talk by having me jump out from behind the curtains, wearing a gray sweat suit just like the one in the infamous 1967 marathon, and yell, "Get outta here, you're not official! Give me that book!" He was certainly surprised and his first reaction was to bop me but when he realized it was a joke, he joined in and enjoyed himself.

I have been lucky in life. I had my parents and Arnie telling me I could anything I wanted. As a female, I was never resigned to just playing with dolls or only being the cheerleader. Yes, I played with dolls and wore dresses but also climbed trees and played sports with a vengeance. After my experience in Boston, I realized there are plenty of women in the world who grow up without that support and without realizing the sky is their only limit. I wanted to reach those women and do something to change their lives.

All you need is the courage to believe in yourself and put one foot in front of the other."

# PART THREE

## *FIRST MARATHONS* ALUMNI
## Who Went on to Run More?

I've done a survey on the percentages of first-timers who go on to run another marathon, but it is a bit unscientific. In fact, the statistical sample is only 37, the number of people I wrote about in *First Marathons*. But it does prove something. Here are the results:

Out of 37, 30 went on run more marathons, five did not respond to the survey, and only two reported no further marathons—yet.

Not bad! Concerning the two who didn't run another: One is only 23 years old so he has plenty of time and still stays in shape by running 5 miles a day. The other is Allan Steinfeld, who has publicly stated he will run the New York City Marathon in the year 2006 to commemorate Fred Lebow's NYC Marathon run while in remission from brain cancer. Lebow was 60 at the time, and that is Allan's mark. He will turn 60 in 2006 and run his first New York City Marathon.

Some, like Richard Bellicchi, swore he would never run another; would rather skydive than run 26.2 miles. He kept running sporadically but his wife, Ellen, went on to run more marathons and one day—10 years after his first marathon—he showed up by her side at the start of the Mystic Places Marathon. He wanted to see if he could still do it. And he did.

Over the years I've heard many unique reasons for running more marathons. The main reason for running the second is to better the finishing time of the first, to prove it wasn't a fluke. Runners who had bad experiences run another to capture the euphoric feeling they missed with the first one. Others run another to try to qualify for Boston, the Granddaddy of marathons.

Once the marathon bug bites, the reasons for running numerous marathons can get quite creative. The favorite is to run a marathon in every state, like members of the 50+DC club. Another is to run 26 marathons, one for each mile of a marathon. Others have to do with years married, number of children, and so on. It can get crazy. Basically, you don't need a reason.

Do it for the sake and honor of the marathoners who can't run anymore.

Do it for Matt Shafner and Larry Smith, who loved the marathon and now are ex-marathoners, disabled with knee problems and hip surgeries. Their accounts in *First Marathons* are tributes to the fact that among the best days of their lives was their first marathon.

Do it for Erich Segal (yes, that one, author of *Love Story*). In *First Marathons* he describes his love for the marathon; he ran a total of forty before an unexpected injury prevented him from running another. He says, "I miss it. Some people dream of becoming president, wining the Nobel Prize, or flying to the moon. My own fantasy is to be running once again through the streets of Boston being cheered by that knowing, loving crowd. So the next time you are due for a workout and it is raining, windy, and freezing, and you are thinking of putting it off, count yourself lucky. Get out there and enjoy the best feeling life can give you."

# BILL BEGG:
# STILL LEARNING AFTER ALL THESE YEARS

*Bill Begg was the brash young doctor in* First Marathons *who ran his first marathon on a bet, with no training, and paid the price. Despite his pain and humiliating finish, he fell in love with the marathon and vowed to do it right the next time. He has since run eight marathons with a PR of 3:58. What keeps him coming back for more is the feeling of crossing the finish line after 26.2 miles. As he states, "It's the greatest feeling in the world."*

After my dismal experience at the Marine Corps Marathon in 1991, I signed up to run it again the following year and trained for six months. I did everything by the book, including a long run of 20 miles. But somehow, my time was two minutes worse! I attribute that to doing the 20-miler two weeks before the marathon. It wasn't enough recovery time; I entered the marathon with sore legs and never felt strong. I had visions of running a 4:30 but didn't even come close. Even though I was disappointed again, I learned something. Actually, I learn something every time I run a marathon. This lesson was about spacing the last long run at least three weeks, preferably four, from the date of the marathon.

I finally reached my goal of 4:30 in my third marathon, which I ran with my wife, Leah. It was her first marathon and I wanted her to have a great experience so I stayed steady and paced her. That made the big difference in my time. I wasn't all over the place like my other two. I also enjoyed training with Leah and we made sure to get in our long runs every other weekend.

My fourth marathon was the Boston 100th in 1996. I knew there was no way I could ever qualify so I ran for a charity. Leah wanted to run also so we both donated to a charity and started training. I wanted this experience to be my best marathon ever, so we trained like professionals. Unfortunately, three days before the marathon we both came down with a stomach virus. Leah was sicker than I was but as she recovered, I got worse. But nothing was going to keep me from this famous event and I went to Boston, sick as a dog. It should be no surprise that the experience turned out to be pitiful. I felt like I was running with a gorilla on my back and eventually hit the biggest wall of my life at Heartbreak Hill. I didn't think I would live through the experience.

I did manage to finish, but it took me over five hours. I actually thought of giving up and calling the search and rescue squad to collect me. I couldn't believe that the one time I trained so hard and so well, did everything right, I got sick. As much as I love marathoning, it never seems to go my way. It just goes to prove that the marathon can throw you a curveball regardless of the best-laid plans.

My favorite marathon was the 2001 Mystic Places Marathon in East Lyme, Connecticut. It was the inaugural run, and five-person relay teams were part of the event. Leah and I wanted to enter the family-event relay division but I couldn't get any of my brothers or cousins to do it with us so I entered our three kids, aged six, five, and two as our other team members. The plan was for Leah to run the first two legs of the marathon, and I would run the last three. We never intended for the kids to run but we needed their presence, and there was no age restriction on the application form.

Leah started out on her segments and I boarded the transport bus with the three kids to meet her at the 11-mile marker. The official balked when he saw the kids and told me no kids were allowed on the bus—but they had their race numbers on so there was nothing he could do. He actually ended up laughing as he looked at my two-year-old with her race number on and knew I had to be a nutcase. The kids were thrilled and excited to be a part of this and cheered us on. Leah and I exchanged wristbands at the 11-mile marker and I ran the remainder of the distance. I was feeling really good and strong and actually ran the last 2 miles at a seven-minute pace.

We never expected to win the family division as several other teams were entered with a full body count of five capable runners. It was just a fun family outing for us. You can imagine my shock when it was announced that we won! That made up for all those other marathons that ended in pain or humiliation. It was one of the best days of my life. For once, everything came together for us.

My best marathon was a 3:58 at Marine Corps in 1999. I love the Marine Corps Marathon and I think that had something to do with setting my PR. I have so many great memories of running that course with Leah and other cousins so it was just a matter of time before I would run well there. It is billed as the "People's Marathon" and lives up to its name.

It may sound as if I am trying to be a hotshot or a hot dog because of the seat-of-the-pants approach I take to my training and my running. But the truth of the matter is that my training takes a backseat to my number one priority, my family, and my number two priority, my job. Whatever is left, I give to the marathon. Ever since graduating from medical school, I've had to work two jobs to pay off my student loans. That was another priority, and I finally paid them off this year. I feel like a new man and have reduced my workload to one job.

I love being a doctor and wouldn't change my life for anything. You never know when it will come in handy. Recently, Leah and I entered the mixed club championships at our golf club, which is sort of like my marathoning because neither of us ever have the time to play and pretty much stink at golf. During the first round, a club member went into cardiac arrest. At the time I was on the 10th hole and ran the fastest mile of my life to reach him. By the time I arrived he was in full cardiac arrest. I administered CPR and every maneuver I could think of until the ambulance arrived. Unbelievably, the paramedic on call was the wife of the guy having the heart attack. She didn't know it was her husband she was responding to until she arrived. I stayed with him on the way to the hospital until the emergency room staff took over. He survived.

I think part of the reason I love the marathon is that I see life and death every day at the hospital. It gives me pause to reflect on what is important in life and for me, it's my family. And second, it's running the marathon. It's the greatest high in the world and I am addicted to it. No other feeling beats it. I want to capture that feeling over and over again, despite the pain, the frustration, and the lack of time for proper training. Crossing the finish line of my first marathon was the greatest thrill of my life. Of course, I feel like the luckiest man alive to be married to Leah, as she shares my passion for running.

I recently underwent back surgery for a herniated disk, and my marathon days may be over. I'm not sure; time will tell. A real thrill for me was bumping into Bill Rodgers at a race and telling him that we had something in common, that we were both in *First Marathons*. He looked at me kind of funny and asked me to refresh his memory as to what my story was about. I told him I was the guy who ran a marathon without training for it. He looked at me and said, "Well, that was an interesting and amusing story, but if you are serious about the marathon that sort of thing doesn't bode well for a long career and you risk hurting yourself if you don't change." Turns out, his words rang true.

If I never run another marathon, I will always treasure my win at Mystic for the family-relay team. While I never really thought about it, my biggest hurdle to becoming a serious marathoner was an obligation to family first. So it seems quite fitting, and ironic, that the only marathon I ever won was the "Five Beggs Relay Team." On that day I realized two goals: For one shining moment I had the feeling of a successful marathoner and was able to share it with my family.

If I never run another marathon because of my back injury, I can honestly say I have no regrets and I am blessed with all the great memories marathon running has given my family.

# ELLEN BELLICCHI: THE COMEBACK KID

When I reviewed my chapter in *First Marathons,* it was like reading about someone I vaguely knew, a girlfriend perhaps that I had lost touch with and barely recognized. I was so driven back then; driven by the clock to run fast, driven by the need to make my fitness centers successful, driven by the desire to be a good mother, and driven to be the fit, energetic woman I aspired to be. I worked myself hard in every aspect of my life. Then it all fell apart during my eighth marathon.

Since my first marathon in 1992, I was running one a year like clockwork. Same marathon, same routine. My marathon training had become part of my life cycle, like some inner clock telling me it was time to start training and get in the long runs. Anyone who knew me—family, friends, employees, neighbors, commuters I passed on my routes—could all predict what I was doing and when I would do it. If I missed a day, or changed my times, they noticed.

But that all changed in 1998. My family moved from our seaside home in Connecticut where I had lived and run for 15 years. I was still adjusting to the move to western Massachusetts when marathon training season started. I missed my familiar routes along Long Island Sound, racing the submarines, feeling the salt air permeating my senses, cool-downs in the water swimming to my raft and checking in with the neighbors who always gave me their support. We moved to be closer to our business. Professionally, it made sense. Emotionally, it tore me up inside. My running life took a turn for the worse and I was miserable and homesick. It was as if I left my best friend behind at the beach.

I never expressed my feelings to anyone. And instead of being a healthy outlet, my running took the brunt of the negativity and every run became filled with anxiety and anger. But I buried the negative thoughts and nagging sense of doubt that this marathon would somehow be different and continued training although my heart wasn't in it.

Then came the heat wave. It was unseasonably hot that summer and I don't do well in heat. I melt. My long runs were laborious and I felt sick to my stomach afterward. Nothing was going right and I attributed it all to the move. I could only hold out hope that the heat wave would diminish by the marathon. It didn't. It was already 90 degrees at the start of the marathon and I knew I was in trouble from the first mile. My breathing was labored and my legs felt encased in cement. For the next 25 miles things only got progressively worse. I was in excruciating pain and had to walk the last 3 miles after vomiting from drinking a Coke too fast. I crossed the finish line in 4:55, embarrassed, humiliated, and defeated, a loser. I vowed I was done with the marathon. Two years went by. I continued to run 30 miles a week, raced in 5Ks and 10Ks, and still defined myself as a runner. But marathons were part of my past.

Along with owning and operating a fitness center dedicated to women, I am also a personal trainer, nutritionist, and motivational speaker. I am the person who challenges, motivates, and gets my clients to set seemingly impossible goals, visualize the goal, be dedicated to achieving the goal, fulfilling the dream, and reaping the rewards of attainment and high self-esteem.

Funny thing was, I could do it for them but I wasn't doing it for myself. I wasn't facing the demons that forced me to abandon my beloved marathons. I hid behind the false claims that they had become too routine, too difficult to run in hot weather, too tough on the body. The real reason had to do with my emotional state and not accepting the fact that life moves on and whether I lived at the beach or the hills of Massachusetts should have no real impact on my desire or ability to run a marathon.

Then I met an angel. Not the kind with wings, but the real kind. I've always believed in angels and define them as people we encounter in our lives that have a profound effect on our path. This angel was actually an employee of mine, someone who knew me well, knew me as a marathoner and how much that used to be a part of my life.

We were at a 5K race and afterward she looked at me and asked why I didn't run marathons anymore. It was a simple question, and my wakeup call. My response seemed to fly out of my mouth as I said, "I couldn't for a long time but now I can, and I will."

In that moment, I ended my grieving period. I needed those two years to distance myself from that horrible experience of the 90-degree marathon and along the way accept my move. Timing is truly everything, and my angel asked the question at just the right time. Why wasn't I doing something I loved? How silly of me. How simple to fix.

Since then I have run six more marathons, sometimes two or three a year, and enjoy every one. What is different is the way I approach my marathons. I'm not running against a clock trying to finish in under four hours. I'm not sleep-deprived worried about work and enduring those long commutes from Connecticut. I am not trying to prove anything to anyone anymore. I am simply putting one foot in front of the other, breathing in and out in a steady, relaxed rhythm, enjoying the scenery, supporting my fellow runners, and thanking my angel for putting my life back on course. Of course I still miss the beach, but this is my life now and I accept it.

In running as in life, all the important lessons are learned during the training season. How I respond through that journey determines the outcome of the finish line; it will either bring joy or disappointment. Since I've come back to the marathon and settled into my new life, it has been filled with joy.

# ROB HEMMEL: A RUNNER BY DEFAULT

*Rob was always athletic, but never a runner. In 1971, a year out of college, he received a call from Uncle Sam to joint the army. He started running to prepare for the grueling week and months ahead of him, but a compound knee fracture from his high school football days resulted in a medical deferment. He kept up the running and over his career he has run 18 marathons, 80 triathlons and 40 duathlons. His last marathon was the 1992 Marine Corps Marathon.*

I used to love to run the marathon. It was exciting, a challenge, and back in the early 1980s, only the crazy, serious runners were doing them. My first marathon was the 1981 Jersey Shore Marathon. It was a different course back then and it was held in December, a freezing-cold day with high winds. More than half the field finished in under three hours. That was the goal to beat. No one did a marathon just to finish.

I finished in 3:27 and immediately knew I had to run another one to better my time. Most of my marathons were run in the '80s, before commercialism spoiled them for me. With 18 marathons behind me and a personal best of 2:53, I had nothing else to prove to myself. By the early '90s, the marathon had become a glamorous enterprise and didn't resemble the event that I loved to compete in.

It just wasn't fun anymore. People didn't race; they jogged or walked. The courses were overcrowded and the challenge wasn't the same. Basically, I lost interest.

The other aspect of marathoning that finally got to me was the amount of time and energy required for a one-day, once-a-year event. It was like putting all my eggs in one basket. One bad turn, one bad day and four months worth of training could be jeopardized.

I was also missing out on too many other things in life due to the training. Getting in the weekly miles and long runs really restricted my life. Back when I was running marathons, the standard marathon guidelines averaged 120 miles a week, which included two 10-milers on most days. I was running schedules based on Shorter and Rodgers. We didn't know anything else.

When I decided to quit the marathon, I concentrated more on my triathlons, which I was doing all along. But soon they started to become popular as well. When I started competing in the Wyckoff Sprint Triathlon, a local event sponsored by the Wyckoff, New Jersey, YMCA, there were perhaps 100 participants, all well-trained serious tri-people. Now it is around 1,000, and has become dangerous because so many untrained people are on the course—and that causes serious accidents, especially in the cycling component. So after a while I gave that up as well.

I moved on to mountain biking, in-line skating, orienteering, and adventure racing, the newest extreme sport. For me it has always been about the challenge and the adventure. Marathon training became a hassle and many of my favorite triathlons were canceled due to insurance costs or lack of organization.

What appeals to me with mountain biking, adventure racing and orienteering is the level of skill required to compete. It also requires a higher level of conditioning; it's a total-body workout. They are very technical sports. You have to know what you're doing at all times or you can be seriously injured.

Winter is now something to look forward to with my all-time favorite sport, cross-country skiing, the ultimate endurance and total-body workout. Whereas most marathoners dread the cold and snow, cross-country skiers thrive on it. Being out in the woods on a mountain trail beats pounding the roads mile after mile. There are just too many other sports that are fun and challenging to be married to the marathon.

I competed in my sixth Hartford Hi-Tec Adventure Racing series this past summer and it was both challenging and fun. Although the basic events are the same—trail running, kayaking, mountain biking, and several special tests, which are usually kept secret till race day—the race is completely different each time. For this event, the secret event was orienteering, something I specialize in. That led into a 5-mile trail run, which ended at a lake that started the next event, kayaking. Only this kayaking was to be somewhat different. One paddler had to sit backward.

Then came paintball target shooting, crossing a balance beam, stepping through "spider mazes," and then my favorite event, mountain biking. However, this too was somewhat different; it was a ride-and-tie version, meaning we could only use two bikes for the three-person team. One of us had to be running the entire time ahead. No problem, as we are all ex-marathoners.

The final mandatory obstacle is scaling the famous 12-foot military wall. Having done this before we had our act together and made it over the wall with great time. It takes team work and technique to accomplish this event.

The Hi-Tec Adventure Racing series are exhausting and thrilling at the same time. No one is ever bored or brain dead, like the feeling you get at the 18-mile marker of a marathon. The team concept makes this the exact opposite of the lonely runner.

I still run every morning and consider myself a runner. And I must admit, the feeling I got from those marathons was a better high than any other sport endeavor I've participated in. I think it boils down to the fact that a marathon is run from a completely different focus. There is no bike or body of water or any other element to content with; just the mind and body. The marathon is one rare opportunity to make such a connection.

My neighbor is training for her first marathon and I've been giving her some coaching advice. She's running the New York City Marathon, a place you couldn't drag me to even if I was still running marathons. Too crowded, to hyped up, too commercial.

Having said all that, I still think I have one more marathon in me. I'm 54, not much older than the average first-time marathoner. Right now I'm recovering from a serious cycling accident I had while competing in a 75-mile race but also training for a winter adventure race, a combination of cross-country skiing, snowshoeing, and trekking. I'm also focusing on ski racing and hope to do a ski marathon this year in Lake Placid.

If I do another marathon, it would have to be carefully selected, far from the madding crowd, and worth my return. Turning 55 would be a good goal for my reentry to marathoning. As I think ahead to the training for this marathon, my other endurance events—although tough and challenging—pale in comparison.

# TED CORBITT: A WILLINGNESS TO SUFFER

*I had the pleasure of catching up with Ted at the 2002 Distance Running Hall of Fame induction ceremonies in Utica New York. Ted was inducted into the inaugural class of 1998.*

After my first marathon, which was the 1951 Boston Marathon where I finished in 15th place with a time of 2:48:42, I not only ran another marathon, but 199 marathons and ultramarathons. I ran Boston a total of 21 times, which included two sixth-place finishes with times ranging from 2:28 to 2:53. In the immediate post-World War II period, most marathons were won with times around 2:37. It was just as tough to win then as it is now in a new century.

I was determined to become a serious marathoner after my first one. Key to my training was the belief that I needed to run 30 miles without stopping to feel comfortable running the 26.2 miles. Having reached that level of fitness, it was natural that after the marathon I would want to run more such races, and a month later I did at the national marathon championship in Yonkers, New York.

In the post-World War II years, the usual site of the national marathon championship was the Yonkers Marathon course, held in May, a month after the Boston Marathon. The championship came too close after a hard run at Boston but there was nothing I could do about that. Also, Yonkers in May can be hot. Add to that a very hilly course and you get the idea that the national championship was a grueling challenge. So it just happened that my second marathon came a month after my first. I finished 13th with a time of 2:48:58. Right after that I ran the Junior National Marathon Championship at Old Orchard Beach, Maine, finishing 10th in 2:47:28. Three marathons in three months; not a bad start to my marathon career.

My second trip to Boston, and my fifth marathon, was the following year in 1952. I finished sixth on a sun-drenched, hot 86-degree day. A month later I ran Yonkers again for the national marathon championship and the final leg of my Olympic trials, setting a personal best of 2:43:23 on that course, finishing third. Not bad considering I had a severe hamstring injury six days prior to the race. My next marathon, 15 months from taking up the sport, was the 1952 Helsinki Olympic marathon. That was not one of my best runs, finishing 44th with a 2:51:09, but it was certainly a memorable one.

The urge to run marathons and ultras was strong in me and began to define who I was. During most of my running career I was working full time and had found a way to incorporate running and training into my life by running to work. I could get in up to 30 miles on my way to work, and occasionally I repeated the distance running back home. Often I also ran at lunchtime and on the weekends which brought my weekly total up to 200 miles. Being married to a wonderful, "old-fashioned" wife was very helpful as she was supportive and took care of our son and the household while I was out running. Now that I am a widower I appreciate so much more what she did for me and the sacrifices she made. Another outlet for my running was taking on more and more responsibilities at the newly formed New York Road Runners club and promoting the "new" running boom in general. I also was very active in racecourse measurement, doing some writing, and always, always, studying my sport to see where I could improve.

Employing the principal of progression, I could run 200 miles a week for months at a time. In my quest to lower my times I did a lot of experimentation, made mistakes, and had occasional successes. There wasn't much reading material or scientific studies to rely on back in the 1950s so I had to make it up as I went along. For years I was plagued by a fear that I couldn't finish the distance. When I finally lost that fear it was replaced by another one: a fear that I wouldn't run fast enough. For me, a glorious performance was finishing in the top 10 of a major race.

Along with my walking and running and a few physical therapy patients that refuse to let me retire, I still like to review road racing courses. Back in the day when standards for measuring courses were not so meticulous, I wrote a book in 1964 on measuring road running courses and it is still used today. Elite runners choose their marathons to some part based on the winning times of the course. Throughout the world, marathon courses get a reputation for the way they are laid out and how easy or hard they are to run. Some are known as fast record makers, such as the Berlin course where Japanese runner Naoko Takahashi broke the women's marathon world record in 2001 with a time of 2:19:46. However, a month later that record was broken by Kenyan Catherine Ndereba with a time of 2:18:47 on the LaSalle Chicago Marathon course, another fast course, and her record was broken in 2002 by Paula Radcliff with a time of 2:17:18, on the same course.

Boston is known for being a downhill run on an often windblown and chilly course. On the other hand, Yonkers was known as a tough, hilly course. In fact, John Lafferty, a marathoner from Boston who ran Yonkers in 1952 said, "The guy who laid this course should be made to run it." And the New York City Marathon course, which I helped plan, is deceptively hilly.

As I look back over my career, injuries and mistakes took their toll, as did the failures and lost opportunities to score in big events. But the successes balanced it all. Looking back on all this makes me wonder why I ran in the first place and whether the bothers were worth it. I do admit I was addicted to running; it was easy for me to leave the house in lousy weather and run 40 miles.

I had an intense urge to run back then that could not be denied. If I could do it all over again, I would. And I would certainly choose to make a different set of mistakes en route.

*Ted's amazing career isn't over. At the age of 81, he walked 240 miles in a six-day race, and then bettered that distance the following year by another 63 miles: 303 miles in six days at the age of 82. Now 83, he continues to inspire marathoners and ultra-marathoners and frequently gives his comments and hard-earned lessons to neophytes of the sport. A gentleman and a scholar, he is truly in a league of his own.*

# GAIL WAESCHE KISLEVITZ: I'M TRI-ING!

*I've run 13 marathons and still love the feeling of crossing the finish line. My first 10 marathons were done for fun; I ran then with my buddy, talking and laughing for the entire 26.2 miles. The last few I've done for speed. I want to know just how fast I can run a marathon, when properly trained. I joined a running club and although the workouts are grueling, my times have come down remarkably. I've also experimented with triathlons, which I think are a great complement to marathon training.*

The orange buoy seemed so far away. Water was rushing up my nose and into my mouth, while slimy eelgrass grabbed at my legs. Someone mentioned water snakes. All around me arms were flailing and legs were kicking and the water was churned like a hornet's nest. What was I thinking? What was I doing here?

Swim, bike, run. Sounds simple. I decided to try a triathlon to break the training routine of distance running. When I asked friends who are triathletes about the event, their feedback was scattered with warnings. "The swim will kill you," they said. "Gotta have the right bike to compete," they noted. "It all takes place in the transition area," I was repeatedly told.

Nonetheless, I decided to enter the Wyckoff Triathlon. Training began in April by joining the local Y to swim, and I soon realized that knowing how to swim and swimming competitively are two different worlds. The head swimming instructor offered to give me advice. Not owning a Speedo was my first mistake. I wore my only one-piece, a little black number split down to the navel, which was very popular back in the 1980s. I was so embarassed by my own image in the mirror that I jumped into the pool and swam as fast as I could to just get it over with and get the heck out of there. I was totally out of breath after four laps. The instructor was polite enough to pull me over and say, "It would help a lot if you breathed while you swam. That, and practice is all you need. And a new suit wouldn't hurt either."

On to the biking. My trusty Trek, although a hybrid and not a road bike, would have to do as I was not about to spend a small fortune on a new one. Having competed in a few duathlons (bike/run), I figured I didn't need all that much training on the bike. A few practices on hills and speedwork and that would be fine. Wrong! What I didn't realize is that most triathletes are serious bikers; it is their main event. A week before the triathlon I rode the course for the first time with my friend and veteran tri-girl Lisa Swain, who usually places in her age division and has a racing bike. No matter how hard I worked, I could not keep up with her. Sorry, but Lance Armstrong is wrong.

It *is* about the bike! My hybrid would do me in. So with a week to go I borrowed (gasp!) a racing bike that was so totally different in all aspects I had to be crazy to use it. But I practiced every day and finally felt comfortable although every once in a while I grabbed the gears instead of the brakes.

Running was going to be my pièce de résistance. But I was warned that after the half-mile swim and 15-mile bike course with killer hills I'd be a bit wobbly on the legs when I started the run. It takes a few minutes for the body to adjust to running after the biking; the blood has to recycle itself to the areas where it is needed, so starting out too fast can cause the wobbles and a dizzy sensation.

Putting it all together was the tough part. Waking up at 5:30 on tri-day to a dull sky and drizzle was not the best way to start out but I was psyched. And nervous. And a bit scared. The gym bag was packed with all the necessary accoutrements of the trade: swim goggles, earplugs, wet suit, the red swim cap issued by the event to distinguish all females, Vaseline to get the wetsuit on and off, bike socks and shoes, helmet, sunglasses, race number attached to the bike, bike/running shorts, running socks and shoes and race number for the running event, a towel, dry clothes for afterward. All that and I almost forgot the bike. Wore the Speedo underneath everything. Laying out the transition gear is an art in itself and I looked around for tips, copying what I saw. Don't want to waste minutes searching for stuff; just grab and go. Decked out in a wetsuit, red cap, and goggles, I stood on the beach with the other women and began to get the first set of doubts. They were complaining about being sandwiched in between the first wave to hit the water, men 30 to 40, followed by the third wave, men 20 to 30. "They'll swim right over you," the women warned. "They're animals," another said. The gun went off and I found myself propelled into Indian Trails Lake following frantically moving bodies. I floundered, unable to catch my breath or get a pace going. A lifeguard floating on a surfboard asked if I was all right and to be totally honest, I wasn't sure myself. He said, "Instead of just floating there why not start swimming? If you get in trouble I'll come get you." With that piece of well-put wisdom, I started swimming and finally caught up with the madding crowd. I thought of my dad who taught me to swim. He passed away three years ago from lung cancer but I somehow felt he was with me out there, encouraging me.

Back on the beach, I ran while stripping off the goggles, cap, and wetsuit and headed back to the transition area. Panic set in yet again when I forgot where my bike was. Five hundred bikes somehow all began to look alike. Running up and down the racks like a loony bug, I was screaming to no one in particular, "Where is my [expletive] bike?" Precious minutes flew by. Why didn't I use some sort of identifier like a balloon or pink boa attached to it as some savvy participants did? A group of women already saddled up and ready to leave acknowledged my panic and took a few seconds to help locate the bike for me. On went the helmet, running shorts pulled over the wet Speedo, socks, bike shoes, and sunglasses.

Once on the bike I began to relax until word filtered back that the lead male biker had been hit by a car and taken to the hospital. It didn't help that the roads were slick from the rain. Not a natural-born speed freak, I did my best and rode smart. At mile 13, a wicked hill dubbed "The Beast" is straight and high at a time when the legs are down and out. Warned to shift into low gear before the sharp curve leading into the hill, I did just that but instead of low gear I accidentally shifted into high and couldn't pedal. Knowing I would fall off the bike, I took the smart approach to the situation and went back down the hill, shifted properly, and started over again. Meanwhile the other bikers were yelling out, "Hey, you're going the wrong way. You have to go up the hill!" More seconds wasted but at least I could pedal. Back in the transition area, off went the helmet, shoes, and socks, and on with the running shoes and socks. Quickly I pulled up the Calvin Klein underwear waistband with the running number already attached and shaved off a few seconds not fumbling with safety pins, a tip from my friend Rob Hemmel, another Tri-vet. Calvin and I raced out of transition and I was so glad to finally be doing something I was good at I could have kissed the ground—but that would have taken up more precious seconds, and I had already wasted several minutes with mistakes so far.

The running course wasn't so bad and I was actually passing people. While running, I focused on my friend Toshi D'Elia who at that very minute was running a marathon in Minnesota trying to break the world record in her age division, 70 and over. If she could run a marathon and attempt a world record at age 70, I could finish my first triathlon. She humbles and inspires me.

Crossing the finish line was thrilling because it meant the trying ordeal was finally over. Friends and families were congratulating the finishers, all soaked with sweat and still wet from the swim but wearing big smiles. After packing up my gear, I walked down to the beach again and took a look at the orange buoy. It didn't look that far away anymore. Next year it will be a piece of cake.

Triathlons can be fun if you work out the kinks and don't make as many mistakes as I did. It's easier than running a marathon, more exciting than swimming laps, and a good way to shake up the monotony of the gym routine. Taking it step by step, it's not as daunting as it may seem from a distance. Anything is possible if you just give it a try.

# MATTHEW SHAFNER: MISSING IT

*Matt will always be a marathoner at heart, even though his knees put an end to his running. He still volunteers at races and loves to reminisce about his glory days of running 26.2 miles.*

My first marathon, when I was 45 years old, took me 4 hours and 20 minutes to complete. I realized that by running a marathon I killed an entire day and decided that I would never even think about running another marathon—a resolve that lasted for all of 24 hours before I started calculating how I could improve my time.

September of the following year I was invited to participate in the Triennial World Congress of Pathology in Jerusalem to lecture on the legal aspects of asbestos disease. I realized I would miss the chance to run the East Lyme Marathon again (now the Mystic Places Marathon) so I signed up for the Ocean State Marathon in Rhode Island, scheduled for the end of November. With that accomplished, my wife Denise and I headed off to Israel and Egypt. The running gear was packed, as I had to keep to my training schedule. And it was pretty exotic training! The constant hills of Jerusalem reminded me of the "Run Around the Block" 15K on Block Island, Rhode Island, which I have done a few times. The hills presented quite a morning workout.

While running the hills, I was joined by a member of the professional Israeli rugby team who was a strong runner. He was an MIT graduate who became a hairdresser in Israel. A few days later while on a tour to a kibbutz near the northern border of Lebanon, I ran with an Israeli who spoke no English. My Hebrew wasn't so good either so we communicated in French as he was from Morocco. I learned that he was an auto mechanic on vacation with his family and wanted to get in his daily 6-mile run. My final run in Israel was in Tel Aviv, along the Mediterranean, which was flat as a pancake, a relief after the hills of Jerusalem and the Lebanon border.

In Egypt we stayed at the Mena House Hotel just below the pyramids of Giza and the famous Sphinx. What a thrill it was to float in the lake-sized pool and look up at the Great Pyramids. In the morning, I ran to the pyramids and beyond on a dirt road through the desert to a small village about 4 miles out. On the outskirts of the village stood an armed guard. We smiled at each other and then he pointed to my sweat-drenched tee shirt, then to his armpit, and finally to end this game of charades held his nose. I don't speak Arabic but I certainly understood this universal gesture and smiled at him. As I ran back toward the pyramids we parted with the only word of Arabic I know, *sukra,* which means "thank you."

Halfway back to my hotel I came across two armed soldiers in combat boots carrying rifles. They strode down from the dunes and began to run alongside me. One was my age and the other much younger. We ran about a mile together when the older man stopped but the younger one kept pace with me, eventually picking up the pace and running faster. Soon we were sprinting full out and it dawned on me I was in a race. It struck me that with no ability to talk to one another and having an armed soldier behind me and one at my side, I had to find a way out of this in a diplomatic fashion. Deciding that discretion is definitely the better part of valor, I brought the race to an immediate halt and started to communicate though body language. Pounding my chest and gasping for air, I made it clear that I was out of breath and he had won the race. He smiled and I extended a handshake to the clear victor, combat boots, rifle, and all and said, "*sukra.*"

My next Egyptian run took place in Luxor. We stayed in a hotel beside the Nile. I was met by a boy around 14, who in his caftan and bare feet ran beside me. We smiled at each other and exchanged mutual "*sukras.*" It dawned on me that my sneakers probably cost more than his family earned in months. This thought gave me pause and I soberly reflected on the disparity of wealth in our two societies.

When I returned to the states I continued to train for my marathon. A few of my buddies, Bill Sanford and Peter Ledger, helped me out on some 20-milers. Without them I don't think I could have made it.

November 1, 1981, was a cloudy day with temperatures in the 50s; perfect marathon weather. Denise and I drove to Newport and parked near Fort Adam, a mile from the start. The Ocean State course was a 6-mile loop followed by two 10-mile loops overlapping each other though the town. The course took us past the great Victorian mansions along Bellevue Avenue, past the Tennis Hall of Fame, through historic downtown Newport, past Fort Adam, and along the rocky Atlantic coastline. It was a beautiful course.

It was a fun time and an easy run. I've never enjoyed a marathon more. I kept a nine-minute pace and finished in 3:56 without any aches or pains, as opposed to my first marathon where I could hardly move afterward.

My third marathon was the 1982 Boston Marathon where I ran as a "bandit," along with the doctors, who are not required to qualify. I knew I was in good company if anything went wrong!

I ran a total of eight marathons and would have kept running them forever but in 1997 I developed severe pain in my left knee. X-rays confirmed a bad arthritic condition. The cartilage cushion that separates the femur from the tibia had narrowed. If I kept running, I would end up with a knee replacement. I decided it wasn't worth it and gave up my marathons.

My last marathon in East Lyme in 1996, I started off with my friend Peter Pantelis, who was then age 73, ten years older than I. He lost me going up the steep hill at mile 4. I finally caught sight of him again at mile 24, and I came up behind him at mile 25. I said, "Hey Peter, lookin' good." He glanced at me and then sprinted 25 yards ahead. I caught up with him again at mile 26, but he sprinted again onto the track and the final tenth of a mile. I tried to catch him a third time, but I had nothing left. I wondered what in the world we were doing—racing at our ages to see who would finish in 150th and 151st place, neither of us breaking four hours. What is this competitive spirit that could grab two senior citizens and push them to some ultimately meaningless win? Win what? Peter and I often laugh about it now. Now that I no longer run, friends encourage me to swim or bicycle or row. Such activities are great aerobic exercises, but they just don't appeal to me—maybe they don't allow for enough social interaction. Walking does—but I still miss running every day. Walking is just not the same. The endorphins simply don't get moving the way they used to. And when a runner blows by me while I'm walking, I say, "Lookin' good" and think about whether I could have done as well in my prime.

I continue to walk 4 miles a day but it isn't the same. It will never be a replacement for running in my life—but when I compare myself to others, I feel fortunate to be able to walk.

# LARRY SMITH:
# MARATHONS TO METAL DETECTORS

*It would have been hard to top Larry's first marathon, the 1978 Athens Marathon —which follows the legendary course of Phidippides—but he did by running another 25 marathons in his career. Unfortunately, two full hip-replacement surgeries ended his running career, and instead of running through airports to catch flights for his international business, he sets off metal detectors instead. Larry adjusted badly to being a non-runner, but is beginning to come out of his funk.*

I ran 25 more marathons after Athens for a total of 26. I ran 19 in the USA, including New York City 11 times and Boston 4 times. I ran three in England (two Londons and one in Rugby) and one each in Brazil, Germany, and Turkey. The most unusual was the Istanbul marathon. It resembles NYC in that you start at one end of a dramatic suspension bridge, only this one connects two continents, not two boroughs of NYC. You start in Asia,cross over to Europe, head out along the Bosphorus toward the Black Sea, turn around and go back to finish in the main stadium in Istanbul. In addition to the 26 marathons I ran 163 other races of distances from 2 to 20 miles. Never ran longer than a marathon, however.

You ask if the glory and glow of the first marathon stayed with me. I'm happy to report it did. I loved running, I loved racing. Only during one period in the middle of my career, when I let myself get out of shape, and at the end when various body parts started failing me did I find it hard to run and race. Running did not change my life but it gave me enormous pleasure and focus. I ran my last marathon in 1996 at the 100th Boston. Fittingly enough, Cedric Grant, who ran my first with me from Marathon to Athens in 1978, was also with me this time as we did the equally famous route from Hopkinton to Boston. I did 3:59 in my first marathon, got my time down to a personal best of 3:03 in the 1981 Boston, and did 5:53 in this last marathon. I walked almost half the distance. I probably should not have entered that particular race but I knew it would be my last marathon. Since I had started in Marathon I figured that ending in Boston, indeed at the 100th Boston, would be a fitting way to close out my career as a marathoner. My knee had already started to go by then and I could not meet the qualifying time. So, when I did not win a lottery entry I had to figure out some legal way to get in. I wanted a place in that race so badly that I joined a running club in Geneva, Switzerland, that had guaranteed entries to the race. I had to pay for an airline ticket I did not use but I did get a legitimate entry number. By the way, I carried with me the same two medals (St. Christopher and St. Michael) that I wore in all my other marathons and mentioned in your first book. I pinned them to a baseball hat on which was embroidered LARRY: BOSTON OR BUST. My two children had given that to me about a year before the race. I retired the medals after the race. First a knee and then two bad hips ended my running career. I have now had total hip-replacement surgery in both hips and I set off airport alarms everywhere. While many kinds of nonimpact athletic activity is permitted and in fact encouraged, running with artificial hips is forbidden. I know that's true because I've sought not just a second, but a third, fourth, fifth, and sixth opinion on that issue. My running days are over. I ran for 28 years and entered races for 22. I never won a race outright but I did win a few age-group trophies and I got to run in great places and meet wonderful people. I adjusted badly to being a nonrunner. When friends learned I could run no longer they would say things like, ". . . But you can swim and bike and walk and go cross-country skiing. There's lots of things you can do." And I'd tell them that if I wanted to swim or bike or do any of those things I would have been doing them the last 28 years and not running. If I could not run, I would not do anything. The result was predictable. I put on 20 pounds and became not only a nonrunner but a nonathlete. I am gradually coming out of that particular funk. I took swimming lessons last year and I also bought books on race walking techniques and training. I find fast walking an acceptable, though not exciting, substitute for running. In fact, I'm now aiming to walk a marathon, only now my goal is no longer to stay under four hours, but to get home under five.

# RAY STEFFEN: NOT YET!

*Ray was the youngest marathoner profiled in* First Marathons. *He ran his first marathon at 19 while still in college. He did well, but it was a tough run. He felt the pain and struggled to finish. He immediately fell asleep in the reunion area and awoke to a bloodstained shirt from bleeding nipples. He hasn't run another yet, but his marathon was definitely a highlight in his young life.*

I haven't run another marathon yet, but I do like to run races and compete in the 5K and 10K. I also run 5 miles a day to stay in shape and that's largely due to the marathon training that got me into this thing in the first place!

I look back on the marathon in awe that I actually did it. I count it as an important accomplishment to be able to complete such an extreme event. Because of that experience, I ended up doing a cycling trip across the country with two college buddies. We cycled from Connecticut to California and I noticed lots of similarities between the two events. There was never a doubt that I could do it because I ran a marathon!

The training was just like a marathon. I had to follow a schedule to get my miles up so I would be comfortable cycling many miles a day. Other similarities included reading up on what to expect from the journey, eating properly, stretching at the end of a long day's ride, and finally the satisfaction of accomplishment after a physically grueling endurance event.

Someday I'll run another marathon.

# PART FOUR

## ADVICE AND SUPPORT

## CHOOSING YOUR FIRST MARATHON

According to USATF, April is marathon month across the country and the world with big-time marathons in Boston, Big Sur, London, Rotterdam, and Paris, to name just a few. But the largest marathons are clustered around October and November, such as Chicago, New York City, Marine Corps and Twin Cities. With over 300 marathon courses in the United States alone, it can be overwhelming for a first-timer to select just one. The obvious factors involve the weather (spring or fall marathon), travel (drive or fly to the marathon), cost (travel, lodging, meals), and size (large with crowd appeal or small with no hassles).

Trying to get into the more popular events such as the New York City and Marine Corps Marathons presents its own wild card. Some runners actually apply to two or three marathons as a backup in case they don't make the lottery of their first choice. Beyond that, you can go crazy looking up the flattest course, the fastest course, altitude settings, crowd factor, course beauty, celebrity sightings, best organization, best postrace food and T-shirts. And there's the Boston factor. If you want to try to qualify for Boston, you should make sure the course you are running is a USATF-certified course. The Boston Athletic Association, the host organization of the Boston Marathon, has a website (www.baa.org) with a list of the certified courses and qualifying times.

There is a good reference book that can help you make your decision. It's called *The Ultimate Guide to Marathons,* by Dennis Craythorn and Rich Hanna. It is full of the information runners crave such as the fastest course (Berlin for international, and Pittsburgh, Houston, Grandma's, and Chicago stateside), most scenic (Big Sur), and a section that ranks the top 20 marathons for first-timers and accompanying criteria on the appropriateness of the marathon for first-timers, such as crowd support.

Also see the excellent website, **www.marathonguide.com.**

A starting point could be the four to six months you will need to set aside for training. If you live in a geographic section of the country where winter conditions bring cold and snow, training through those conditions and the accompanying ice and windchill factors can make those long runs miserable, and dangerous. Fall marathons are popular because the training occurs during the spring and summer. Having said that, summer training can be brutal—but at least there isn't the ice factor, and you can always get up early to beat the sun.

The ideal strategy is to match your training weather as close as possible with that of the marathon. CM Jenkins realized too late that the Country Music Marathon, in Nashville, Tennessee, would have a different type of weather than he trained in. "I did not realize that Nashville would be a weather change for me. All my long runs were done on cool days in the early spring. I didn't realize until too late that it's always hot in Nashville. I didn't prepare for running in the heat."

The next important decision is size. Most first-timers go for the big ones, with New York City and Chicago having the largest numbers of finishers, both exceeding 25,000. Don't underestimate the allure, and importance, of crowd support. It's nice to know your friends and families will be waiting at the finish, but you'll also need some cheering and reassurance that you aren't dead yet for the other 26 miles. David Lavalle realized this too late when he chose the Ocean State Marathon (which was his backup when he didn't make the New York City lottery). "During miles 22 to 25, there were no spectators. Gone were my cheering fans, my rock, my foundation for getting through this journey. I felt abandoned and lost and miserable."

Jen Sage and Richard Friedrichson selected marathons close to home and on the smaller size. For Richard, who lives in Nebraska, traveling to Lincoln for the Lincoln, Nebraska, Marathon with an average number of 1,300 participants was big enough. "This was all so new to me. I was in complete awe that a marathon would draw this many people." Jen, from Virginia, wanted to bring her family so she chose the Virginia Beach Marathon close by and they all piled in the car and went to Mom's marathon.

Whether you travel by car or plane, packing creates another layer of anxiety, as there is no going back for forgotten items. You also have to pack for all types of weather. The forecast may call for sunshine but you could wake up to rain. It may be 40 degrees at the start but 60 degrees midway. Pack enough layers for all types of conditions.

If you need a hotel, make sure it is located close to the start of the marathon and all the marathon activities, and that you book well in advance. Even if you are lucky enough to choose a marathon in your backyard, be prepared for extreme traffic—as Dale Chrystof, a native of Chicago, found out the morning of the Chicago Marathon. "As I drove to the race on Lake Shore Drive, following the instructions from the race brochure, the exit I was supposed to take was closed due to the marathon!"

With marathons becoming more popular and mainstream, race organizers are catering to the entire family. Because of this trend, a new category of marathons has emerged, the Destination Marathon. The Walt Disney World Marathon is probably the consummate family marathon, as there are enough activities, fireworks, rides, and amusements to keep the family entertained while you are off running 26.2 miles for four or five hours. They won't even know you're gone! The Rock 'n' Roll Marathon organization (www.rnr-marathon.com) has also seized the new trend and markets their marathons as a combination of running and entertainment, with 2,000 cheerleaders and 40 bands lining the course and a postrace rock concert with headliner groups.

There's something to say for small, hometown marathons where everyone knows your name and there isn't the jousting of 30,000 other runners. The Steamtown Marathon in Pennsylvania, the Hartford Marathon in Connecticut, and the Napa Valley Marathon, all with about 1,000 finishers, have their fans and supporters and a growing number of runners who are attracted to their friendly, hands-on attentiveness. Robert Sawyer chose the Napa Marathon after conquering the Los Angeles Marathon. "I chose the Sutter Home Napa Valley Marathon because of its beautiful scenery and the fact that it is billed as low-key."

No matter what marathon you choose, do your homework. Check out the website to view the course. Is it a point-to-point? At what mile does any elevation occur? Are there adequate water and aid stations? Do you have to be bused to the start and if so, what time do the buses leave? Where is the family gathering site? Is there a baggage claim area (necessary for point-to-point courses so that your baggage arrives at the finish)? What were the race-day weather conditions for the past few years? Some marathon websites have virtual tours so you see the entire course. And finally, keep in mind that race brochures are designed to entice you to enter, so they may overlook a few details or create pretty sentences to disguise the real facts. *Rolling scenic hills* can most likely be interpreted as "killer hills."

As you run more marathons, mix it up. Some marathoners choose to run the same course ad infinitum. It's familiar. They get comfortable. But if you are going to invest in marathons, it really is fun to try different courses, big and small, far and near. It adds to the excitement and brings some novelty back into the picture.

And speaking of pictures, a finish-line photo is a must for the first marathon!

# WHAT TO PACK IN THE MARATHON DUFFEL BAG

Start making a list of all the items you want to bring to the race a few days in advance so you won't forget any details in the a last-minute packing frenzy. Include the following must-have items: dry socks, warm-up pants and jacket, a dry shirt, a skullcap (helps retain body heat) band-aids (for those postrace blisters), flip-flops or other comfortable slip-on shoes (more comfortable after the race, especially with those blisters), ibuprofen, a camera, a protein-packed snack (think Power Bar, apple, banana, trail mix), a sportsdrink (keep hydrating all the way home), and a face towel (26.2 miles of grime and sweat isn't pretty).

Body glide is something to consider if you tend to chafe anywhere. It's better than Vaseline and a heck of a lot easier to apply. And men may want to consider Nipguards. Male nipples do bleed, and it can be painful. If you don't believe it, just watch the finish line of a marathon and see the bloodstained shirts go by on the men.

You may want to carry a few extra dollars with you for taxi, subway, or bus fare. After finishing the New York City Marathon one year with no ride home, I hopped on a bus before realizing I had no money at all, not even exact change. The bus driver took one look at my race number and let me ride for free. But just in case this doesn't happen in every city, have some spare change.

Lastly, make specific plans with your family and friends for a reunion area. Most of the larger marathons like New York City have established family reunion areas with instructions on how to get to them.

## WEATHER AND THE MARATHON

When it comes to running marathons, the one thing you can't control is the weather. Too many runners waste energy worrying about weather conditions. If you are physically and mentally prepared to run a marathon, the weather should not stand in your way.

According to Lewis Maharam, M.D., medical director of the New York City Marathon, the ideal conditions for a marathon are cool—no warmer than 55 degrees—calm, and overcast, with little or no precipitation (though a light rain can actually help on a warm day). Most major marathons are scheduled for the spring or fall, when such conditions are most likely to prevail—though of course, that's no guarantee that they will. The Boston Marathon, scheduled for mid-April, has seen snow squalls, temperatures ranging from the 30s to the 90s, and severe winds. In 1939 Boston took place in the middle of a nor'easter with a partial eclipse of the sun. The 1976 race has been nick-named the "Run of the Hoses" as the extreme heat had spectators along the route hosing down the sunbaked runners. World-class marathoner Toshiko D'Elia remembers standing at the start line of that race alongside legendary Dr. George Sheehan, who told the crowd, "Be careful out there. The heat can kill you."

Sheehan's warning was actually quite correct. Hyperthermia, when the body temperature rises to over 102 degrees and can't cool down, is a risk to runners. The body accumulates too much heat, which can result in cramping, nausea, fainting, and even fatal heatstroke. During the 1998 East Lyme Marathon in East Lyme, Connecticut, the temperature rose to 90 degrees, despite the fact that it was late September. More than a few runners took a cool dip in Long Island Sound, which borders the course. A 70-year old man finally made it to the finish, only to collapse with heart failure. An ambulance was already there but he wouldn't get in until he received his finisher's medal. He survived, but only because he received immediate treatment.

Another sign of hyperthermia that is sometimes ignored is an increase in sweating, which leads to a decrease of body fluids that can't be replaced. Runners should start every race, regardless of the weather, fully hydrated and drink one cup of sports drink every 20 minutes. It's also a good idea to con-sume extra salt before a marathon to maintain the body's sodium levels, which assist with fluid balance.

Running in the cold, wind, or snow can bring on the opposite problem—hypothermia, when body temperature drops too low. Staying warm while run-ning cold can be a challenge, especially if it is cold, windy, or wet—or worse, all three. Runners who walk for prolonged periods of time in the cold without the proper clothing are especially at risk for hypothermia, as are runners with low body fat.

Wearing layers of warm clothes that can be tossed or tied around the waist as the run progresses and body temperatures rise is the best way to go. At the end of a long run or race make sure to have warm clothes available to change into. This is especially important at mega-marathons like New York City, Chicago, or Marine Corps, when it will be some time before you get back to a place where you can shower or bath. Make sure your family or friends who are meeting you in the reunion area have a duffel bag filled with warm clothes including a skullcap, gloves, and fresh socks.

Don't think that bad weather will cancel your marathon. It won't. The race must go on. According to USA Track and Field, no major marathon has ever been canceled due to bad weather. Even the 2001 Antarctica Marathon, though postponed due to 100-mile-per-hour winds, was ultimately run—around the deck of a ship!

Race directors do their best to safeguard runners from extreme weather.

Carey Pinkowski, race director of the LaSalle Banks Chicago Marathon, moved the date from late October to Columbus Day weekend to avoid the freezing temperatures that can descend upon Chicago later in the season. One year saw snow and temperatures in the 20s on the day of the marathon before it was moved up. Race directors also work closely with their medical directors and the emergency services crew to make sure the team is equipped to handle extreme weather conditions.

Runners can do a number of things to ensure a safe and healthy run. Keep in mind that predictions aren't always accurate (which can work in your favor as well as against), so arrive at the race prepared for any type of condition. Even if it is 80 degrees at the start, bring a pair of warm-ups for afterward. A summer squall is usually accompanied by severe dips in the temperature. Consult past race-day conditions (usually available on the race website) so you have an idea of what to expect.

If possible, try to train in all types of conditions. Don't stay indoors on a wet day. Go out and experiment; it won't seem so scary on race day if you've done it before. Train in the heat as well, even if you have to go indoors and run on a treadmill.

As far as clothing for a marathon, the number one rule is to avoid cotton. Save that new marathon cotton T-shirt for after the race. Cotton retains moisture, resulting in cold, clammy skin on cool days and possible overheating when it's warm.

And finally, always experiment with any kind of sports drink *before* the day of the race. Don't end up like a number of other first-timers vomiting on the sideline from gastro problems brought on by bars, gels, goos, and drinks that react badly in your stomach. This is no time to fool with the gastrointestinal system. It will get you in the end!

# THE THREE STAGES OF THE MARATHON

## BY RICHARD BENYO, JONATHAN BEVERLY, AND MARK CONOVER

*This essay originally appeared in the September-October 1998 issue of* Marathon and Beyond *magazine, a bimonthly publication for long-distance runners: www.marathonandbeyond.com. Reprinted with permission from 42K(+) Press, Inc.*

"The marathon," Frank Shorter once said, "is half over at 20 miles." Serious marathoners agree that the marathon begins as a diehard race at the 18- to 20-mile point; the journey to that point is just that: a journey to a battlefield where the runner confronts the remaining distance and his or her own soul.

Although what occurs after 20 miles is of extreme importance to the outcome of the race, the condition in which you arrive at the battleground has a profound effect upon the outcome.

If you consider the physiology and tactics of marathoning, the race breaks down into three segments:

1. The start to roughly 7 miles: Find your pace; set your position; warm up the muscles, lungs, and mind; hold yourself in control.

2. Miles 7 to 18: Usually the smoothest portion of the marathon, where your deep muscles are warmed and you establish a rhythm, and where it is easy to "blow up" by running how you feel, because you usually feel good through these miles.

3. Miles 18 to the finish: Dig down and go for it.

Three sub-three-hour marathoners run you through the three stages of the marathon, and it is no mere coincidence that as you move from stage 1 to stage 2 to stage 3, the lower the writer's PR.

# SECTION 1: MILES 0 TO 7
# PACING IS EVERYTHING

## BY RICHARD BENYO

There are essentially three things a runner needs to know about approaching a marathon:

1. You cannot run what you have not practiced during the build-up to the marathon. Certainly, the excitement of the race situation pumps you up to the point that you can potentially run the best race of your life, but that which has not been practiced beforehand cannot be applied to the race.

2. There is no such thing as a "bank" into which you can deposit time and

miles in the early going that will deliver dividends in the final miles. Actually, the opposite is true: Go too fast too early and you're guaranteed to be bankrupt by the end of the race.

3. The secret to running a successful marathon is summed up in one word: pace.

My favorite story about the converse of good pacing comes via Derek Clayton, the fierce Australian who held the world's marathon record for 14 years: 1967-81 (2:09:36, set in Fukuoka on December 3, 1967, and 2:08:34, set in Antwerp on May 30, 1969). It was the early miles of the 1969 Antwerp Marathon, in which Clayton would break his own world's record. He went into the race with the idea of going very fast, and he went out of the blocks that way, but very much under control. As he went through the 10K split in 30:06, there was an unfamiliar Kenyan with him. Clayton turned to the runner as they sped along. "Do you know what your best 10,000-meter time was?" Clayton asked.

"Well, that's it," the unfamiliar runner replied.

Clayton laughed.

"You've got to be in it to win it," the runner said, defending his strategy.

"Well," Clayton finishes the story, "he wasn't in it for long, I can tell you."

One of the most common laments I hear about pacing, or rather, about the lack of pacing, is this chestnut: "I run like I feel. I've never been able to run an even pace."

Of course, that attitude is ridiculous. "Can't" and "won't" are two entirely different concepts. Running an even pace takes self-control and discipline. If you can be disciplined enough to put in the miles needed to race a marathon, you can call upon that discipline to learn even pacing. The concept of even pacing isn't an alien thing.

Arthur Lydiard, the father of successful modern distance running, lists proper pacing among the 11 essential factors needed for a runner to reach racing potential.

Joe Henderson, currently West Coast editor of *Runner's World* and in 1970 (when he said this) editor of that magazine, put it this way: "Generally, it's pace that kills, not distance."

"I'm pretty sure one's best race times are achieved as a result of even pacing," Bill Rodgers says. "If I've had any success in racing, this is one of the major reasons why. In my training and in my racing, I've tried to run at a steady, rhythmic pace."

"A factor in marathon racing that is of supreme importance is the even pace," says Manfred Steffny, editor of the German running magazine *Spiridon*. "In no other sport will you gain so much from an ability to apportion your energy carefully. Poor pacing is disastrous; usually it takes the form of going out too fast."

Jon Anderson, the 1973 Boston Marathon winner, puts it this way: "If one is to race effectively, he must realize what pace to begin the race at—this is the key to being able to finish the race effectively."

Even pacing begins months before you arrive at the starting line. Like everything else about running, pacing can be practiced. Since pacing is a matter of running miles in a predetermined time, and since training for a marathon involves running lots of miles, you can practice pacing with every training mile you log.

Unless you are running at a track, where the distances are precisely marked, measuring workout courses accurately is essential to determining pace. Most essential is marking the first mile of each course.

The focus of this article, however, is not learning pacing so much as applying pacing to the early miles of a marathon so you save yourself for the later miles. The point is, pacing is everything. Period.

Let's jog through the first 7 miles of the marathon, beginning with the countdown 30 minutes before the start.

## MINUS 30 MINUTES AND COUNTING

Between 15 and 30 minutes before the marathon start, it is a good idea to gently jog a half-mile at a shuffling pace (3 to 5 minutes per mile slower than your planned race pace). This warm-up will begin to loosen the big muscles of your legs, and it will gradually shift your breathing from anaerobic to aerobic, making the initial miles of the race more comfortable.

Between 10 and 15 minutes before the start, shed your outer clothing and either secure it in your car (if it's an out-and-back or loop course) or bag it and stow it on the sweats bus.

From 5 to 10 minutes before the start, do half a dozen 40-yard pickups (easy sprints); begin gently, and then, as your legs respond, increase the speed and power; jog 15 to 20 seconds between each pickup.

Five minutes before the start, find your place in the starting field. Many marathons have pacing standards on the side of the starting field indicating the pace that segment of the field hopes to maintain throughout the race. At other races, the start announcer will give you directions for lining up in an appropriate place in the field based on your planned pace. Unless you are able to run 26 five-minute miles in a row, do not place yourself near the front of the field. If you are unsure about where to line up, ask one of the other runners. It is usually good advice to line up on one side of the field or the other, where you'll have some space to maneuver and not be trapped in the middle of the field.

The ability to get rolling at the start is, naturally, a much bigger problem at mega-races like New York, Marine Corps, Honolulu, or Los Angeles than at the marathons that feature 1,000 runners or fewer. At a big marathon, it will take a while before you even see the starting line, while in a smaller marathon you'll likely cross it in thirty seconds or less.

While you are waiting for the starting signal, shake some of the tightness out of your arms and shoulders; gently lift your legs, one at a time, to your chest (this gently stretches the muscles and tendons); blow the air out of your lungs and take a few deep breaths, filling your lungs with fresh oxygen.

## THE START!

At most marathons, a countdown from the starting area is chanted by the assembled runners, so you will have a good sense of when the race is about to begin. Be prepared to punch your chronograph at the signal of the start, even though you will not immediately move. Your finish time is based upon the time elapsed from the starting signal. In some large, sophisticated marathons where runners are corralled by qualifying times, adjustments are fed into the computer to reflect more accurately the time the specific groups of runners crossed the starting line. And, of course, with the introduction of the ChampionChip, accurate times are pretty much assured for each runner, although the chips are not yet used at many marathons because of the extra expense.

If it takes you more than three minutes to reach the starting line, reset your chronograph to zero and restart it when you cross the starting line. In a large field you'll hardly move at all at first. Then a shuffling begins with some forward movement and periodic stops as the front of the pack moves down the course, opening space for runners coming up from behind to fill in. Don't panic. Move as the opportunity permits. Shuffle forward smoothly. Even when you begin to move somewhat regularly, try to walk fast initially, saving your running muscles.

Once the field moves forward enough to allow you to roll into a shuffling jog, do so, but don't push too hard. If you see an opening in front of you, flow into it. If an opening is ahead and to one side, check to see if anyone else is coming up to fill it. If no one is, move gently into the opening. Take pains to make all moves smoothly and well planned so you don't run into or trip other runners, or be stepped on yourself.

The first mile of any marathon can be rather confusing and also somewhat frustrating; you don't want to waste all your pent-up energy by immediately trying to get into a running rhythm. In reality, the close quarters during the first mile tend to "save" more marathons for runners than ruin them. The tightly packed field makes it difficult for you to get pulled out too quickly. If you are shuffling along on the side of the field, and it is clear for 20 yards ahead, roll into the opening, but don't sprint into it. Conserve, don't waste energy.

Gradually, as the runners in front move farther ahead, there will be more and more space for you to maneuver. Gradually you'll be able to increase your pace. Do not attempt to make up within the first mile the time you may have lost at the start!

## MILE 1

When you reach the first mile, check your time. If you are several minutes slower than you had hoped to be, don't panic, and don't attempt to make up the difference over the next mile. The idea is to get back on your pace over the first 5 miles if the field is not too congested, or over the first 10 miles if it is. Readjust your time goals if it took you an unreasonable amount of time to reach the starting line.

If you had planned to run at an 8-minute pace, and you reach the 1-mile mark in 10 minutes, plan to run between 7:45 and 7:50 for the next 9 miles. This will put you back on an 8-minute pace by mile 10. If the field is small and you got out smoothly, immediately try to get into an easy rhythm. During the first mile it's better to err on the slow side than to go faster than planned. Considering the tremendous physical conditioning you are in at this point, the first mile may very well seem incredibly pedestrian, but don't give in to the urge to pick up the pace. At 20 miles, your 8-minute pace will not seem so pedestrian, and it may even be a struggle to hold it.

If you reach the first mile a bit on the fast side, immediately slow yourself to what you feel is the proper pace. Don't slow down below your planned pace to average out your first 2 miles so they equal your planned pace. Just put the few extra seconds away and forget about them. If you ran a 7:45 first mile, for instance, and you planned to run 8:00, plan to reach mile 2 at 15:45.

If you took more than three minutes to get to the starting line and you reset your chronograph to zero as you crossed the starting line, run the race according to your chronograph and not according to the official time. Your first goal, after all, is to complete the marathon safely.

If you had set a specific time goal that now seems impossible because it took you so long to reach the starting line, you have two options. Accept that you cannot regain the lost time and run on your own chronograph, ignoring the official clock. Then you can still strive to achieve your time goal. Although the published results won't reflect it, you'll know what you did. The second option is to try, if you are feeling good when you reach the final 10K, to regain some of the lost time.

It's not worth jeopardizing your entire race by attempting to make up more than three minutes within the first 10 miles. This inability to get to the starting line quickly in a mega-marathon is a prime drawback for the first-time marathoner.

## MILES 2 THROUGH 7

Late in the race, it becomes almost impossible for many marathoners to do even the most simple math. This is not the case during the initial 10 miles, so take advantage of the segment by settling in, finding your breathing and running rhythm, and doing the necessary math and pace adjustments you need to get into your planned pace.

You'll find yourself running the same pace as many of the runners around you. If you are shooting for a popular time goal (3:00 or 3:30 or 4:00), there will be whole clumps of runners rolling along together. They are attempting to feed off one another and to stay on pace to reach their goals.

If during the first 7 miles you want to join such a group mirroring your target pace, that's fine. If you do join them, run at the edge of the group. Its leaders will typically change periodically. If you are a new marathoner, don't lead and don't get absorbed to the point where you feel hemmed in or where you become lulled by the group mind. If you are sensitive to it, and if the group you are with is an experienced one, you can feel the energy coursing back and forth. It is always easier to run the initial 7 to 10 miles with one or more other runners than it is alone, especially if headwinds prevail.

However, there is a tendency when running in a group to allow the group to dictate your pace, seemingly relieving you of the responsibility of staying on top of your planned race. But you need to continue to monitor your own pace at each mile marker. If the group begins dropping behind or getting ahead of your planned pace, gradually leave them and get into your own groove.

Some groups converse as they roll along. Don't join in. Save your breath for later in the race. If someone addresses a question specifically to you, answer as simply and precisely as possible. If it's your first marathon, it's fine to add, "This is my first marathon so I want to listen and learn," but don't become engaged in a conversation.

You want to stay on top of all of your body systems, so monitor your physical condition from head to foot at least once a mile: How's my breathing? Can I hear my footsteps, or are they silent? Am I drinking enough? Could I urinate right now if I wanted to? Am I too hot or too cold? Should I remove a layer of clothing now that I'm warmed up so I don't overheat? Am I using my arms as I practiced at the track? Is that a passing twinge I feel on the outside of my left knee or have I experienced it before? If I move to the other side of the road, will the different slant of the road alleviate the twinge?

Begin taking fluids from the very first aid station onward. When you approach aid stations, slow down, take your fluids, and walk briskly through the station area as you drink. Do not attempt to drink on the run; fluid splashed on your T-shirt won't do you any good. Walking gives your running muscles a temporary break, and, more importantly, you remain hydrated.

Drink, and then flow out the other side of the aid station and roll back into a run. Eventually you'll catch back up with your group or get back onto your pace. (If you are running in a group, make sure that you're not hemmed in as you approach an aid station—you don't want to miss your chance to grab a cup.)

If it's a cold day, drink one cup of water at the first aid station. If it's a hot day, drink two cups at the first aid station. You want to begin taking fluid as early as possible, since it takes about 45 minutes even for plain water to be emptied from the stomach and properly processed through the body where it will do some good. Even if it's cool, your working muscles are using a tremendous amount of fluid to cool themselves. Don't be lulled into dehydration just because you are enjoying cool weather. You are still perspiring. You need fluid during a marathon no matter what the temperature.

Don't use electrolyte replacement fluids during the first 10 miles—take only water. You don't need other fluids yet, and if you take electrolytes too early, the sugar in them could interfere with your body's attempt to switch to using a greater proportion of fatty acids from the bloodstream.

Once you get beyond 10 miles, your body will begin lusting after sugar in as simple-to-process a form as possible, both to fuel the working muscles and to keep the brain, which requires tremendous amounts of simple sugars to function properly, stable. Here, between 7 and 10 miles, is the place to begin taking electrolyte drinks. You can drink it alone or, if the drink is too concentrated, drink a cup of water to dilute it.

By the time you reach 7 miles, your muscles should be warmed through and through, even to the middle of your dense thigh and calf muscles. Within the next dozen miles, you should experience some of the smoothest, most effortless running of your life. During this period, however, you must be careful not to succumb to the urge to run the way you feel, which usually means running too fast because you feel so good. In real estate, it's location, location, location; in marathoning, it's pace, pace, pace.

# SECTION 2: MILES 7 TO 18
## MANAGING THE MIDDLE MILES

**BY JONATHAN BEVERLY**

If the marathon is a 20-mile training run followed by a 10K race, we need not waste time on a separate section for the middle miles. We can view them simply as an extension of the first 7 miles, with the marathoner's only task to endure the accumulating time and distance. Accepting this model, one of my friends calls them "the stupid middle miles."

Repeatedly, however, I have been surprised at the crises of body and mind that occurred during these "stupid miles." I found myself shocked and unprepared when the ragged edges of fatigue surfaced through my veneer of cool composure. More than once I wanted to call "Time Out!" somewhere around mile 12. Like life, however, the marathon allows no time outs, so I have always pressed on, trying to manage these crises literally on the run.

The difficulty of the middle miles is this: They are neither the beginning miles, where control is the clear priority, nor the final miles, where the mandate of survival lends crystal clarity to the task at hand. The middle miles are a transition, where elements of both the beginning and the end exist concurrently, where ideals meet harsh reality, and where the runner must make critical decisions and commitments.

If, as Fred Lebow used to say, the marathon is a metaphor for life, then the marathon's middle miles can be compared to the middle years of life. Like the middle miles, these years may seem benign and unimportant compared to the formidable demands of childhood or the struggles of old age; research and literature on the life's span devote the majority of their attention to these bookends. Yet the middle years fill the bulk of one's life, and the skill with which they are managed determines the satisfaction of the final years—indeed, the success of a life itself.

The crises of the middle years start when we begin to doubt our life's direction. This internal ambiguity is unavoidable as we age. While in our youth we drove forward with clear goals, we now find ourselves divided and uncertain. Part of us wants to continue to explore and expand the limits of our world, while another wants to settle and establish continuity and community. We enjoy the authority and confidence of age yet fight to maintain the energy and recklessness of youth.

## BALANCE THE CONTRADICTORY

Our natural reaction is either to ignore these problems or to try to solve them by fully embracing one side and disregarding the other. "The serious problems in life, however, are never fully solved," Jung wrote. "If ever they should appear to be so it is a sure sign that something has been lost." We must learn the trick of balancing seemingly contradictory concerns and priorities.

Similarly, we find ambiguity and conflicting priorities in the marathon. Like the life challenges they mirror, they cannot be solved, but must be balanced against each other. The first of three challenges stems from the marathon's demanding length.

### 1. Establish a Rhythm While Avoiding Stagnation

By the middle miles of the marathon, we begin to fully understand how long it is. We barely remember the start and cannot yet imagine the end. To survive and succeed, we must develop strategies to pace ourselves physically and emotionally. But we face a danger of falling into a rut and losing contact with the markers that guide us toward our goal.

By our middle years, life also feels interminably long: days blur into months, tempting us to stagnate in a well-worn routine. When the big picture eludes us, we must establish disciplines that enable us to endure less inspiring days, to pay attention to details, and to care about excellence in our work and relationships.

The marathon also demands a few clear disciplines. We need an efficient stride that consumes miles with minimal effort. Maintaining regular fluid intake should be second nature; the ability to sustain a steady pace must be as sure as a musician's scales. We can only develop these disciplines during the hundreds of miles leading up to race-day.

On race-day, ideally we want our legs to maintain the same rhythm over the entire course. But the distance betrays us: The same muscles repeating the same motion will fatigue before the day is through, requiring us occasionally to vary our efficient stride. On a hilly course, practice altering your stride going up or down. When running the Jersey Shore McMarathon, a very flat course, I switched to a higher knee lift for a few hundred yards when I felt muscle fatigue, then settled back to my low, marathoner's stride.

## CONSERVING ALL ENERGIES

Success in the marathon, however, requires that we conserve more than physical energy. As in life, the mental and emotional demands of our days drain us deeper than any physical tasks. We must also learn the discipline of running on cruise control, relying on our practiced form to carry us forward while we reserve our emotional energies for the demanding miles to come. This "autopilot" mode gives us the freedom to dissociate and enjoy the event while it monitors the level of effort and ensures all needs are being met.

Personally I have little difficulty going on autopilot, sometimes achieving this state even during the middle of a workday. During more than one marathon, however, I let the autopilot run too freely and found that I had gradually lost pace throughout the middle miles, arriving at the end too late to push for my goal. On a few occasions the autopilot has pushed too hard, like an absentminded driver with a lead foot.

Since the autopilot can sabotage our goals as well as preserve them, we can't fully "check out." We have to balance the need to tune out with the ability to monitor our progress. I like to imagine this as a program running in the background that flags me with any problems while I run in energy-saving "suspend" mode.

Many race factors can serve as flags for our mental program: Play mental games with splits, updating the formulas and recalculating each mile. Pick landmarks on the course map and use them as checkpoints. If you ran the first miles correctly, you should be catching other runners—when you find yourself behind the same group for several miles it often means you are slowing down, and that fact should wake you up. Thank a volunteer: It will break your trance and make someone's day. These mental breaks provide an opportunity to evaluate and adjust our strategy during the middle miles, which is the second challenge.

### 2. Adjust to Realities While Overcoming Obstacles

The strategies of the middle miles are dependent on several factors: race-day conditions, the results of the first miles, and your physical and mental toughness. Since none of these can be completely known in advance, evaluation must be conducted and decisions made in midstride, requiring you to balance honest appraisal with courageous resolve.

The middle years also inspire a time of evaluation and reckoning. We realize that we cannot be everything we thought we could be at 21—that the choices and circumstances of our lives have set a course, and we must either adjust to these realities or consider starting over, perhaps at a disadvantage.

Some say this process begins the day we recognize our mortality. In the marathon it begins the moment we realize, "This is going to be work!" If this happens earlier than expected (and it always seems earlier than expected), it may cause a crisis of confidence. Whatever goals we carried to this point are threatened. We naively dreamed that we could cruise through this without difficulty.

"We wish to hear only unequivocal results," Jung wrote, "and completely forget that these results can only be brought about when we have ventured into and emerged from the darkness." The darkness begins with the doubts of the middle miles, which must be confronted before the deep darkness of fatigue sets in.

Often the first hints of darkness are not an indication of impending doom. Many marathoners report having bad patches—when an easy pace suddenly becomes ragged and strained, when something hurts, or when we lose focus and motivation. Learning to ride out these bad patches is a mark of a successful marathoner.

### RUN THROUGH THE ROUGH SPOTS

Compared to a 10K, where one bad mile is a significant portion of the race, the length of the marathon weighs to the runner's advantage during tough miles. If we don't panic at the first sign of difficulty, we can back off a notch and ride through it. A mile or two reveals whether it is serious, and when the rough spot passes, we will have lost little. Sometimes all that is necessary is an internal adjustment to the increasing difficulty as the miles add up.

The marathon does, however, require a blunt and thorough evaluation: "Have I overextended myself in the first miles?" we must ask. "Do the conditions (heat, humidity, wind, crowds) necessitate altering my goal? Am I injured? Sick?" The marathon does not permit delusions past the middle miles. We may ignore the signs that we should adjust our goals and strategies, but we will pay for it later.

Some indicators are concrete and non-negotiable. The temperature in the 1993 New York City Marathon climbed to the mid-70s before I reached halfway. A year earlier I had run in similar conditions in Pueblo, Colorado, ignored the early signs of dehydration, and suffered debilitating cramps as my reward. Having learned my lesson, in New York I cut the pace enough to allow me to finish strong: not a record, but far ahead of my stumbling Pueblo debacle.

Any preexisting condition will resurface by the middle miles, often forcing the most difficult choice: to drop out. I spent the night before the 1982 Maine Coast Marathon drenched in a fever sweat. Even though on a PR pace at mile 18, I stepped off the course rather than face the last 8. A friend went into the 1997 Boston ignoring a knee pain that had plagued him for six weeks. He reported afterward that he "came through 10 miles in 60:08 [his goal pace] and then had a nice walk along the marathon course from mile 12 to 17." Both of us decided that the cost of ignoring these conditions was greater than the reward of finishing this race.

The evaluation that continues throughout the middle miles—balancing the necessity of adjustment with the courage to overcome difficulties—requires both emotional control and competitive will. Learning to balance these emotions is the third challenge.

### 3. Stay Calm While Gearing Up

A marathoner enters the middle miles tightly controlled and emotionally detached—casually observing and monitoring the body to keep it from pushing and wasting energy. At mile 18, the same marathoner emerges an aggressive competitor poised to attack the last 8—totally committed to the task, pushing farther and reaching deeper than at any point in life. The middle miles are a gray continuum of both.

Again the marathon parallels life: We find in the middle years the imperative to plan and save for our final years but do not want to arrive at the end with reserves that should have been enjoyed when we had youth and energy. We want to burn brightly but are afraid of burning out too soon.

In the marathon, we need to balance control and competitiveness. Erring on either side leads to disaster or disappointment. At Boston's "100th" celebration, the cumulative adrenaline was overpowering. After 7 miles of holding back, I surrendered to the energy within and around me. I'd rather not talk about the final miles. In contrast, at the 1995 Vermont City Marathon, I found myself running a careful, controlled pace at halfway, but over two minutes behind my goal. I made an instant transition to competitor, running a negative split PR, but was left with tantalizing questions of what might have been.

Ideally, we want to maintain an even pace and gradually transition our mental state to meet the changing demands of the task. One of the keys is to break away from friends or other runners that we have socialized with during the first miles. While companions can help in the early priority of keeping the tone calm and easy, they can distract you from the task of preparing for the final miles—miles that everyone must face alone.

### TALK TO YOURSELF—REALLY

Accomplishing this transition requires changing how we talk to ourselves. Over the course of the middle miles, our words of calm ("Relax. Have fun. I am in control. This is just a long run.") transform to statements of affirmation and determination. ("I am fast. I am tough. I am smooth. I am prepared for whatever it takes.")

If we are going to succeed in this challenge, we must know and believe in our goals. The mind requires a persuasive reason to depart from its natural tendency to avoid pain. If we wait until the moment, we will have trouble convincing ourselves that the cost is worth it.

Well before the marathon—days and even weeks earlier—we must mentally work through the full race, deciding why we are running, what we wish to accomplish, and what accomplishing this will require, that is, the "cost." Once we have settled the cost and prepared ourselves to go the distance, we wrap this raw desire with a smooth shell of emotional calm to preserve it for when it is needed. Thus prepared, the strategy in the middle miles becomes the task of gradually removing layers of calm control to reveal the solid core of resolve with which to face the final miles.

# SECTION 3: MILES 18 TO 26.2
## 18—PERHAPS YOUR LUCKY NUMBER

### BY MARK CONOVER

The final 8 miles of the marathon will test you in ways you can't imagine. Only after you get there will you know how you'll feel. And only after you know how you feel will you know how to react. The way your mind and body react during the final 8 miles may not always be pretty, but chances are once you've finished and assessed the race, you'll be satisfied. I will provide examples of what you may experience from mile 18 to the finish based upon personal experience. In all instances, there is a definite cause and effect.

The previous two authors have already prepared you for the ride along the way to the 18-mile mark, discussing a possible cause (impatience) that may result in a rather dismal effect (simply known as "hitting the wall"). I will discuss this scenario first since this effect is what one tries to avoid, but which you will most likely face more than once during a marathon career.

My example comes from my third most memorable marathon, which was actually my first-ever marathon, the 1976 Livermore Marathon, which I ran as a high school junior.

The running boom was at its peak, and as a result, people of all ages were running lots of miles. In California, schoolboys were breaking nine minutes for two miles on a regular basis, mostly because these guys were already doing college-type mileage and intensity. For a schoolboy to run 80 to 100 miles a week wasn't unheard of then as it is now. Even the less genetically gifted were pumping out the miles. How cool, then, for this undeveloped youngster to join the craze and run a marathon . . .

I had finished my second cross-country season as a varsity runner, becoming the number one runner on our team. I had five weeks to go for the marathon, so I immediately upped my weekly mileage from 50 to 90 miles. I reached 108 miles two weeks before the marathon, then rested for a week. My longest run was 14 miles.

I remember how easy the marathon felt—until about 8 miles. I was running sub-6:00 miles and realized early on that I was no longer taking in the scenery or feeling giddy and euphoric with the flow of endorphins that had lulled my body earlier in the race.

By the half marathon, I was a mask of ultimate concentration: furrowed brow, oblivious to the beautiful green pastures surrounding the flat country miles. I was feeling like a gnarled old tree trunk trying to run a 6:30 mile.

You see, at that age, I had yet to consider pacing for 26.2 miles. I was happy to pass pre-Algebra, so why should I have to figure out that to run a 3-hour marathon, which was my goal, I needed to run consistent 6:55 miles, not the 5:40 to 6:00 miles that I had begun to lope through as soon as the gun went off?

By 22 miles, I was oblivious to my own feet striking the ground. The only thing I recognized were other runners passing me like I was standing still. Hell, by 23 miles, I was standing still, hunched over with the worst side stitch I've ever experienced.

## THE DEATH MARCH

I walked nearly a mile, then started jogging it in, looking ahead on the long, straight, tulle-fog-infested road for any sign of a finish line. My legs were reduced to moving bones with muscles so depleted of glycogen and so laden with lactic acid that it's a wonder I was able to finish at all. My mind was numb, kind of like what happens if you have to listen to a jackhammer all day long. Actually, my whole body felt like a jackhammer—a shattered one.

I reached 25 miles and had the wherewithal to know I would break 3 hours, but I wouldn't look good doing it. As I trudged to the finish at the Lawrence Livermore Lab, where at one time work had been done on creating the atom bomb, I felt like the physicists must have left one bomb behind, and it fell on me—right around the 18-mile point in the race.

I ran 2:54:51, tired, sore, and downright ornery: "Hell no, Dad, I ain't walking to the car. Go get it and pick me up while I lie here on the sidewalk—"

One of the hordes of more intelligent marathoners on that day who whipped past me looked a lot like a young guy my age. You can imagine how delighted I was to find out that it was a 14-year-old girl who set the national age-group record with a 2:52.

Yes, while this tale may attest more to the impetuousness of youth, I've seen many seemingly sound adults ignore proper pacing in the early stages of a marathon. As a result of bad pacing, you can still finish your marathon, and you may even reach your time goal, but the price you pay will be a visit to hell, especially during the miles beyond 18. You'll have no glycogen for fuel because you will have used carbohydrates from storage too early to meet your intense energy needs to deliver oxygen to the working muscles.

Along with depleted glycogen will come the formation of lactic acid, the only way your body will have left to attempt to secure oxygen for the working muscles—an avenue that produces whole tanker trucks full of this evil by-product.

Other effects from stupid pacing—or rather, lack of pacing—range from zero blood sugar, which will impair your ability to concentrate, to post-marathon depression and injury. In the wake of your disappointing marathon, you may not feel like running for months. In my case, I became injured and couldn't train or race again for a long time. I ended up missing my junior year of high school track with sciatica, which I attributed directly to my first marathon.

Aside from having to drop out, the experience I related is one you should strive to avoid at all costs. I have never had such a tedious 8 miles since then. But my next experience typified the majority of my dealings with miles 18 to the finish, save one special marathon, which I'll discuss later. For now, I'll discuss a race strategy and circumstances during the race that are commonplace and result in relatively predictable feelings after mile 18.

## WITH KNOWLEDGE COMES GOOD PACING

By 1987, I had become a seasoned veteran, nearly becoming one of those nine-minute two-milers my senior year in high school (I never ran more than 70 miles a week after that ill-fated Livermore Marathon), a national champion collegiate runner, and an Olympic trials qualifier at 10,000 meters on the track. My new goal was to qualify for the 1988 Olympic trials—in the marathon. I chose the California International Marathon in Sacramento as my qualifier.

Not only had my body accumulated a wealth of strong training miles since my first marathon in 1976, but my mind had also accumulated a wealth of knowledge about pacing and preparing for the marathon. Thus, after three months of weekly tempo runs and a few 20-milers, I felt ready for a sub-2:20 marathon, the time needed to run in the Olympic trials four months later.

The day before the race was stormy. The morning of the race was even worse. I remained calm and realized that my pre-race plan of starting conservatively was going to be everyone's plan. On a day with driving rain and gale-force winds, surely no one would go out at a suicidal pace. Even if they did, I wasn't going to follow.

As a pack of 25 or so went through the halfway mark at a modest 68 minutes, I felt very relieved and relaxed. Just as I had hoped, my breathing was easy, my mind focused, and my legs fresh. At about 16 miles, an Irish runner made a move, and the field was suddenly down to six lead runners, including myself. I was beginning to feel less comfortable as I entered the zone where the real racing begins.

At 18 miles, my legs were heavy, a sign that I was probably savoring my last few miles of glycogen. From there on I would have to focus on remaining efficient and economical with my stride. I made a conscious effort to make sure I latched on to one of the other runners, thinking to myself that if I treated the last few fatiguing miles like a hard tempo run with a training partner who was feeling a bit more chipper then I was, I could at least get pulled to a solid finish.

Thankfully, my intuition paid off, because by 21 miles, I had entered a zone where I could still run efficiently, but my mind wasn't as focused and my ability to consciously be aggressive was waning—a classic sign of blood sugar and glycogen depletion.

Now it was up to whatever mental resolve I had left in order to latch onto someone and run, robotlike, simply focusing on putting one foot in front of the other in tandem with another human being.

The Irishman who made the move at 16 miles fell off the pace at 21 miles, and a Canadian who was a marathon veteran seemed to be running away with the race. But a Kenyan about 5-foot-3 became my running buddy, and off we went in tandem, running for second place. With each passing mile, my brow became more furrowed, and my concentration focused on merely being able to concentrate, rather than concentrating on how to win my race against the Kenyan. My legs began to get that pounded-like-a-jackhammer feeling. But I hung on to the diminutive African runner, memorizing every contour of his muscular shoulders, to which I had become attached like a limpet.

By 25 miles, I wasn't thinking very clearly, but I knew I only had a mile to go. At that point, I lost much of my mental resolve, and as my head lifted against fatigue, the Kenyan pulled away to beat me by 10 seconds. I placed third, but more importantly, I ran 2:18 to earn a trip to the Olympic trials.

## THE "DREAM" RACE

I was very satisfied, but I realized that with the marathon, you are bound to feel heavy-legged and unfocused from 18 miles to the finish. It's the degree of heavy legs and cloudy mind that determines whether the whole race falls apart or whether you salvage a respectable performance.

And as this article preaches, it's how fast you run the earlier miles that will determine this degree. But there's no getting around it—you're going to fatigue after 18 miles—or are you?

That's the beauty of the marathon. You prepare as best you can and run the race. You get to see what happens. What happened to me in my next marathon, the 1988 United States Olympic trials in New Jersey, is the stuff of which we runners dream.

By the time I reached the 18-mile mark, I was leading. Not only was I leading, but, along with Ed Eyestone, I was pulling away from the field. I was actually feeling better from 18 miles to the finish than I felt earlier in the race.

As we reached the 20-mile mark, I was completely focused, my mind very alert and cognizant of my surroundings. I remember looking at my reflection in store windows, doing a "form check." I was telling the motorcycle cop in front of us to give us more room. In other words, I was feeling like I was on an easy 8-miler rather than battling it out in the biggest race of my life. Why did the latter miles of this marathon run so smoothly compared to other marathons I ran?

I can think of several reasons, all of which you can learn from and take with you to your next marathon.

First, in the months leading up to the race, I didn't train like an idiot. I didn't do too many long runs (a mistake we all make in our preparation), fast runs, miles, or races. I trained with extreme moderation. I knew I had built up a tremendous base after I was able to run 2:18 in lousy early-December weather in Sacramento.

Instead of immediately gearing up for the trials, I took a month off, not running until after Christmas in preparation for the April trials race. I never ran more than 85 miles a week. I ran one long interval workout a week, a shorter, quicker interval workout every other week, five races from 5K to 15K, and only four runs longer than one hour and 45 minutes. With a one-week taper, I came to the trials eager, nervous, and ready to see what would happen.

My legs felt fresh, my mind clear, my stride efficient, and my glycogen stores intact. I never felt any discomfort until after I was finished. Only then did my muscles ache with lactic acid and my intestines grumble with what-ever physiological trauma they bore the brunt of after running 26.2 miles at 5:03 pace per mile.

Another saving grace for me was my ability to negative split the race. I ran my fastest 10K portion from 20 miles to the finish. I hadn't planned on this, although certainly every marathoner dreams about it. I think the combination of a manageable pace through 18 miles coupled with being undertrained allowed my legs to stave off any formulation of excessive lactic acid. My body wasn't torn down before the race even started, as is often the case for most marathoners.

## USE FAT AS FUEL

This allowed my body to run efficiently for a longer time compared to my other marathons. The pace and condition of my body were sufficient enough to allow less energy-consuming fat to be used as fuel by the muscles rather than carbohydrates, which, once tapped into in the form of glycogen, means your fuel and energy meter are running on borrowed time. Start the meter too early and you'll begin to shut down, which is what often happens from 18 miles to the finish. Remember the jackhammer feeling of pounded legs? That's the sign that you've run out of glycogen.

I've had several other good marathons in my career, but none so thrilling and exhilarating as the 1988 Olympic trials. Never again have I been able to enjoy the final 8 miles of a marathon. I'm almost positive this is because since then I've showed up at the starting line as "damaged goods"—a person whose body was already torn down before the race even started. In these instances, glycogen reserves were spent early, meaning that I had to dig deep mentally to salvage a good race during the last 8 miles.

Overtraining is one reason we become damaged goods. Too many miles without proper buildup, too many hard workouts, and too many races can cause overtraining. If you feel excessively tired, especially mentally, then you are probably overtraining. In my opinion, too many long runs over too short a period of time will bring you to the start as an overtrained marathoner.

Long runs, like the marathon itself, exact quite a toll from the body. Unlike going into the marathon, runners don't usually go into their long runs rested. Thus it's like getting the jackhammer effect at 18 miles every single week! The body can't stand such constant stress. My suggestion is to wait until about two months out from your marathon before you run longer than 17 miles. I would run only four of these, one every other week. Never exceed 20 miles. Do your last long run two weeks before the marathon. If you do too long a run every week, especially from too far out from your marathon, you're not going to give yourself a fighting chance once you hit 18 miles in the race.

Hopefully, we all get to experience a euphoric final 8 miles of a marathon. If not, we settle for the next best thing, which is the ability mentally to persevere and tell ourselves to finish strong in spite of having a weakened mind and even weaker legs. The thing to avoid is the complete "bonk," where mind and body succumb to the adverse physiological effects that can take their toll during the final 8 miles. The degree of unpleasantness at the end of the marathon is directly proportional to the degree of the bonk. Slowing to a walk, for example, isn't as bad as having to stop altogether.

Our bodies are amazingly resilient and intelligent (despite what non-marathoners say). Reasonably fit people have internal mechanisms that will prevent them from doing irreparable damage after the bonk occurs.

We know running the marathon won't kill us. Thus, we take on the challenge, immersing ourselves in the training process that is meant to guide us through a satisfying marathon. By paying close attention to the process, which begins months before the big day, and by heeding that most important word—patience—you will come through the final miles with flying colors, bound for glory.

About the Authors:

RICHARD BENYO was executive editor of *Runner's World* magazine from 1977 to 1984. He is a full-time writer with 16 books to his credit, all in the areas of fitness, health, and sports. He's run 37 marathons, and in 1989 he and running partner Tom Crawford became the first athletes in history to run from Badwater in Death Valley (the lowest point in the Western Hemisphere and the hottest and driest spot on earth) to the peak of Mount Whitney (at 14,494 feet, the highest point in the contiguous United States) and back, a distance of 300 miles. Rich enjoyed the experience so much that he returned to the course in 1991 and 1992 but has since seen the error of his ways.

JONATHAN BEVERLY has been running since he was a freshman cross-country runner in Maine 20 years ago. The marathon has fascinated him from the beginning, luring him into skipping track his junior year to run the inaugural Maine Coast Marathon. After several years away from the event, Jonathan has now run 13 marathons, with a PR of 2:46:04 set at Pittsburgh. He is currently editor-in-chief for *Running Times* magazine.

MARK CONOVER has been a runner for 23 years. Along the way, he was a California state high school track meet medalist in the 2 miles in 1978 and an Olympic trials marathon winner in 1988. Mark's most cherished accomplishment came in 1996 when he ran in the Olympic trials marathon after a two-year battle with Hodgkin's Disease. Mark coaches runners of all abilities via e-mail (mconover@slonet.org) or phone (805-541-2833) and is the assistant track and cross-country coach at Cal Poly San Luis Obispo. Mark is also involved in raising funds for leukemia research.

# REFERENCES

Jeff Galloway, *Galloway's Book on Running*
Jeff Galloway, *You Can Do It*
Glenn Town and Todd Kearney, *Swim Bike Run*
Gordon Bakoulis, *Getting Real About Running*
Craythorn and Hanna, *The Ultimate Guide to Marathons*
Gail Kislevitz, *First Marathons*
Kara Douglass Thom, *Becoming an Ironman*
Neal Jamison, *Running Through the Wall*

# MARATHON COURSES DESCRIBED IN STORIES

**Atlanta Marathon**, Atlanta, Georgia (Page 211)
(404) 231-9064
www.atlantatrackclub.org

**Big Sur International Marathon**, Big Sur, CA (Pages 39, 51)
(408) 625-6226
www.bsim.org

**Boston Marathon**, Boston, MA (Pages 66, 97, 135, 173, 215, 233, 242)
(617) 236-1652
www.bostonmarathon.org

**Hartford Marathon** (Page 129)
(860) 652-8866
www.hartfordmarathon.org

**La Salle Banks Chicago Marathon**, Chicago, IL
(Pages 19, 21, 69, 75, 119, 250)
(312) 904-9800
www.chicagomarathon.org

**Grandma's Marathon**, Duluth, MN (Pages 162, 195)
(218) 727-0947
www.grandmasmarathon.com

**Marine Corps Marathon**, Washington, DC (Pages 113, 175, 203, 225, 230)
(703) 784-2225
www.marinemarathon.com

**Country Music Marathon**, Nashville, TN (Pages 31, 90)
(858) 450-6510
www.cmmmarathon.com

**New York City Marathon**, New York City, NY
(Pages 9, 17, 57, 84, 105, 137,168, 175, 179, 191, 208, 220, 223)
(212) 860-4455
www.nyrrc.org

**Shamrock Sportsfest Marathon**, Virginia Beach, VA (Page 145)
(757) 481-5090
www.shamrocksportsfest.com

**City Of Los Angeles Marathon** (Pages 132, 151, 174)
(310) 444-5544
www.lamarathon.com

**Walt Disney World Marathon,** Orlando, FL (Pages 95, 247)
(407) 939-7810
www.disneyworldsports.com

**The Mystic Places Marathon,** East Lyme, CT (Pages 72, 223, 239)
(203) 481-5933
www.jbsports.com

**Ocean State Marathon,** Narragansett, RI (Pages 99, 233)
(401) 885-4499
www.osm26.com

**Twin Cities Marathon**, St. Paul, MN (Page 47)
(952) 925-3500
www.TwinCitiesMarathon.org

**Napa Valley Marathon** (Pages 156, 247)
www.napa-marathon.com

**Lincoln Marathon**, Lincoln, NE (63, 246)
402-435-3504
   www.lincolnrun.org/marathon.htm